With a Dauntless Spirit
Alaska Nursing in Dog-Team Days

With a Dauntless Spirit
Alaska Nursing in Dog-Team Days

Edited with an Introduction and Commentary by
Effie Graham
Jackie Pflaum
Elfrida Nord

University of Alaska Press
Fairbanks

© 2003 University of Alaska Press
    Box 756240-UAF
    Fairbanks, AK 99775-6240
    fypress@uaf.edu
    www.uaf.edu/uapress

This publication was printed on acid-free paper that meets the mini-
mum requirements for the American National Standard for Information
Science—Permanence of Paper for Printed Library Materials ANSI
Z39.48-1984.

Publication design and production by Sue Mitchell, Inkworks.
Cover design by Dixon J. Jones.
Cover photos: Top: The *Bear* (reprinted with permission from Anchorage
    Museum of History and Art, #1381-164-16). Bottom, left to right: dog
    sled courtesy of Robert Stevens; Red Cross Nurse Madeline de Foras
    (reprinted with permission from Alaska Nurses' Association collec-
    tion, #78-27-03N, Elmer E. Rasmuson Library, University of Alaska
    Fairbanks); Augusta (Gussie) Mueller, courtesy of the North Slope
    Borough's Inupiat History, Language, and Culture Commission; Alma
    Carlson (reprinted with permission from Alaska Nurses' Association
    collection, #18-27-12N, Elmer E. Rasmuson Library, University of
    Alaska Fairbanks).

Library of Congress Cataloging-in-Publication Data

With a dauntless spirit : Alaska nursing in dog-team days / edited by Effie
Graham, Jackie Pflaum, and Elfrida Nord.
    p. cm.
    ISBN 1-889963-61-5 (cloth : alk. paper)—ISBN 1-889963-62-3 (pbk. :
alk. paper)
    1. Nurses—Alaska—Biography. I. Graham, Effie A. II. Pflaum, Jackie.
III. Nord, Elfrida.
    RT34 .W55 2003
    610.73'092'2798--dc21
                    2003002157

To

Catherine (Kitty) Gair
and the Alaska Nurses Association Committee
who collected these stories before it was too late

Contents

Acknowledgements

M ANY PERSONS HAVE BEEN involved in the evolution and production of this volume, and this over a very long period. It began in 1956 with the Alaska Nurses Association, its committee on nursing history, and particularly Catherine Gair, then president of the association. The evidence of their work is concretely present in the extensive files preserved in the archives of the Rasmuson Library at the University of Alaska Fairbanks.

Connie Blair Brehm, while on the University of Alaska Anchorage nursing faculty, described the archival collection to Effie Graham, exciting her interest. Nancy Yaw Davis, anthropologist, encouraged Effie Graham to pursue this area as a post-retirement project. Ruth Benson of Fairbanks assisted by reading materials, helping select, and editing lengthy ones. Gail McGuill, president of the association in the early 1990s, wrote a letter of personal support and of the support of the association. Marjorie J. Hill of Maine read and helped edit other materials.

Relatives of the nurses in this collection—the Newsome Bakers of Clallam Bay, Washington, Glannie Wiehe of Prairie Valley, Kansas, Mildred Ruthruff of Snohomish, Washington, and Ted Keaton of Marysville, Washington—actively gave their support to this project. Byron Bruckner of Fairbanks provided a link to Mrs. Wiehe, which then led to an audio tape and letters.

Library support, public and university, was important. These include the staff of the archives in Fairbanks, the Alaska section of the Loussac Library in Anchorage, the Betty Anderson Library of the Intercollegiate Center for Nursing Education in Spokane for early nursing texts, the Alaska State Library in Juneau, with particular thanks to Kay Sheldon. The National Archives both in Washington, D.C., and in its office in Anchorage provided both written materials and photos on a federal level. The Anchorage Museum of History and Art gave help from its extensive collection of early photos, the Neville Museum of Brown County, Green Bay, Wisconsin, and the Inupiat History, Language, and Culture Commission in Barrow, Alaska, provided photos relating to Stella Fuller and Augusta Mueller. Robert Stevens, aviation historian, of Seattle, provided some early general photos of Alaska scenes. The School of Nursing at the University of Alaska Anchorage provided extensive support. Jean Waldman, nurse historian for the American Red Cross Museum, was helpful.

Theta Omicron of Sigma Theta Tau provided a monetary gift, making it possible to move the manuscript into its final stages. Marguerite Lambert provided the support at this stage. Nancy Fischer of Palmer, Alaska, did early transcriptions of tapes and the typing of early drafts. Lynn East of Tucson, Arizona, provided encouragement and skill in her assistance with photos and maps, and sample displays of a finished document.

Thank you all.

Introduction

WOMEN ARE OFTEN OVERLOOKED in stories from Alaska's past, but many women's services were essential to health and welfare on a continuing basis in isolated villages. These women were the teachers, who more frequently were women, and the nurses, who almost always were. This collection presents the first-hand accounts of six nurses as they lived and worked in rural Alaska between 1907 and 1947, in an environment requiring unusual tolerance of isolation, temperature extremes, and rudimentary living conditions.

A 1954 report described nurses serving the rural population in Alaska:

> The itinerant nurses traveled by dog-team and later by "bush plane," experienced dangers and hardships which their stateside colleagues could scarcely comprehend; they lived in the most primitive conditions. For the most part they matched the rigors of the environment with a dauntless spirit.[1]

In 1956, the newly organized Alaska Nurses Association (AaNA), with unusual foresight, began collecting memoirs, letters, and photos that would document the experiences of early nurses. These documents, now protected in the archives of the Elmer E. Rasmuson Library at the University of Alaska Fairbanks, have remained a hidden treasure. The AaNA archive is the resource for four accounts in this collection.[2]

Reading the archival material was sometimes tedious but often exciting. The letters and memoirs gave an immediacy to the past and revealed the nurses' individual personal traits and problems. From health care challenges to holiday celebrations, the people and events described came to life.

The selection of accounts for this collection was based on two criteria: that the writer be employed in her professional role as nurse and that the focus be on her own experience and not that of others. An effort was made to verify facts, shaded as they would be expected to be by the time and place. The nurses in this collection had the major portion of their experiences before World War II and present a history before the technical, medical, and social changes of the war heralded a new era.

The first reminiscence is by Lula Welch, a nurse who married a doctor. Together they managed the health care of patients in two small mining camp hospitals on the Seward Peninsula during gold-rush days. When she was in her late eighties, in response to the 1956 AaNA request, she wrote the memoirs that are presented here.

The letters of Augusta Mueller and Gertrude Fergus provide the heart of this collection. These young women wrote long, journal-like letters home. Their letters had been saved and were submitted by the women themselves when the 1956 AaNA request was made. In presenting their letters here, we did not include text of a repetitive nature and personal references. Regrettably, because of length much could not be included, but we retained most descriptions of their work.

The letters and reports by Stella Fuller[3] contrast in style. She had the most professional nursing experience on arrival in Alaska, with a creditable career in public health nursing.

Her letters and reports are to her Red Cross superiors. She had great hopes of establishing nursing services in a poorly served area of immense size.

Both Alma Carlson and Mildred Keaton spent many years as itinerant nurses, Carlson in western and northwestern Eskimo villages, and Keaton in the southeast, on the Yukon River, and in many other parts of the territory. Their initial contributions to the 1956 AaNA request were meager. Keaton was in the process of writing an autobiography of her Alaskan experiences, which she eventually left, unfinished and untitled, with the archives.[4]

Alma Carlson considered her contribution fulfilled when she submitted a portfolio of photos and related comments. Recently, a fortuitous contact with her niece[5] yielded several letters Carlson wrote in the 1930s and a tape recording Carlson made at the request of her family in 1975, the final year of her life. There is a benediction quality to this tape, and it is appropriate to place her comments at the end of this collection.

Chapters One and Two are a prelude to the personal reports. Chapter One summarizes nursing roles and the living and employment conditions as they affected the nurses and their patients during the first half of this century. Chapter Two gives a contextual history of Alaska with reference to health care. Each nurse is then featured, with a short personal history followed by their letters or memoirs. Maps locate regional sections in relation to Alaska as a whole, and photographs illustrate the person, time, and place.

The first-hand accounts of these women, who ventured forth with a sense of service, duty, and compassion, are a part of Alaska's history, so far under-reported. Nurses of today may be encouraged by these stories from the past and general readers may appreciate the lively accounts of these hardy persons. Readers will encounter incidents reflecting early and mid twentieth century attitudes. In doing so they will have glimpses of paternalism toward a different culture, and carelessness with artifacts and remains. They will also view some medical and nursing practices no longer considered acceptable today.

Endnotes

1. *Alaska's Health: A Survey Report,* by Alaska Health Survey Team, Thomas Parran, chief (Pittsburgh, PA: Graduate School of Public Health, University of Pittsburgh, 1954), 94. This survey was commissioned in 1953 by the Bureau of Indian Affairs, Department of Interior. It revealed the serious health conditions of Alaska Natives, particularly in the area of tuberculosis.

2. The Alaska Nurses Association began a history project in 1956 when Catherine (Kitty) Gair was president. Other committee members involved in the project were Bertha Johnson, co-chair; Jeanne Ridley; Betty Buchanan; Ann Zaldaris; Blanche Findlay; Hannah Chestnutt; Jessie DeVries; and Gail Avery. Solicitations were made by word of mouth and by advertising. The letters and memoirs collected were eventually transferred to the archives of the Elmer E. Rasmuson Library at the University of Alaska Fairbanks in 1976. They were expanded over the years, much under the leadership of Doris Southall. Rie Muñoz wrote a brief but factual history of nursing in Alaska using the archival materials as a major source, titled *Nursing in the North: 1867–1967,* published by the Alaska Nurses Association, 1967. The archival materials used in this volume were selected from the first solicitation of 1956.

3. Elfrida Nord, chief of the Section on Nursing, Department of Health and Social Services, State of Alaska (retired), made these letters available for use in this volume.

4. Keaton completed the work for the benefit of her family. Entitled *No Regrets, the Autobiography of an Arctic Nurse,* it is available from her niece, Annette Tucker, 914 Fourth St., Apt. 14, Snohomish, Washington, 98291-2858. Send $22 (includes shipping).

5. Glannie Weihe of Prairie Village, Kansas, is the daughter of Alma Carlson's sister, Annie.

Women Who Could

L IVING AND WORKING IN rural Alaska in the first half of the twentieth century provided nurses an exceptional opportunity for professional independence. This could be both stressful and liberating.

Early nursing school socialization practice was the basis of some of the stress. The nurses who provided their letters and memoirs for this collection graduated from diploma schools of nursing.[1] These schools were modeled after those first established in England in 1860, then in the United States in 1873. By the early years of the twentieth century they had proliferated in the United States, providing much of the care of hospitalized patients.[2]

Diploma schools provided two, and later three, years of education within the hospital setting. Curricula had been standardized by the 1920s with precisely described courses and required practice.[3]

Twelve-hour work days were common. By the 1920s, state examination and licensure had been instituted, assuring the public that performance requirements had been met. Although Alaska did not initiate licensure until 1941, careful employers of nurses followed the federal example of requiring current licensure in some state.

Approved schools of nursing did not exist in Alaska until after 1950. Qualified nurses had to be imported. A few
hospitals provided some training programs; these were not
related to the national scheme and provided no mobility for
graduates.[4]

Nursing textbooks from this period give little or no instruction for any autonomous functions of nurses.[5] Rather,
they are full of detail on various procedures, simple and
complex, relating not only to the physical care of patients
but in assisting in medical treatments and careful observation
of symptoms. There is emphasis on the need for nurses to be
good and caring people: cheerful, honest, unselfish, and obe-
dient. In a historical analysis of American nursing during this
early period, Reverby noted, "The nurse as an individual,
and nursing as an occupational group, were to conform to a
given set of rules. Judgment as to appropriate behavior and
stance of nursing were based on the acceptance of orders."[6]

Many small hospitals (six to thirty beds) existed in Alaska
before 1940.[7] The buildings were of frame or log construction, with an operating room, laundry, and kitchen in addition to patient rooms. There were rooms for staff, who could
be on call twenty-four hours a day. In mining camps, in small
towns and Native communities, the hospitals were sponsored
by subscription, religious groups, the fishing or mining
industries, or by the federal government. In the days before
air transportation, these facilities were reassuring to isolated
peoples. Representative hospital nurses in this collection are
Lula Welch and Augusta Mueller.

Usually a hospital had at least one physician, who was
often absent. The doctor could be called to serve surrounding
areas or the position could not be filled at all for long peri-
ods. Then the nurse became the medical provider. The use
of "standing orders"[8] helped, but this required diagnosis, a
decision-making skill not taught in the nursing curriculum.

Skilled observation was taught, but always for the purpose of reporting to the physician who then gave orders for treatment. The dilemma, both cognitive and emotional, emerging from this conflict is apparent. In a recent study of nurses working on American Indian reservations in the 1930s, Able noted that one of the main problems recalled was doing things they had been forbidden to do in usual practice.[9]

Beginning with the early years of the century, stimulated by a variety of charitable and volunteer groups, such as the American Red Cross, some nurses moved from hospital work into home care of the client, health teaching, and developing departments of health.[10] These nurses became known by various terms such as visiting nurse, industrial nurse, school nurse, village nurse, or field nurse, all under a more complete umbrella term of public health nurse. In 1929 this field of nursing was defined as:

> an organized community service, individual, family, and community. This service includes interpretation and application of medical, sanitary and social procedures for the correction of defects, prevention of disease and the promotion of health and may include skilled care of sick in their homes.[11]

Village or field nurses, originally part of federal service in Alaska, were phased into a variety of agencies. Before 1931 medical care was provided under the Alaska School Service of the Bureau of Education of the Department of Interior.[12] At first, nurses were hired as "sanitation teachers"[13] [Figure 1.1]. They taught in the classroom but also provided dispensary, emergency, and home health care services in the village. These nurses received contracts no different than other teachers. Variability was covered under the general statement, "teachers are required to perform such duties for the benefit of the Natives or for the interests of the Alaska School Service as may be assigned to them by the district superintendents."[14] Relationships with the school system continued into the 1920s and early 1930s, although the position title was changed from "sanitation teacher" to village or field nurse.

Four of the nurses in this volume—Stella Fuller, Gertrude Fergus, Mildred Keaton, and Alma Carlson—had their primary responsibilities in the field of public health nursing, although they moved between hospital and community. Three of them were employed by educational officers.[15] There is no evidence that their job descriptions were more complex than those of the sanitation teachers. Their letters and memoirs reveal the broad and creative ways they interpreted their roles.

The employment of Elinor Gregg[16] [Figure 1.2] in 1924 as chief nurse at the federal level for the Office of Indian Affairs

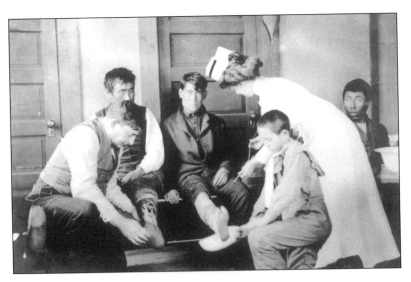

1.1 Sanitation Teacher Ada Van Vranken in 1909. She was hired by J. H. Romig, MD, to demonstrate this role on the Kenai Peninsula, spending time in the villages of Seldovia and Tatitlek. Reprinted from the National Archives, Washington, DC (RG75, E806, Box 28).

eventually provided more structure to nursing; job descriptions were developed and salaries were standardized. In her memoirs she says of Alaska:

> I did not give Alaska much thought, though I knew the nurses at-large made two extended trips a year, one by dogsled in winter and one by gas boat in the summer. They had been functioning without professional supervision for years under the Office of Education, and I had plenty to do without doing more than recruit if Dr. Fellows asked for more nurses.[17]

By 1931 the Office of Indian Affairs had Alaska medical care under its jurisdiction, and once a medical officer had been assigned to Alaska, his office began developing job descriptions and other regulations for nurses. Early drafts and final documents in 1935 were similar to those developed by Gregg for Indian reservations and approved by her. A set of these job descriptions is included in the Appendix.[18]

For nurses already functioning in field or village nursing roles, setting up a system and regularizing roles may have been reassuring, but there was at least one related comment. Mildred Keaton, who had been self-directed in her work schedule since 1923 when she arrived in Alaska, wrote in her autobiography:

1.2. Elinor Gregg. As chief nurse for the Office of Indian Affairs, she visited Alaska for an extensive tour in 1936. This included Barrow and other isolated areas. Courtesy of Jackie Pflaum and the Gregg Family.

The medical director made out an itinerary for us dog sled nurses such as one or two days in a village based on the population of the village, with never a day allowed for an epidemic anywhere which might necessitate the nurse back-tracking, or an emergency, or layovers when too stormy to travel, he of course, never having traveled by dog team.[19]

Nursing autonomy was clearly defined on a theoretical level in a deceivingly simple statement by Virginia Henderson in 1955. Although revised somewhat since, it is still relevant and useful today. Henderson stated that the unique function of the nurse is:

> To assist the individual, sick or well, in the performance of those activities contributing to health or its recovery (or to peaceful death) that he would perform unaided if he had the necessary strength or knowledge. It is likewise her function to help the individual gain independence as rapidly as possible.[20]

This statement shifted the focus from the nurse to the individual cared for, allowed for variability, and gave autonomy to both the nurse and the patient. Henderson did not deny that nurses also assist physicians in the treatment program and act as members of the health care team, but of the unique function "she initiates and controls; of this she is the master."[21] This, from a highly respected nursing leader, was permission for nurses to depart from their earlier socialization, from "women who shouldn't to women who could."[22]

Endnotes

1. There is one exception: Gertrude Fergus graduated from the nursing program at the University of Cincinnati.
2. Philip Kalish and Beatrice Kalish, *The Advance of American Nursing*, 3rd ed. (Philadelphia: J. B. Lippincott, 1987), 35–36, 70–75, 108, 197.
3. I. Stewart, *Standard Curriculum for Schools of Nursing*, 4th ed. (New York: National League for Nursing Education, 1922).

4. Mabel Leroy, "Nursing in Alaska," *American Journal of Nursing* 23 (November 1923): 925–928. The Native hospital in Juneau trained several Native nurses.

5. Two examples of standard nursing textbooks from this early period are: Isabel Hampton Robb, *Nursing, Its Principles and Practice*, 3rd ed. (Toronto: J. F. Hartz, 1909) and Bertha Harmer, *Textbook of the Principles and Practice of Nursing* (New York: Macmillan, 1923). Harmer describes the personal characteristics of nurses, pp. 3–7.

6. Susan M. Reverby, *Ordered to Care: The Dilemma of American Nursing 1850–1945* (Cambridge, UK: University Press, 1987), 202.

7. Within the period of this book, and in the northwest area of the territory only, reference is made to hospitals in Council and Candle (Welch), Unalakleet and Nome (Fergus), and Noorvik, Mountain Village, and Bethel (Carlson).

8. An example of "standing orders" is the publication Medical Handbook, produced by the U.S. government for use by teachers and others in isolated communities, written by medical doctors E. Krulish and Daniel Neuman, (Washington, D.C.: U.S. Government Printing Office, 1913).

9. Emily K. Abel, "We are left so much alone to work out our own problems: Nurses on American Indian Reservations during the 1930s," *Nursing History Review* 4 (1996): 43–64.

10. Kalish and Kalish, *The Advance of American Nursing,* 171–191, 266–292.

11. *Public Health Nursing* (October 1929): 80–85.

12. Barrell Hevener Smith, "Bureau of Education: History, Activities and Organization," in *Service Monograph* of U.S. Government (Baltimore: John Hopkins Press, 1923), 47. In 1884, the education of Alaska Native children was assigned to the Department of Interior, Bureau of Education. The BOE expected their Alaska school teachers to assume the functions of community leader, counselor, censor of morals, arbitrator in disputes, local observer and reporter of conditions, defender of the peace, public nurse, consulting physician, and census taker. In 1916 the overwhelming burden on the teachers' time and need for skills well beyond their training led to separation of funds for education and medical care of Alaska Natives.

13. J. H. Romig, district superintendent of Southwest Region, Alaska, to E. Brown, commissioner of education, and W. T. Lopp, chief of the Alaska Division, Washington, D.C., Letter 11 February 1911, RG 75, Box 28, E 806, National Archives, Washington, D.C.

14. P. P. Claxton, Commissioner of Education, to Esther Gibson, Alaska Medical Service, Letter of Appointment as Sanitation Teacher, 30 October 1916, RG 75, Box 77, National Archives, Washington, D.C.

15. Fergus consulted with a Mr. Range, a district superintendent; Carlson was hired by an education official to develop a traveling nurse service in western Alaska; and Keaton was interviewed by W. T. Lopp, chief of the Alaska Division, in Seattle.

16. Elinor D. Gregg, *The Indians and the Nurse* (Norman, OK: University of Oklahoma Press, 1965), 152–168.

17. Ibid., 152. (F. S. Fellows was the medical director in Juneau for the Office of Indian Affairs.)

18. Letter to the United States Civil Service Commission, Washington, D.C. 8 June 1938. (Author unknown.) Regarding appointments to the Alaska Division of the Bureau of Indian Affairs. Medical Service Nurses, Alaska Division of the Bureau of Indian Affairs, RG 75, Box 257, National Archives, Washington, D.C.

19. Mildred Keaton, unpublished autobiography (no date). This reference relates to her Kotzebue experience. Alaska Nurses Association Collection, Archives Series 13-4, Box 33, File 520, Elmer E. Rasmuson Library, University of Alaska Fairbanks.

20. Bertha Harmer, *Textbook of the Principles and Practice of Nursing*, revised Virginia Henderson, 5th ed. (New York: Macmillan, 1955), 4. This book has been completely revised since the 1923 edition.

21. Ibid.

22. Dorothy Schneider and Carl Schneider, *American Women in the Progressive Era: 1900–1920* (New York: Facts in File, 1993), 246.

2

The Times and the Context

THE SIX NURSES DEPICTED IN this book practiced in Alaska from the early 1900s through the 1940s, primarily during the 1920s and 1930s. It is important to place their presence within the larger context of Alaska, its people and politics.

The population served by these nurses was predominantly Alaska Native. Gertrude Fergus and Alma Carlson cared for both the Inupiat- and Yup'ik-speaking Eskimos. Stella Fuller served various indigenous groups in a large territory encompassing the Kenai Peninsula, the Aleutians, and the Alaska Peninsula. Augusta Mueller worked in the northern Eskimo, Inupiat village of Barrow. Mildred Keaton served the Aleuts, Eskimos, interior Alaska Indians, and the Indians of the south-coastal panhandle during her long career (1922–1972).

The two main Eskimo groups, Inupiat and Yup'ik, had been nomadic and enduring for millennia, learning to live with limited food supplies and environmental extremes. The Aleuts, related to the Yup'ik although less nomadic, were distinctive for their remarkable maritime adaptation to the islands of the Aleutians.[1] The tribal subunits of Athabascan-speaking Indians were widely scattered throughout the Alaska interior. They were nomadic within that region with cultural characteristics very different from Eskimos. The

Indians of southeast Alaska, the northernmost group of the Northwest Coast culture, the Tlingit and Haida, were well known for highly stratified social groups and the quality of their artwork. Alaska Native culture changed slowly through the centuries, but contact with Europeans dramatically altered the Alaska Native way of life.

Geographically, Alaska appeared on the larger world scene in 1741 with its discovery by Vitus Bering, a Dane and member of the Russian navy. For the next 126 years, Russian influence was felt in varying degrees. Russians were mostly interested in fur trade.[2] The Russian penetration of the Aleutian Islands followed a pattern of making slaves of the Aleuts and exploiting the islands until the fur supply was exhausted.[3] The year 1799 was pivotal in Alaska history when the czar's government began to manage Alaska as a commercial concession chartered to the Russian American Company. For the next sixty years, Russian groups attempted to establish a significant presence in Alaska. They were met with strong resistance from Tlingits, and although they were able to establish a foothold in Sitka they were never able to

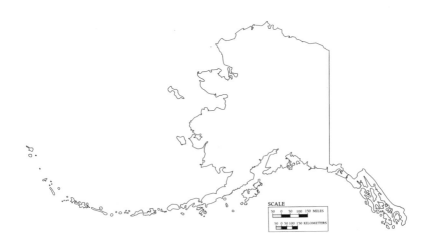

SCALE
50   0   50   100   150 MILES
50   0   50 100 150 KILOMETERS

exercise control over other Tlingit and Haida villages. Russian trading expanded up the coast of western Alaska but over time foreign competitors severely restricted the Russian expansion. The entire Russian-American venture became a financial burden.[4]

In 1867, the United States purchased Russian America.[5] After the American flag was raised at Sitka in October 1867, the few health services that had been established for Alaska Natives deteriorated. The Russian hospitals at Sitka and Kodiak were closed. For more than ten years the only medical help available was from the military physicians headquartered at Sitka.[6]

From 1867 to 1884, Alaska had no civil government and was under the military jurisdiction of the army and then the navy. The Alaska outpost was manned by a rugged breed of soldier who contributed to the difficulties of the Native groups. Results of the military presence included teaching the Tlingit how to make homebrew or "hootchinoo." In the villages of Kake and Angoon, villagers who sought to rectify any injustices were shown a display of military might and their houses were shelled, destroying canoes and provisions.[7]

After the American purchase, a few whites began filtering into Alaska as prospectors, storekeepers, prospectors, and whalers.[8] The Bureau of Indian Affairs, which usually oversaw affairs related to aboriginal people, refused to serve Alaska primarily because of scarce resources, negative publicity, and lack of reservation status for Alaska Natives. Beginning in the late 1870s, the surgeons of the U.S. Navy and Revenue Marine Service ships began to provide intermittent services to the Alaska Natives in the more distant coastal areas of the territory.[9]

In the far north, the Inupiat had already been exposed to Yankee whalers.[10] Whalers had a dramatic impact on life in the Bering Straits region. In the winter of 1878–1879, the destruction of the bowhead whale and walrus by whalers, combined with bad weather, led to starvation among St. Lawrence Islanders. In the shadow of the whalers came traders, bringing a variety of food and manufactured items, including flour, sugar, coffee, tobacco, sewing needles, guns, and alcohol as well as epidemics.[11]

Increased coastal exploration and whaling also attracted other people such as missionaries and schoolteachers.[12] These individuals had a vision of establishing missionary-educators in villages to carry out the Christianization and education of Alaska Natives. The focus on education was consistent with policies toward American Indians developing in the rest of the country. When it became evident that religion would not solve what they viewed as the Indian problem, education became the solution.[13]

Education services were authorized as early as 1887 by Sheldon Jackson, the first general agent.[14] He negotiated an agreement among all the mission boards in Alaska to divide the territory into districts and to accept responsibility for specific areas. The Office of Education gave the first impetus to provide medical service to the Natives of Alaska. Beginning in the 1890s, several of the mission groups initiated regular medical services in remote areas of Alaska when medical missionaries took up residence and established small hospitals in some of the larger Native communities.[15]

With the discovery of gold in the Klondike came a new global discovery of Alaska. Fortune hunters flocked from all parts of the world to one of the greatest of gold rushes. As the gateway to the Klondike, Alaska prospered. New towns and businesses sprang up to meet the needs of men going to the gold fields. Miners exploring in search of new gold sources beyond the Klondike advanced the opening of Alaska's gold fields.[16]

Alaska experienced its own gold rush on the Seward Peninsula in 1899. By October the rush was on and more than three thousand prospectors were working at Nome.[17] By the summer of 1900 Nome was a tent city with more than twenty thousand men working its golden sands.[18] Across the Seward Peninsula, town after town followed the discovery of gold: Candle, Council, Deering, and Bluff. What once had been a wilderness frontier was now interspersed with small communities. Nome's boom was accompanied and followed by gold strikes in different parts of Alaska: the Kenai Peninsula, Wiseman, Iditarod, and the Tanana Valley. For the Alaska Natives, the inability to stake mining claims clarified their vulnerable, second-class status under U.S. laws. This led to a strong determination on their part to obtain citizenship so they could obtain and protect property rights.[19]

The gold rush era closed just before World War I. As a result of the rush, the population doubled and was dispersed broadly throughout the land. Trails interspersed with roadhouses took travelers from Valdez to Fairbanks, from Seward to Iditarod and Nome. Telegraph links informed villages. Gold left a legacy of transformation. Miners, traders, and others had blazed trails, founded settlements, and forged economic ties with the rest of the country.[20] None of the Alaska Native groups were able to escape the ravages of disease. The Alaska Native population declined to its lowest point in 1910 when the census recorded 25,331 persons.[21] Yet that census recorded the largest population in Alaska history to date, 64,356, even though the excitement of the gold rush was over. People could find work at mining camps, at canneries, or on public construction projects.[22]

Congressional interest in Alaska had also grown with the gold rush.[23] In 1912, Congress passed the Second Organic Act, creating a territorial government. Congress simply delegated power over certain local matters to the territorial legislature, which could pass laws affecting sanitation, quarantine, public health, supervision of banks, registration of vital statistics, school attendance, relief of the destitute, and the general welfare of the citizens of Alaska.[24]

However, strong restrictions were placed on self-government. Control of Alaska resources, including land minerals and fisheries, all remained in federal hands. Matters relating to divorce, gambling, the sale of liquor, and incorporation of towns were exclusively the province of Congress. The territory was not permitted to borrow money, and its taxing authority was restricted to one percent of the assessed value of property. However, as limited as it was, the act of 1912 signaled the potential of Alaska as a future state.[25]

Relative political calm followed the passing of the act. Women were enfranchised; provision was made for the aged and indigent pioneers with the establishment of a Pioneers' Home at Sitka for males and a pension scheme for females.[26] Native villages in southeastern Alaska were given some rights of self-government and provisions were made to extend the rights of citizenship to Indians.[27] Education received much attention, and a territorial board was formed to coordinate the school system, although these were not schools for Native children. The territorial policies perpetuated segregation in schools.[28]

In 1913, the territorial governor was named as the commissioner of health. Laws spelled out the duties of the commissioner and his deputies and provided for the organization of boards of health in the various school districts of the territory. In 1915, the United States Bureau of Education was officially given the responsibility for health care of Alaska Natives. The bureau had already been providing medical care funded from the school budget and had also founded several hospitals.

The first federal hospital for treatment of Alaska Natives was constructed in Juneau in 1916 and signaled a new era of federal responsibility. During World War I there were few services and fewer practitioners providing care. When the worldwide influenza epidemic hit Alaska in 1918, only ten physicians were assigned by the Public Health Service.[29] To combat the killing disease, several villages on the Seward Peninsula posted guards to prevent anyone from entering their boundaries.[30]

As further evidence of a declining population and declining services, the 1920 census recorded only 55,036 citizens. The drop in population was very disconcerting to Alaskans.[31] World War I is regarded as the chief factor because men left for army enlistment. Other factors were higher wages elsewhere and a sharp drop in the demand for Alaska copper and salmon.[32] Mining towns decreased in size while shipping towns increased. The decline in population was mainly among single white men and the foreign-born. The native-born as well as females, both stable elements of population, were increasing. The number of homesteads tripled between 1915 and 1925. Alaska saw the final vestige of boom days and settled down to a slow, steady, permanent growth.[33] While the 1920s were lusty, expansive, and confident years in the rest of the country, Alaska was experiencing relative stability for the first time even though authors such as Ernest Gruening labeled the period the "twilit twenties."[34]

Transportation was a key factor in Alaska's development. Watercraft of all kinds moved people and supplies into remote areas for exploration. Navigable water defined the limits for development before to overland transportation and air travel. Water routes also provided a way of serving medical needs, since a major portion of the population lived near water.[35] The greatest boon to Alaska transportation was the government railroad. President Woodrow Wilson authorized the first railroad commission in 1912. Wilson directed the line to run from Seward to Fairbanks. Construction difficulties were formidable and the project was not completed until 1923.[36]

The important role of transportation in Alaska is illustrated by the serum run to Nome during the winter of 1925. Diphtheria was suspected and the community urgently requested antitoxin to combat the disease. In response, serum was rushed from Seattle to Nome: by ship from Seattle to Seward, aboard the Alaska Railroad from Seward to Nenana, and by dog teams from Nenana to Nome. Twenty mushers and their dog teams relayed the serum the 674 miles between Nenana and Nome in 127.5 hours.[37]

Following World War I, the American Red Cross augmented its Rural Health Program by sending nurses to work along the Alaska Railroad corridor and on the Aleutian Chain. The decision by the Red Cross to establish a countrywide program for public health was based on the opportunity to use its organization and the interest and enthusiasm generated by many men and women enrolled in its war work programs. Along the railroad corridor, some communities organized American Red Cross chapters to train people in emergency first aid, to provide home nursing care, and to distribute information on nutrition and illness prevention.[38]

The expansion of airplane travel and the telegraph increased the ability to provide health service more efficiently. The decades of the 1920s and 1930s were critical in the emergence of the airplane as the transportation of choice for the territory, which is more than twice the area of Texas. Airplane travel over the vast distances between Alaska communities became possible.[39]

Just as Alaska had not shared in the American prosperity of the 1920s, it suffered less from the trauma of the 1930s, although it wasn't entirely unaffected by the Depression. Mining employment declined and the value of fish fell with the overall drop in commodity prices. Several actions of the Roosevelt administration were helpful to the territory. The price of gold was raised and there was a steady industrial recovery without great upheavals. The Public Works Administration sponsored a variety of projects, and a number of public buildings and bridges were constructed. Certainly the Matanuska Colony resettlement project, designed to move rural populations away from areas of poverty and into a new location of potential productivity, was considered a success.[40] [see Figure 2.1].

The Indian Reorganization Act of 1934 represented a dramatic shift in American Indian policy. This act clearly recognized the legitimacy of Indian self-determination. The act enabled several Native communities to incorporate and to

2.1. Madeline de Foras, Red Cross Nurse at the Matanuska Colony. She accompanied the colonists on their sea voyage north in 1935 and assisted with their health care during their first months as colonists. Reprinted, with permission, from the Alaska Nurses' Association Collection (78-27-03N), Elmer E. Rasmuson Library, University of Alaska Fairbanks.

draw up constitutions for self-government. Yet overall the effect of the New Deal on Alaska was not profound.[41]

In 1931, the Bureau of Education at last gave up its irregular position of providing medical care to the Alaska Natives. Despite the fact that appropriations for medical services had increased over fivefold since 1918, the bureau had made few visible gains in the health field. In March of 1931, medical functions of the Bureau of Education were turned over to the Alaska Native Service (ANS), the Alaska Office of the Bureau of Indian Affairs.[42]

Little change in policies, staffing, and facilities was immediately noticeable, largely because annual health expenditures remained low.[43] Yet, under the Alaska Native Service several facilities were newly built or remodeled. By 1936 there were six hospitals, ten doctors, and twenty field nurses for thirty thousand Native residents as compared to fifty doctors and twelve hospitals for thirty thousand white residents.[44] The severity of health conditions among the Alaska Natives was demonstrated by a survey of mortality published in 1934.[45]

The impetus provided to the territory by the Social Security Act of 1935 did little to improve the health of Alaska Natives. Almost all of the services were directed toward the Caucasian population. During the 1920s through the 1940s, a variety of approaches were used to accomplish rural health care delivery. From 1926 to 1935, the *Martha Angeline*, a floating clinic, served the Native villages along the Yukon from its home port of Nenana to Kotlik. In the 1940s the MS *Hygiene* traveled throughout southeast Alaska.[46]

Alaska was profoundly changed by World War II, which broke out in September 1939. The war irrevocably altered the pace and tenor of Alaskan life. The modernization of the Alaska Railroad and the expansion of airfields and construction of roads benefited the civilian population as well as the war effort. Between 1940 and 1950 the civilian population increased from 74,000 to 112,000, another profound expansion in Alaska's history.[47]

Endnotes

1. Steve Langdon, *The Native People of Alaska*, 3rd ed. (Anchorage, AK: Greatland Graphics, 1993).
2. Claus-M. Naske and Herman Slotnik. *Alaska: A History of the Forty-ninth State* (Grand Rapids, MI: William Erdman's Publishing Co., 1979), 27.
3. Langdon, *Native People of Alaska*, 24.
4. Donald Craig Mitchell, *Sold American: The Story of Alaska Natives and Their Land, 1867–1959* (Hanover, NH: University Press of New England, 1997), 23.
5. Richard E. Welch, "Buying Alaska: The Myth of Icebergs in Interpreting Alaska's History," in *Interpreting Alaska's History: An Anthology*, edited by Mary Childers Mangusso and Steven W. Haycox (Anchorage, AK: Alaska Pacific University Press, 1989), 141–157.
6. Robert Fortuine, *Chills and Fever: Health and Disease in the Early History of Alaska* (Fairbanks, AK: University of Alaska Press, 1989).
7. Langdon, *Native People of Alaska*, 87.
8. Ibid.
9. Fortuine, *Chills and Fever*.
10. "North Slope Now," *Alaska Geographic* 16, no. 2: 43–55.
11. Langdon, *Native People of Alaska*, 88.
12. "North Slope Now," *Alaska Geographic 16*, no. 2: 47.
13. United States Commission on Human Rights. "A Historical Context for Evaluation," in *Native Americans and Public Policy*, edited by F. J. Lyden and L. H. Leggars (Pittsburgh: University of Pittsburgh Press, 1992).
14. Fortuine, *Chills and Fever*.
15. Ibid.
16. Naske and Slotnik, *Alaska: A History*, 71–76.
17. "The Golden Gamble," *Alaska Geographic* 24, no. 2.
18. "Alaska's Seward Peninsula," *Alaska Geographic* 14, no. 3.
19. Langdon, *Native People of Alaska*, 90.
20. "The Golden Gamble," *Alaska Geographic* 24, no. 2: 84.
21. Langdon, *Native People of Alaska*.
22. Joan M. Antonson and William S. Hanable, "Alaska's Heritage," in *Human History 1867 to Present*, Alaska Historical Commission, Studies in History, no. 13 [no pagination], Alaska Historical Society for the Alaska Historical Commission, Department of Education, State of Alaska.
23. Naske and Slotnik, *Alaska: A History*.
24. Clarence C. Hullery, *Alaska: Past and Present* (Portland, OR: Binford & Mort, 1958), 306.

25. Ibid., 307.
26. Ibid., 308.
27. Naske and Slotnik, *Alaska: A History.*
28. Ibid.
29. C. E. Albrecht, "Public Health in Alaska: United States Frontier," *American Journal of Public Health* 42, no. 6 (June 1952): 694–700.
30. Antonson and Hanable, "Alaska's Heritage."
31. Ernest Gruening, *The State of Alaska* (New York: Random House, 1968), 227.
32. Ernest Gruening, *State of Alaska* (New York: Random House, 1954), 20.
33. Henry Clark, *Alaska: The Last Frontier* (New York: Grosset & Dunlap, 1934), 182.
34. Gruening, *The State of Alaska,* 1968, 227.
35. Naske and Slotnik, *Alaska: A History.*
36. Clark, *Alaska: The Last Frontier,* 185.
37. Antonson and Hanable, "Alaska's Heritage."
38. A. Brainerd, *The Evolution of Public Health Nursing* (Philadelphia: Saunders, 1922).
39. Naske and Slotnik, *Alaska: A History.*
40. Ibid.
41. Kenneth Philip, "The Alaska I.R.A.," in *Interpreting Alaska's History: An Anthology* edited by Mary Childers Mangusso and Steven W. Haycox (Anchorage, AK: Alaska Pacific University Press, 1989), 358–377.
42. Elinor Gregg, "A Federal Nursing Service Above the Arctic Circle," *American Journal of Nursing* 36, no. 2: 128–136.
43. Robert Fortuine, "The Development of Modern Medicine in Southwest Alaska: The Growth of Health Services," *Alaska Medicine* (April 1971), 51–59.
44. Gregg, "A Federal Nursing Service," 128–136.
45. F. S. Fellows, "Mortality in the Races of the Territory of Alaska: With Special Reference to Tuberculosis," *Public Health Reports* 49: 289–298.
46. C. Smulling, "Hygiene: Alaska's Floating Health Unit," *Public Health Nursing* 39 (May 1947): 258–261.
47. Naske and Slotnik, *Alaska: A History.*

3

We Saved Some Lives:
Lula Welch

Hospital Nurse, Mining Camps, Seward Peninsula, 1907–1918

LULA JAMES, THE ELDEST of four girls and one boy, was born in Jeffersonville, Indiana, to parents Plez and Anna Bell James (ca. 1874).[1] When she was eight years old the family moved to Anaheim, California, where her father opened the first bank in Anaheim. At age twelve she was enrolled at Irving Institute, a private school for girls in San Francisco, graduating in 1892.[2] Here she made contacts that opened up possibilities for an acting and stage career. Lula James spent time in Chicago and Los Angeles playing Shakespearean roles.[3]

Forsaking an acting career, Lula entered nurses' training at Los Angeles County Hospital. There she met Curtis Welch,[4] a Yale medical school graduate completing his internship.[5] Upon graduating from nurses' training, Lula married Curtis. They eventually opened a hospital in Oakland, California, working side by side until the 1905 San Francisco earthquake.[6] In Los Angeles, quite by accident, Curtis Welch met a Dr. Anton who wanted to give up his practice at a mining camp hospital in Council, Alaska. In 1907 the population of Council was around 600 in the summer and about half that in the winter.[7]

Dr. Anton conveyed his enthusiasm for Council to the Welches. They paid him one thousand dollars for the practice and sailed from Seattle to Nome on the *Victoria* on July 1, 1907.[8] After eight years, the Welches moved from Council to Candle to operate Fairhaven Hospital. They remained in Candle until the United States became embroiled in World War I. Curtis Welch wanted to join the Medical Corps but had to find a replacement for his practice first. A replacement was found and the Welches arrived in Seattle at the height of the 1918 influenza epidemic. Despite all his efforts to report at Fort Dix for Army service, the Armistice was signed before Dr. Welch got into uniform.

They returned to Alaska in the spring of 1919 for ten more years. Lula assisted her husband as office nurse and anesthetist. The Welches had the opportunity to see the first airplane land in Nome in August of 1920, to meet Roald Amundsen and his crew,[9] and to help in the famous diphtheria epidemic that hit Nome in 1925.[10]

In July 1926, the Welches were present for the christening of the *Martha Angeline*.[11] They surveyed the health conditions of Natives along the Yukon River for the chief of the Alaska Division of the U.S. Bureau of Education. After one summer aboard the *Martha Angeline* they returned to Nome for two years. They retired in Santa Barbara, California, where Dr. Welch died in 1945.

Lula Welch moved into Wood Glen Retirement Center in 1958.[12] Her activities included studying Shakespeare's writings and playing bridge. Wood Glen residents said, "The thing we all love about her is her interesting conversations and her truly genuine interest in her fellow human beings."[13] Responding to the Alaska Nurses Association request in 1956, Lula Welch sent her memoirs of Council and Candle from 1907 to 1918.

Memoirs by Lula Welch
(1956)

Council, Alaska, 1907–1916

DURING THE SAN FRANCISCO earthquake, Dr. Welch and I were running a small hospital in Oakland. Immediately after the quake we were swamped with refugee patients. Our lease was up the last of the year and as property became infinitely more valuable the rent went up, so we sold out and closed up the hospital. We heard of a mining contract in Council, 80 miles from Nome, that was for sale, and since we were footloose we decided to try it for a year, or at the most for two years, and sailed from Seattle on June 1, 1907. We were the greenest cheechakos I am sure that ever arrived at a mining camp. We had a long trip by boat to Chinic and up the Neukluk River by scow, hauled by a temperamental engine, and then with horses on the bank towing us. We almost froze—we were not dressed properly, and if there hadn't been a lot of old sourdoughs aboard who

3.1. Lula Welch. Reprinted with permission from Metcalf Collection (#91-013-188), Archives, Elmer E. Rasmuson Library, University of Alaska Fairbanks.

loaned us fur robes and woolen socks to pull on over our shoes, we would really have suffered.

The practice we had bought consisted of a drug store filled with every drug imaginable left by the first doctors who had come and gone, and we had as a partner a very proper and stilted Englishman whom, in the nine years we were there, we learned to love.

The so-called hospital consisted of a three-bed ward upstairs and a bedroom for us. Dr. R. slept in an alcove off the office downstairs. Back of this was the kitchen. When we bought this, we were told we would have a cook who would go over with us from Nome, but she proved to be otherwise engaged so I was elected to cook. I knew very little about cooking and had opened few tin cans. The kitchen had a very small stove; wood was piled alongside of it. There was a table and some chairs and a barrel in the corner for water. One window was very small and the dark paper on the wall hung in shreds. When I looked at this I burst into tears. It seemed impossible but here again the sourdoughs came to our rescue. They cut another window on the other side of the kitchen, papered it, and we bought a new stove. There were about 500

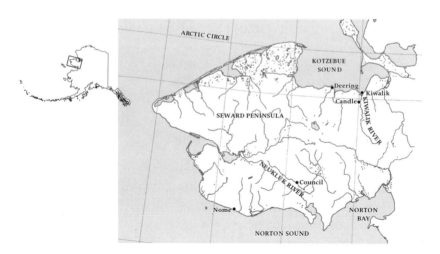

miners distributed along Ophir Creek, all the miners paying for doctor and hospital insurance. At the freeze-up, mining is discontinued and most of the men leave camp and come back in the spring. Dog teams were our only means of travel from the freeze until the middle of June. During the summer we had no serious cases, only some broken bones and minor injuries, so I really had little nursing to do. The government sent in medicines for the Eskimos, and the doctors cared for them gratis. Most of them had TB and they were always shooting themselves or each other accidentally. I had several obstetrical cases. I went to their cabins and took care of them for at least a week of twenty-four-hour duty. All the cases we had there were normal. Once in the middle of the winter we were called to a Mrs. B.'s who was in labor. We had only coal-oil lamps and the husband came in to hold one so the doctor could see what he was doing. Mr. B. promptly fainted. Down he went on the floor, lamp and all. I grabbed the blanket and got the lamp out and then had to get a flashlight and put aside the anesthetic I was giving her for her last few hard pains.

Since we burned only wood in Council, [see Figure 3.2] it was a task keeping fires going. In another case, when the doctor had been called out on a trip [see Figure 3.3] to see a patient, he decided to stay all night since it was storming badly and 20 below zero. A neighbor came for me to see a woman who was having a miscarriage. When I got there she was in labor and crying, and her little girl who was two years old was screaming. Since the wind was blowing a gale, the stove was red hot—I kept the man who came for me to attend the stove—she finally delivered a four months dead fetus. The wind was so bad we could not keep the stove under control. I stayed the night with her until her husband returned in the morning. We cremated the fetus in the stove. The woman recovered without incident.

One morning an Eskimo child came in and asked me to go to see her mother. Her mother was married to a white man. Eskimos never ask for help in childbirth unless something is very wrong. When I got there the woman was on the floor and an old Eskimo medicine man was holding her head up by the hair. I told him to help me get her on the bed, and when we went to lift her up found the baby on the floor, too. As soon as I got her on the bed I sent the girl for the doctor. I cut the cord and tied it and one of the other children took the baby by the fire. Then I saw a strange thing. At first I thought it was the placenta and tried to deliver it but it was the uterus with an hour-glass contraction. When the doctor got there we put hot cloths on and finally got it up into place and then the placenta was delivered. She was exhausted and I stayed with her the rest of the day. All she wanted to eat was some frozen tom cod, but I finally got some soup and some milk down and she was up and around in a few days. Finally, the government gave us the job of teaching and care of the Eskimos. I visited them every few days and tried to teach them something of cleanliness and sanitation but it was uphill work.

Another time a white man phoned from Chinic, fifty miles away, that an Eskimo woman had shot herself in the foot. It was very much swollen and she was suffering a good deal. He was sending her up by dog team. I put on my little Arnold sterilizer[14] with dressings and a gown and towels in case we had to amputate. Then we wondered where we would do it. Finally, the grocer next door, who had a large store, said, "why not do it in the store?" So we carried a table over and I had everything prepared when she got there. Bowls of disinfectant and sterile water were set up. I was giving the anesthetic—it must necessarily be chloroform[15] since we had to use coal-oil lamps—I had my table ready and the doctors' instruments boiled, and the commissioner asked if he might look on since he had never seen an operation. We said yes, of course. And we told him to stand back of me. Just as the doctor made the first incision the man fainted and fell against me, knocked everything on the floor. I kept my patient slightly anesthetized until the instruments were boiled again and some men righted things, but since the patient had been three or four days in a bad condition, she died the next day.

In the winter of 1915, one dark and stormy night a man's voice said, "I'm bringing T. S. to the doctor. He is suffering terribly with pains in the belly." That might mean a number of things so we had to wait until he came to make a diagnosis. It wasn't hard—he had a strangulated hernia. While he was on the way up, I did the best I could to prepare something in case of operation: put on my little Arnold sterilizer, and needles and knives in alcohol, and got other instruments ready to boil. This winter we had moved into the big ward. Where to operate if we had to? Finally decided to move from our room so got several men to help. Took out our bed, dressing table, couch, chairs, and we moved into something of a storeroom. Dr. Welch operated on him and he recovered without incident. He is still living. I stayed on with him until morning and then went to bed, and one of the men in camp came over while I got some sleep. This happened on January 26. The patient left the hospital on February 26.

By this time pick-and-shovel mining was replaced by dredges. Then we had very few men on the payroll—not enough to support two doctors and a nurse. We had about decided to return to Oakland when a call came from Candle. The doctor there wanted to leave and the nurse was getting married, so we said we would go as soon as the breakup. We both hated to leave after nine years in Council. I even loved my Eskimo children and we had made deep friendships.

3.2. Town of Council. Reprinted with permission, from Anchorage Museum of History and Art (#B72.27.62), Anchorage, Alaska.

3.3. Curtis Welch, MD, with dogs in Council. Reprinted with permission from Metcalf Collection (#91-013-196), Archives, Elmer E. Rasmuson Library, University of Alaska Fairbanks.

Candle, Alaska, 1916–1918

I went first, since the nurse wanted to leave on the same boat that I went up on. The doctor there would stay a few weeks longer, so my husband could get our things together and see about shipping them. What a trip that was: by wagon forty miles to a roadhouse, and there I was met by a friend with a horse for me to ride the other forty miles. After a few days in Nome, I took a gasoline boat for Candle. There were five or six men aboard besides the captain and mate. The cook they had hired got drunk and didn't show up and neither did the supplies, so we went without them. All we had to eat for four days was some fried potatoes, chocolate bars, hardtack and tea. Our first meal was in Kiwalik at the mouth of the Kiwalik River. We took an outboard motor eight miles up to Candle. Candle was much like Council only more remote. The hospital was larger: a downstairs drug room and office, bedroom, living room and dining room and kitchen all together in one big room[16] (see Figure 3.4). A ward with three beds, a smaller room with two beds for women, and an operating room all heated with coal stoves and coal oil lamps were upstairs. The hospital was run by a board of directors and a manager. There were some two hundred people in the camp. Each family who wanted hospital insurance and doctors' care paid $4.50 a month. The doctor not only had to take care of these people but other camps within a radius of 150 miles. The nurse and doctor were paid $3,500 and food. An Eskimo was furnished for chores and when needed one to help in the kitchen. When I arrived there were no patients in the hospital so I had a chance to look things over. Here I had to learn to use coal, but after nine years I had learned to cook. Dr. Welch arrived after three weeks.

I had no real hard work until winter and then I learned what hard work was. As the days grew shorter and winter set in there were lamps to be filled, stoves to be kept going, supplies to lay in. When it really froze up we had a reindeer brought up into the cache and cut up. The hindquarters we cut into roasts, steaks, and chops. The forequarters I used for soup, and I kept a ten gallon kettle filled with broth for emergencies. Loaves of bread froze immediately. When the river froze up, men cut fifteen tons of ice in large chunks and piled it around the hospital for water during the winter. In the summer we had running water for three months. Every morning during the winter an Eskimo brought tubs of ice into the kitchen. There was a large fifty-gallon tank connected with the stove, usually filled with snow for hot water, and then there were three twenty-gallon tanks near the stove. I washed the ice with boiling water and put [it] into one tank for drinking. I piled the other two tanks full of ice to use for washing, etc.

My day began with getting breakfast, carrying trays up to my patients, then I attended to the water, and then patient care. If I was lucky, an Eskimo girl washed dishes. Of course, I had to cook three meals a day. The first winter I had three obstetrical cases. I always slept in the room with them and had to keep the stove going. I took the babies to bed with me to keep them warm the first twenty-four hours, then the mother took them to bed with her. We had twelve obstetrical cases while we were there. Most of the babies were born in the winter and it was often fifty below.

On March 25, 1917 in Candle—winter again—Mrs. R. who was in her seventh month of pregnancy came in with slight pains. It was stormy and she thought she would come in early in case she should come in with real labor in the night. We put her to bed with a sedative, hoping she would go on to term. The next night about 9 P.M., during a very bad storm and thirty below zero, Mr. Seppala brought in Mr. B., who had fallen into a buzz saw. He was in bad shape, one leg almost completely severed, the other broken in several places, ribs broken. His whole body was bruised and he probably had internal injuries. We had a telephone message that he was on the way, so I had time to get the operating room ready. We took him into the operating room after a hypo and some rest, amputated one leg above the knee, and since he was in bad shape we did what we could with the other one and got him to bed. I sent for Mrs. Evans[17] to stay with him, and I went to bed in Mrs. R.'s room, but not for long because her pains began again. She was in labor until the next afternoon by which time Mr. B. had developed what the doctor thought was perhaps a bad infection, I had to deliver her. She had a five pound baby, very thin and very weak, but still alive. I wrapped it into a rabbit's robe and blanket and warmed water bottles and took care of the mother, gave her

3.4. *Fairhaven Hospital in Candle. Reprinted with permission from Alaska Nurses Association Collection (#75-167-484N), Archives, Elmer E. Rasmuson Library, University of Alaska Fairbanks.*

a sedative, and dropped into bed and took the baby with me. When I awoke it was dead. Mr. B. died that night. On April 2, after Mr. R. had picked out the small grave through the ice and frozen ground, we took the little baby to the cemetery on the hill back of the hospital and buried it. He had made a little wooden coffin and under the direction of his wife and lined it with white satin. In those days we kept our obstetrical cases in bed from ten to fourteen days. Many times I was up most of the night with the babies. Some of the mothers couldn't nurse their babies and all I had to give them was Carnation milk but they all seemed to thrive on it and we lost none. When things quieted down and I had a week, maybe two without any patients, I got caught up with the washing and ironing. My washing machine was an old wooden one and I had to have an Eskimo turn the handle. I also got a chance to get some sleep.

My husband made regular monthly trips around to the surrounding camps by dog team in winter, by boat and horseback in summer. In the spring of 1917 he had left on his first summer trip. Not long after he had gone, two men came in carrying a woman whom they said they had found on the floor of her cabin. She was in her eighth month of pregnancy. Her husband had gone out the night before to his camp and asked a neighbor to look in on his wife in the morning. She evidently had had many convulsions—her mouth was very much swollen where she had bitten her lips. The first I did was to try to get hold of the doctor. I caught him at Deering and he started back to Candle. I put my patient to bed, of course. She had several more convulsions before the doctor got there. I had sent for Mrs. Evans and got the operating room ready, and when the doctor got there he delivered her as quickly as possible of a dead fetus. She remained unconscious for two days, and one morning when I thought she was dying she opened her eyes and recognized her husband.

But she did not regain complete memory for weeks. She stayed with me from June 23 until July 16.

One night during the next winter an Eskimo man came in with another Eskimo who had shot himself in the elbow. His arm was swollen to three times its size, and he had been on the trail three days. They had put a tourniquet on his arm above the elbow but never loosened it. His arm was gangrenous and the doctor amputated it just below the elbow. Last time I saw him he was carrying a gun again.

In the three years we were in Candle our only deaths, besides Mr. B., were violent ones. One man who cut his throat was alive but almost ex-sanguinated. If we could have given him blood transfusions we could have saved him, but maybe it was just as well since he had already shot himself twice.

It would seem as if most of my nursing consisted of housework, washing and ironing and cooking and cleaning, but it was always twenty-dour-hour-duty. Even nursing was hard on account of scarcity of water in winter, no bathtubs, and no modern devices to help us with the work. Of course, we had no X-rays. I wonder how we got on with no blood transfusions, no antibiotics, and only a small sterilizer. But it was a great satisfaction to think we did and that we saved some lives and made those who suffered comfortable.

We were in Alaska for twenty-three years, and I gave all of my husband's anesthetics, chloroform necessarily because of the inflammability of ether.

We were in Candle during the war and my husband was very anxious to get into the service. He tried for a year to find a doctor to take his place. Most of the young men were already in the service, and the older doctors taking their place, but at last one was available. He came up in July 1918, and we left for Nome. We borrowed an outboard motor to go to Kiwalik from a friend who owned a store there, which he kept opened in summer only, and told us to stay there until our boat came. During the evening a storm came up. We were afraid the boat would be damaged so we went to pull it on the beach. After a long and hard struggle we got its nose up on the beach, went into the store and into bed. All of a sudden the house began to shake, everything that was loose in the room rolled on the floor, and we both sat up and said, "Earthquake!" There was no one anywhere near us and we spent another miserable twenty-four hours waiting for the boat to come. We left Nome on September 28 and got to Seattle October 4, into the awful flu epidemic. We left for New Haven on October 11. Dr. Welch got into the army after his physical examination, ordered his uniform, and was told that he would be sent to Fort Dix. Peace was declared November 7, armistice signed on November 11, and so we were footloose again, but not for long. We had a wire asking us to come back to Nome since the doctor who was leaving had nearly died of the flu, so back we went in the spring of 1919 for ten years.[18] There were no planes then.

Endnotes

1. In a 1956 letter to Kitty Gair, Lula Welch writes that she is eighty-two years old.

2. M. R. Kennedy, "Northland Doctor's Wife," series of eleven articles May 1965–May 1966, *Alaska Sportsman* (May 1965): 19.

3. *Wood Glen News,* no. 13 (October 24, 1962), Metcalf Collection, Lula Welch File, Archives, Elmer E. Rasmuson Library, University of Alaska Fairbanks, Fairbanks.

4. Ibid.

5. Kennedy (May 1965): 19.

6. *Wood Glen News.*

7. Ibid.

8. Kennedy (May 1965): 19.

9. Kennedy (February 1966): 34.

10. K. A. Ungermann, *The Race to Nome:the story of the heroic Alaskan dog teams that rushed diphtheria serum to stricken Nome in 1925.* (New York: Harper and Row, 1963).

11. Kennedy (May 1966): 18.

12. At the time of the Kennedy interview for the subsequent series of articles in 1965–1966, Lula was 90 years old.

13. Ibid.

14. An Arnold sterilizer was a small live steam sterilizer that could be used on a regular stove, shown and described in G. J. Sanders, *Modern Methods in Nursing,* 2nd ed. (New York: W. B. Saunders, 1922), 456.

15. Chloroform was safer with an open flame. The alternative, ether, had flammable properties although there was a wider margin of clinical safety.

16. Almer Rydeen noted in a letter to Catherine Gair (5 April 1956) that the Candle Hospital, named Fairhaven, was built in 1906 at the cost of somewhat over $3,000, with funds collected by two miners who went door to door. When the collected funds ran out, people contributed some of their own furnishings. The first doctor was paid room and board and $2,000 a year. Single miners paid $2.50 and married ones $4.00 a month for medical and hospital care. Rydeen noted that they rarely had a graduate nurse on staff; they didn't have the funds and nurses were not available. He remembered Lula Welch, whom he called "Mrs. Dr. Welch." The hospital survived for almost twenty years (Alaska Nurses Association Collection, Hospitals File, Box 17, Archives, Elmer E. Rasmuson Library, University of Alaska Fairbanks, Fairbanks).

17. Mrs. Evans, a nurse who was leaving to be married when the Welches arrived. She helped when extra help was needed. (Lula Welch to Catherine Gair, letter 8 April 1956, Alaska Nurses Association Collection, Catherine Gair File 1955–1956, Folder 720, Box 35, Series 14-1, Archives, Elmer E. Rasmuson Library, University of Alaska Fairbanks, Fairbanks).

18. Kennedy (March 1966, May 1966); Ungerman, *Race to Nome,* 96–97, 100.

We had More Fun
Than Enough:
Augusta Mueller

Missionary Nurse, Presbyterian Hospital, Barrow, 1922–1926

CONTRASTING WITH THE REMINISCENT tone of Lula Welch's memoirs is the day-to-day reporting in a series of letters written by Augusta (Gussie) Mueller, missionary nurse in Barrow. She wrote these between 1922 and 1926 to her family in New York state and to an older nurse friend, Miss Knust. Her letters, colored with a variety of colloquialisms, show that Gussie did not allow the opportunity for new experiences to escape her. Only half of her letters are presented here, mainly those that describe her nursing practice.[1]

Augusta Mueller was born in the Bronx, New York, on July 15, 1899, the daughter of Louis and Elizabeth Mueller.[2] In 1920, she graduated from the School of Nursing of the Metropolitan Hospital, Welfare Island, New York.[3] In her writing, Gussie referred to this very large institution as "the Met." In Barrow, Gussie was known as a nurse from New York "who could give anesthetics."[4]

The village of Barrow is the most northerly in Alaska and the most northerly inhabited point on the American continent. In 1920, Barrow had a population of 354 (346 Natives and eight whites).[5] Letter mail arrived four times a year and parcel post once a year. In winter the sun is not seen for two months, and in summer the sun does not leave the sky for two months.[6]

The Presbyterian Mission was established in Barrow in 1890.[7] The hospital was built in 1921 in advance of the arrival of Dr. Henry Greist, a medical missionary; his wife Mollie, a nurse; and their son, David. Also arriving at the same time was the chief nurse, Florence Dakin.[8] Augusta Mueller refers to these people frequently in her letters.

The church along with the parsonage were the most conspicuous buildings; the schoolhouse adjoined the teacher's residence. Scattered about were Native dwellings and a few frame houses. About a half-mile away were the warehouses and store buildings of Charlie Brower's establishment and more Native sod and driftwood dwellings, called igloos. Charlie Brower was the oldest and most influential white resident in Barrow, having arrived there in 1884.[9]

Augusta Mueller's work as a missionary nurse included many church-related activities. In addition she participated in the Barrow community. She spoke some Eskimo, could find her way around the village in a snowstorm, visited Native homes, owned and used a kayak, learned to use a shotgun, and carried babies inside her garments Native-style.

4.1. Augusta Mueller at Barrow. Reprinted with permission from Russel and Lesley Cramer Collection (#94-02-068), Inupiat History, Language and Culture Commission, Barrow, Alaska.

After leaving Barrow in 1926, she returned to the New
York city area for the remainder of her life. In a 1956 letter
to Catherine Gair, Gussie wrote that she was busy with "my
job, church work, a six-room house in Bayside and a cottage
with a half acre of land sixty-five miles out on the island."[10]
In 1963 she wrote that she had retired after forty years of
nursing: "institutional, Barrow, office, Public Health, and in
Employee Relations of Industry."[11] The same year that she
retired, she revisited Barrow, having kept in touch with her
Alaska acquaintances.[12] She died in January 1968.

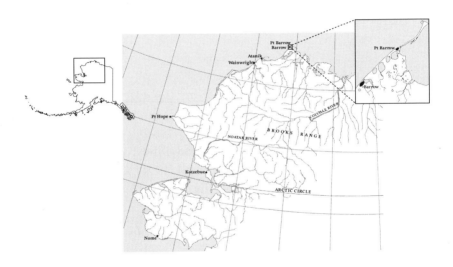

Letters written by Augusta (Gussie) Mueller, 1922–1926

Barrow, Alaska
August 21, 1922

Dear Folks:

We tied up to the ice at 11:50 this morning and about 4 P.M. some Natives came aboard. The village is six miles out. They said there was a "lead" ten miles up the coast that we could get in by launch but when the *Bear*[13] [Figure 4.2] got up there it had closed in, so we're headed back for the ice wharf. Had a lot of fun out on the ice this morning as soon as we tied up.

Great high drifts of ice and snow and almost froze to death. The ice is beautiful, though, and the sun is just wonderful, shining on it. Captain is quite proud. He's the first ship up this far this year. I'm mighty glad I'm here all right.

August 23

Surely wish I could be home to tell you how I got here from the *Bear*. When the *Bear* got back to a good place that she could tie up to at about 9 P.M., the Natives said they'd go back and try to get dog teams through. Since I wanted to get to the hospital as soon as possible, I trotted along.

I put on my knickers and took my parka, a stick, and heavy gloves. I'll say we went some. Left the ship at 10:30 and we went steady, except for three five-minute rests to get drinks, until 3:30 A.M. Jim[14] said we went at least twelve miles. It was up hill and down, jumping over cracks in the ice and going twice as far to get where the ice would hold.

By 1:30 my legs were beginning to give out and we were just in sight of the beach. I'd shed my parka almost as soon as we started. It was lots of fun, though, and the way we got a drink was to lie flat on the snow near a pool of snow water, crack the top crust of ice and just suck up the water. It's the best tasting water and was cold. I was so hot when I lay down the heat of my body melted the ice and I was sopping wet, and when I got up it froze.

When we were near enough to see the buildings [see Figure 4.3] and boat, the cracks got wider and I was so stiff and sore, but I had to jump or swim, so I jumped. We also had to wade through water that had ice at the bottom. There are easier things to do. We went the last half mile in boats and had a five-minute walk. I could hardly navigate.

The next day the ice broke enough for the *Bear* and the *Herman* to get in. They got all the mail off and my baggage and Dr. Greist's supplies, and then the ice started to close in again so we haven't seen another ship. All the hospital grub and supplies are on the *Holmes* so we're on plain fare till it gets in. Have plenty of well cooked food, though.

August 24

Today I've been fixing up my room; some job. Have it mostly done now and I feel quite happy. My stiffness is going, too. We have a cook from the *Herman* with possible appendicitis, a Native from Wainwright with pleurisy, a Native baby—a dear little fellow—with pneumonia, and three other kids. The Natives certainly are nice and I sure love the babies.

In the mail were a lot of missionary boxes and I never had so much fun as I did unpacking them. There was everything but the kitchen stove in them. Miss Dakin[15] had a lot of

4.2. The Bear. *This steam and sail powered ship is photo-graphed here east of Barrow at Demarcation Point in August 1921. Reprinted, with permission, the Anchorage Museum of History and Art (1381-164-16).*

4.3. Barrow, 1921. Reprinted from National Archives, Alaska Region, Anchorage, Alaska.

letters and packages of her own so I unpacked all the other boxes and listed the contents. We got a lot of soap, towels, wash cloths, dolls, toys, hospital supplies, games, pencils, and a million and one things.

September 5

We're sort of out of luck; the *Letty,* on her way to Banks Land, passed today—the ice has been open for two days now—and told the people at the station that the *Holmes* and *Fox* both unloaded at Wainwright and headed south two days ago. If we do get our food, as I guess we will, all the most important things will be frozen: the fruit, milk, potatoes, and almost all the canned goods. The staple foods will get up all right so we won't have to go hungry.

Anyone who says this hospital isn't needed ought to be here now: we have three babies with pneumonia; one boy, Patsy, with a high temperature—don't know just what the matter is; Susie from Wainwright with all sorts of aches; Phoebe, an old lady from Barrow, with I guess flu; two boys with TB [tuberculosis] knees from Wainwright. Whenever there are babies in the hospital their mothers have to stay with them or they yell their heads off, and since they don't understand English, it's better to keep the mothers with them. We're filled up, and then some.

September 9, 1922

Dear Miss Knust:

How are you and how did you get through the hot summer that I escaped? It's cold up here now; even the lagoon has frozen over. The boat with our food stuff unloaded at Wainwright, 120 miles away by dog team, because of the dangerous ice.

I'm as happy as a bug in a rug here in the hospital. Miss Dakin is as dear as she can be and I just love her. Dr. Greist could be much worse, although he is rather overbearing, but as long as Miss Dakin and I pull together things will run smoothly. We were some busy for a few days with three awfully sick pneumonia kiddies. They're all doing nicely now and we're so happy about them. Conditions are much better than you'd expect to find way off one thousand miles from the Pole. We have electric lights, a furnace that keeps the place real comfortable during the day, and plenty of bedding when night comes. We have a good Native janitor who keeps the cans full of ice so we have plenty of water, and we have a tank connected with the big kitchen range so we have hot water during the day. Helen,[16] a Native girl, does most of the cooking and the washing and ironing. We have an electric washer and mangle. We're rather low on food stuff but have plenty of reindeer meat and fish until they can bring the things up with dog sled this winter. Reindeer meat is sure good. Miss Dakin and I have separate rooms; then there are three two-bedded and one three-bedded rooms for Native patients and a single room if we should get a white patient, a big dispensary and nice operating room, big kitchen, dining room, and laundry. It's as cozy and comfortable as it can be [see Figure 4.4].

Miss Dakin has the Sunday School so I'm going to try to start a Junior Christian Endeavor. All teaching and things have to be interpreted to the majority of the people. Once I get them started I'll just have the leader for the week come over and I'll help with the topic. Now I've got to prepare the topic from some old Sunday School papers from 1920 and 1921 and have Lucy interpret for me. It's rather difficult but I suppose it will get easier.

So far I just love everything up here and the outlook is favorable to keep up liking everything, too. Please write whenever you have a chance. The letters will reach me eventually.

Heaps of love,
Gussie

October 1, 1922

Dear Folks,

It was some cold going over to church. I haven't my fur boots yet so my legs were rather chilly. It's about 20 above zero today, too, much warmer than it was this week. Dr. Greist said it was four below the other night. I don't lose a bit of time getting dressed in the morning either. Last night Dr. Greist brought a piece of rubber-like substance, it was black and, except for being gummy, it looked like coal. It is the oil that is found up here, pure petroleum. It's in regular lakes about thirty miles east. It burns like a candle. We put a big piece in the stove and it burned like coal and gave off quite a bit of heat, too. It's funny stuff.

Monday we saw the whale boats coming in with a whale. They were in single file [see Figure 4.5] and looked too pretty for words, the sails all the same, and the sky and ocean were beautiful, too. I made surgical supplies most of the day while Miss Dakin sewed for the kids. Needless to say, I'd rather do anything but sew. Prepared Susie for operation and in the evening printed pictures,[17] they turned out pretty good for

4.4. The Barrow Hospital in 1921. Reprinted, with permission, The Anchorage Museum of History and Art, Eide Album (1370-28-360).

a first attempt, but I need another printing frame. Miss Dakin has three; you can get so much more done with more than one frame.

Tuesday we started to get ready for the operation and then went over to the station to see the whale, but they'd only brought the whalebone in. It's awfully queer looking stuff, about five feet long and in layers. There are over five hundred bones in the head, I think Mr. Brower said. They're one next to the other and the hairy part is inside so the whale strains his food, or something like that. They look like big teeth, looking at the end of them.

Doctor operated on Susie; it took him two hours. I was some tired giving the anesthetic. She had quite an operation, is getting better, but surely had some pain for quite a while after she got out of the anesthetic. Mrs. Nichols[18] came over for a while in the afternoon, after everything was over. We were some tired [see Figure 4.6].

October 19, 1922

Dearest Miss Knust,

This morning the mercury touched zero. It went up to twelve by noon, but after sundown, about 4 P.M., it was two above zero again.

About 5:30 it was dark except in the southeast where the sky was all aglow still from the sunset. The north was white with northern lights and right above us, brighter than I've ever seen it, was the Big Dipper. You can't imagine how beautiful it all is and I can't possibly describe it. I just love it, though.

The hospital is light at present. We don't know for how long so are making the best of the opportunity to get letters written to go off on the November mail. Here's what I did today. Got up at 7:20. It's no joke to get up in a cold room with the temperature at zero. Finecombed Ralph's head before he

4.5. Whale boats in a single file as Mueller saw them. Reprinted with permission from Anchorage Museum of History and Art (#B70-28-305), Anchorage, Alaska.

4.6. Medical and school staff, 1922–1923, Barrow. L to R: Henry Greist, MD, Jim Nichols with Betty Nichols, Augusta Mueller, Mollie Greist with David Greist, Florence Dakin, and Helen Nichols. Reprinted by permission, Inupiat History, Language, and Culture Commission, Barrow, Alaska, Henry Greist Collection (#G215).

went to school (he's a TB knee case), had breakfast, washed a lot of bottles and cleaned up the dispensary in general until nine, took Anton's (our P.O. carcinoma of mesentery case) TPR and got him out of bed, let his bed air while I made my bed and straightened up my room, darned a pair of stockings (I do wear more holes than I can keep sewed up), made Anton's bed, and got Helen to wash up his room. Then just as I got ready to sit down and sew, one of the Native boys, Guy, came in with a toothache, and from then until lunch time I waited on Dr. Greist while he prepared two teeth for fillings. After lunch I made lemon pie and in the midst of that Dr. Greist came in with a lot of letters of instructions he'd gotten from the "Board" he wanted us to hear. I sat on pins and needles until my pie was ready to come out of the oven.

Tonight I went over and took notes for my Junior Christian Endeavor work Sunday. The children are getting very much interested in it and I have them take almost entire charge of the meeting. One reads or talks in English and one in Eskimo and whatever I say is translated into Eskimo. They love to sing hymns and have rather sweet voices.

Thank you for your prayers, we need them up here to have patience with these people who are still only children and need to be led to the Right. I love all my work up here and have not regretted for a minute that I came.

With all my love to you,
Gussie

Monday, November 6

I didn't feel very much like doing anything so took life easy all morning. In the afternoon whom should Mr. Brower bring over but the celebrated Captain Amundsen.[19] I told Miss Dakin her floor was highly honored because Mr. Brower had his own coat and Capt. Amundsen's ahtega,[20] and where did he put both of them, but on the floor. I stepped on them going over to the window. Imagine stepping on a celebrity's coat back in the States. He certainly is a jolly man and can talk. He wears a very dainty wrist watch and we started talking about the time. He said Mr. Brower was kidding him about his watch. He gave this one, as he said, all sufficient reason for his wearing a wrist watch. "I have to get up very early in the morning. It is the dark season and I am in a sleeping bag with all my heavy fur clothing on. I wake up, I wonder what time it is. I fish around, go through three or four layers of clothes and finally discover it is still three hours to rising time. Maybe another man could go to sleep in that time, but not me, I am wide awake after the exertion of finding out the time. If I have a wrist watch ..." then he just looked at it and yawned and shut his eyes. That was more expressive than any words could be.

Then he described how he'd started up here by reindeer team. He said they did everything but go, so after going four miles in an hour he decided to use dogs. He talks broken English, or rather has a strong Norwegian accent, but certainly is as nice as he can be.

He went all through the hospital with Miss Dakin and thought it was some hospital. We think so, too. He is going to Nome, starting out for Kotzebue Thursday and is going to stay there to get the correct time and be in communication with the States by wireless until May, when he is going to come up in his aeroplane. We white folks are all anxious to see the Natives on their first sight of a plane. He is going to make the lagoon his lighting place. Believe me, I'm going to save a film or two for some pictures. Just think of getting pictures of him and of his plane just before leaving for the Pole. I'm glad I'm here, all right.

I've written over seventy letters for this mail and am about written out. If some folks don't hear from me on the next mail then tell them I can't write without an inspiration of getting some letters and they don't get here until the next mail goes out. Send mail any time because it will get up here somehow. Until the latter part of August, from June, or rather May, there are boats going up to Nome and all the mail goes there and as far as Kotzebue. It stays at Kotzebue after the *Bear* leaves there until this mail that Ned is going after this week.

December 28, 1922, 5 A.M.

Dear Miss Knust,

I'm up taking care of a mighty sick pneumonia case. He's been quite a bit better since midnight but I didn't dare go to bed because he had been so restless.

I had the busiest, yet merriest, Christmas I ever remember having. Between sick patients and preparing for the church Christmas, Miss Dakin and I were all in, neither of us getting much sleep and both working as hard as we could. Saturday morning, I'd been up all night with Morgan, our sickest pneumonia case, and May, Luther's mother, who has taken some care of him since Morgan came in, decided to have a baby. At 5 A.M. I found out she was having pains and at 5:40 everything was over but the charting. A six-pound girl, whom we have named Carol. At present she surely does live up to her name, she carols continuously. I did everything but choke her tonight. I'd just get Morgan quieted when she'd yell, and she may be small, but, oh, what a pair of lungs. Luther is better, but so very weak. He's only two years old and ran a temperature of 105.4 for quite a few days. Morgan is four years old. He is a sweet boy but so very sick. Last night I stayed up, too. Kept the furnace going but that's some job, going down in the cold cellar p.r.n. (as needed) to fire the furnace. It's about twenty-six below zero. Tonight I have him in the kitchen and am keeping the doors closed and the range fire going. It makes it rather comfortable. Abel (Morgan's father) has been asleep on the floor since midnight. Both he and the youngster's mother have done all they could to help us take care of him. Usually, the Natives (whether through ignorance or just plain contrariness, I don't know) work against us when their children are sick, but Abel and Rachel have been just fine.

Friday, the 22nd, was the church entertainment. I didn't get to the entertainment but did get over for the gifts. Every Native received a package, a box of candy and peanuts and some popcorn. They were all as happy as they could be. Both Miss Dakin and I received a package with photographic paper and developing tablets from Mr. Hopson,[21] and oogaruk[22] soles. We don't know who the soles came from. Sunday the white folks were invited to the Nichols' for luncheon. Miss Dakin made me go and she stayed with Morgan. I'd hardly had any sleep but went over and had a dandy time until three o'clock when I had to go to Christian Endeavor. I could have let Roscoe manage alone but it was the Christmas topic and I do thoroughly enjoy my Christian Endeavor work, so I went over. Mrs. Nichols gave me a box of homemade candy and Miss Dakin two geese; these are some presents given up here.

Monday we had our hospital Christmas. The hospital is all decorated and there are four artificial trees. After the work was done Miss Dakin gave out the presents. Roscoe gave me two ivory needles he made; Helen, a pair of doll's fur pants; Miss Dakin, a basket for my crocheting, a calendar, three handkerchiefs, pins, and candy. At three o'clock, Morgan seemed well enough to leave with his father and mother; we went to the station. As tired as we were, we just had the best time and the best dinner. We had seven courses: soup and crackers, crab salad, baked fish, sauce and mashed potatoes, reindeer roast, baked ham, creamed onions, spinach, olives, sweet pickles and pickled beets, plum duff, three kinds of cake, three kinds of Jello, mince pie, vanilla and strawberry and pineapple ice cream, coffee, and wine or grape juice.

After supper, David Brower and Steve Hopson took turns playing the Victrola. Tommy Brower taught me to play pool and we played the rest of the evening. Mr. Brower gave Mrs. Greist, Mrs. Nichols, Miss Dakin, and me each a basket woven of whalebone. They are odd things and certainly are pretty. They were filled with awfully good candy, too. I don't know why he did it, but Tommy Brower gave me an exquisite pair of walrus tusk tips. They'll make wonderful handles for a carving set when I get home.

I'm beginning to get impatient for the mail. If Ned hurries he ought to be back in two weeks. If he doesn't he surely ought to be back in twenty days. I just think about it all the time, as much as I try not to. I wonder who is going to write, what, and why, and I do want to hear from home. My nephew is six months old already. I hope all these patients get better and we don't get any more in until the mail gets in and we get our letters read.

We expect the Cramers[23] up from Wainwright Friday or Saturday. Poor Lesley is the only white woman in Wainwright and her husband and Captain Amundsen's pilot are the only white men. Captain Amundsen was here one afternoon last month. We enjoyed his visit so much. He's in Nome now until May when he expects to fly up here from Wainwright and then start his trip across the pole. I am going to save some films for that event all right.

It's six o'clock. Certainly wish 7:30 would come. I'm tired enough to sleep on a picket fence.

Loads of love,
Gussie

February 4, 1923
Dearest Miss Knust;
Your letter of October 19 reached here January 14 but the other one and the card didn't arrive until the twenty-seventh.

Ned came with just a little of the mail. He had had a hard trip, lost five of his dogs (froze to death). He had to go right back with the "out" mail. Johnson had lost seven dogs and we'd almost given up hope of getting the mail he was carrying, but we finally did. You can't imagine how glad we were.

The SUN came back the twenty-fourth. I was so happy I nearly jumped out of my shoes. You know how you feel back in the States when you have some stormy weather and don't see the sun for a few days, how good it seems when it finally does shine? Well, just multiply that feeling by about 299 and you'll know how I felt. The sun left about the nineteenth of November and, although we didn't have absolute darkness, we didn't see that golden globe. When it came back everyone was excited and now it stays up quite a while, but I still haven't gotten used to the wonder of it.

4.7. The "Station" in Barrow. The Barrow Refuge Station was the headquarters for Charles Brower's business. Reprinted by permission, Alaska and Polar Region Archives, Elmer E. Rasmuson Library, University of Alaska Fairbanks (#66-10-56).

I've been having good times lately going to the station [see Figure 4.7][24] and playing pool. Tommy Brower comes for me and brings me back, as I don't know the place well enough to go out alone when it's dark. There are no landmarks here unless you know the direction of the winds and the snow-drifts. All the snow is exactly alike, only some places you have to sit down and slide and other drifts you crawl up. When the wind blows, the lights from the buildings are in-visible fifty feet away.

March 10

I started this letter quite a while ago but so many things came up that I didn't get back to it again. We had quite a sick baby the middle of February just when everything was thawing. (There is an annual thaw in Alaska, at least this part, and there is some work trying to get things dried up after it.) Doctor operated on it (the baby) twice for a bad abscess but it developed meningitis and died.

Doctor did a trachelorrhaphy [see Glossary] on a Wainwright woman. She was a scream coming out of the anaesthetic. She speaks English quite well and almost had us doubled up laughing at her.

Doctor started out for Wainwright February 21 but came back because of the hard trail. He needed another team so asked me if I wanted to go. I sure did and did some tall hustling to get ready. Borrowed all sorts of things from Mrs. Greist and got up at 4 A.M. to start off. About a dozen things turned up wrong so we didn't get started until 7:30 A.M. Some trip. We were four days and three nights on the trail. One day we traveled twelve hours and another fourteen hours. We slept in a tent when the mercury was about thirty-five below zero. The first night out I nearly froze to death. Cooking out is sure hard in the Arctic: the dishes, food, and everything is frozen. First of all, snow has to be melted on Primus stoves[25] so we could put the bread on to thaw. Then

it's a case of cook and eat before everything freezes solid
again. It's lots worse to pick up something real cold than
something hot, because the cold things stick and pull the
skin clear off. The last night of our trip down we slept in an
igloo at Atanik. There were ten adults and four children, two
of them sick, all in a room about twice as big as our rooms at
the Met. We were arranged like this:

We sure were packed tight, but it was good to get a warm
place to sleep after fourteen hours on the trail. We got to
Wainwright at six P.M. the next day. The Cramers seemed
glad to see me. I was the first white female Lesley had seen
since the boats left.

Captain Amundsen has his quarters about five miles from
Wainwright. He is in Nome now but his pilot, Lieutenant
Omdal, is there. He's a young chap about twenty-seven
years old, good looking, and as nice as he can be. One of the
Cramers, and sometimes both, took me down every day I was
there except one, so I had a dandy good time and got to know
the lieutenant real well. He says even if Captain Amundsen
doesn't fly over the pole, he's going to. It's a twenty-hour
flight.

The Cramers decided to come back with us, and a Native
was bringing a sick man to the hospital, so four teams started

out Monday morning. We were in Wainwright just a week. It took us five days and four nights to get back. We had fifty-two-below weather and the trail was hard. Some of the dogs were frozen and all their feet were bleeding. It was awful. One night we slept three miles out of Atanik in a tent, the second night in a deserted cabin that was full of snow and frost, and when we got all our Primus stoves going all that stuff melted and the place sure was wet. The third night, when it was fifty-two below, we wondered why everything was frozen up. Even the stoves refused to work. We knew it was cold but had no idea just how cold it was. Lesley, Russel, and I went into a tiny igloo. At home it would be considered a large dog kennel; about as big as an ordinary bathroom and the only way to get in is to drop in a hole and crawl on your hands and knees. There were two children and nine adults in there and not enough air to talk about, but it was warm, so we didn't care. Doctor had a little girl up from Wainwright and I shared my sleeping bag with her. That night in the tent I thought she'd frozen, she was so cold; so I spent the rest of the night seeing that she didn't freeze. The last night we reached Appiyah's cabin, or igloo, and thirteen adults and two children shared that place. We were packed like sardines but had driven through a terrific storm and couldn't pitch the tent nor build a snow house. I guess none of us acquired any lice, even though we expected to. I ate enough reindeer hair to make a mattress. I froze my cheek and nose quite badly but they're both getting well, although my face certainly wouldn't pass in a beauty show. I ate some blubber and some frozen raw fish; both taste pretty good, especially the blubber, if you're cold. It's regular canned heat.

The mail ought to be in tonight and I have quite a few letters to write before Thursday, besides my home letter. I sure am glad I went on the trip, although I wouldn't care to repeat it again, for a little while at least, unless I went with a lighter pack and more dogs.

Will close now, with
Heaps & heaps of love
Gussie

October 12, 1923

Dear Miss Knust,

Received both your letters and your box. The box was just wonderful. Thank you so much for everything in it. I'll tell you a secret—I ate the candy right up. It sure tasted good, fresh candy, and I love that kind and hadn't had any for more than a year. The flowers are on my dresser and look so very nice. I read the book, too, as soon as the excitement died down. Hadn't had anything to read for a long time. I borrow books from all over.

I wish you could see the stars up here when our dark season is really here. There hardly seems room for them all and the Big Dipper is right overhead. Our days are gradually growing shorter. Last month we had some wonderful moonlit nights and the northern lights were bright, too.

We weren't a bit cold all winter. Had plenty of coal. We got coal from the States. By the time it's in our basement it costs the board about eighty-five dollars a ton. We won't be cold for two more years for we got up two hundred tons this summer on the *Holmes*. There is a coal mine at Wainwright but the coal isn't very good quality. They use it at the school house there, though.

My junior C. E. [Christian Endeavor] is coming along nicely. I just love the kiddies. The Eskimo language is very hard to learn since it's an unwritten language. My vocabulary has not increased very much. I do know a few words, like *al-lapah,* "cold;" *adee,* "pain" or "it hurts;" *pechuk,* "all gone;"

micaruk, "little;" *micaninny,* "baby;" *anaklit,* "did your bowels move?;" *capseni,* "how many or how much;" *illowit,* "say it!" (spelling not guaranteed—mostly phonetic). I do know a few other words but couldn't carry on a conversation.

Roscoe, my interpreter, has gone outside, or rather to Sitka, Alaska, to the Sheldon Jackson School. Percy,[26] another dandy lad, is my interpreter now. He is also our janitor.

Wish you could have seen little Carol. She's the prettiest baby here. Is a quarter breed but the white blood is strongest. She was so cunning. Her family have all gone East. They left the oldest boy here. He is Mr. Van der Sterre's house boy. Surely is a caution. Peter Van der Sterre,[27] the school teacher, is too, and was questioning Adam as to his family. Adam wanted to tell Peter his mother had had twins so he said his mother "catch'im doubles." I thought I'd never stop laughing when Peter told us that.

We are just getting over a terrible flu epidemic. It was awful. Three weeks ago I gave a three-hour anesthetic for a double herniotomy. Admitting Andrew for that certainly started things, for two days later we got in a boy about twenty with a bad case of pneumonia. He was as cyanotic as could be and moaned with each breath. Just as he started to improve the tiniest bit the epidemic broke. We have room for nine patients but had fourteen. Had three cribs in the O.R. and the babies' mothers slept on the office floor. We had office hours for outpatients every day from 8:30 A.M. until after 1:30 P.M. They were all so very sick. School shut down and an annex was made there. They had six adults with pneumonia over there and Natives cared for them. An old man died in his igloo. Rivicik, an old timer here, died at the school house and they moved another woman from there just in time for her to die here in the hospital. We lost an eighteen-month-old boy, a perfect little fellow, and a three-year-old girl, little Dorcas, who we had here this summer with typhoid. A woman was admitted with a very bad case of pneumonia and five months pregnant. She aborted and is getting along fine, although we didn't expect her to live through the night. Grant, the first case we had, is walking around now. The operative case caught a flu bug somewhere and coughed his incisions open and he's still in bed. We have two sick laddies now; one is a quarter breed from Pt. Barrow and is the weakest, sickest looking thing you ever saw. She's a contrary little thing, too; won't take medicine nor stay put on her side. We don't know if she'll pull through or not. Little John is getting well and bad. He's a cute little monkey, is only about eighteen months old, and as bright as a new dollar. I sleep on a mattress on the floor of the O.R. with John and Olive, and John will wake up and peek out of his crib. If I'm not looking at him he'll sit up and yell, but if I am he'll duck under the covers and begin to cough most pathetically. He's always hungry. We just love him but he doesn't like to be petted. His mother made me a lovely pair of fur-lined slippers. They are white deer skin outside, and have seal soles and dog skin trimming. They're as warm as toast. I have a sealskin pair lined with deer skin that I wear all the time at night. I certainly won't want to wear civilized shoes. It's getting cold enough now to wear fur boots outdoors and I just love them.

Doctor Greist was sick and Mrs. and David[28] both had pneumonia. The Nichols went outside on the *Bear*. It was a lucky thing because Betty certainly would have gotten it, too. We miss them lots. We like Peter, though. He comes over quite often and we play cards. Miss Bannan[29] was quite sick and Miss Dakin had the intestinal form of flu. I only had a sore throat one day, but don't feel sick with it, just couldn't swallow solids. Had soup and milk toast all day. Doctor gave me ammonium salicylate.

It knocked my stomach slightly out of kilter but didn't affect my appetite, which is still as good as it was in the "Met" days. Somehow I can't realize I'm getting old. I don't feel a bit older than I did in 1917; certainly don't feel any more dignified. I wonder how I'll ever get enough gumption up to lecture in 1926.

Morgan and Luther both got well. Morgan had to be operated on for empyema [see Glossary]. Luther learned quite a little English before he left the hospital.

During the height of our flu epidemic a family came in from inland. The woman was nearly insane with pain from an abscess under her ear. We were so tired and worn out. The O.R. was being used as a nursery and everything was upside down, but Doctor had to operate immediately. Esther, the patient, weighs about 250 lbs. She is a dear old crone; we have lots of fun with her and her husband Horace. Neither speaks a word of English but I talk a blue streak to them and they rattle off a stream of Eskimo and Helen and Percy, who understand both of us, nearly go into fits laughing.

Doctor thought, account of the flu, that chloroform would be the best anaesthetic. I had to give it standing at her side instead of at her head and it made it very hard. Her heart went bad and I quickly switched to ether. She came out fine but I sure was scared for a little while. I hate to give chloroform except in obstetrical cases. She's doing nicely now. Doctor had taken out the tubes and only has a piece of gauze as drainage. Esther is as happy and grateful as she can be. The other day Doctor irrigated it with a twenty-five percent alcohol solution of iodine and it hurt the poor old soul so that she put both arms around me and hugged me so hard she near busted my ribs.

The flu sure did put me back in my letter writing. I have a heap to write and the mail goes out November 1 this year instead of the fifteenth as it did last.

I get the *Trained Nurse* and Miss Dakin gets the *Nursing Journal* so we get both of them. We trade when we finish.

We are going to have sauerkraut and sausages tonight for supper. I can hardly wait. It's the first time we've had sauerkraut since I've been here. We get it in cans. I never knew so many things came canned. I never liked sweet potatoes at home but I like the canned ones real well. This year we also got canned grapefruit. Haven't tasted it yet but they say it's good.

Please write us often as you can.

December 21, 1923

Dear Miss Knust,

Peter and I were on the church decoration committee. I was chairman. Mr. Riley[30] came over to help, too. I had gotten the Natives to get all the stuff out to trim the tree and decorate and told them to come back and have a fire built by 6:00. I got there at 6:30 and there was no light or fire. I lit a lamp and started to sort out some of the bills and things when Joe finally arrived to start the fires. I nearly froze for a little while but I did want to finish up that night so I stuck to it. About 8:00 the crowd came and then I took life easy—just bossed the job and left about 10:00 when it was nearly finished.

Mrs. Greist hadn't all the corn popped so Saturday I said I'd help her out and take it over here to pop. (I wasn't going to be bothered with David if I could help it.) Leo, one of the herd boys, and I popped continually for five hours, we filled three hundred-pound sugar sacks. Helen and Harriet were popping for the hospital and Helen kept the stove red hot. Gee! but it was warm work. We had more fun, though, than enough.

Sunday we were all busy, too. We forgot it was Sunday for once.

We had only three patients and they were all well enough to go over to the church Monday afternoon. The entertainment was just great. The kids talked right up, even though a lot of them didn't know what they were saying. Peter Van der Sterre was Santa Claus and he made a fine one. While the gifts were being distributed the stove blew up. No one was hurt and there was very little excitement. The men carried the stove and pipe out and, to look at the children, you'd think nothing had happened. They're the best kids anyway.

Tuesday was a real honest-to-goodness Christmas. Peter came over to breakfast and after that we got our presents. They were all great. After we'd opened and admired and exclaimed over ours we tended to the kids. The hall was packed with them. Each one received a gift of some kind, and candy, peanuts, and popcorn. They stayed until one o'clock when we had to chase them out because we had to get dressed to go to the station for dinner [see Figure 4.8].

4.8. Christmas at the Station, 1923. Left to right, back row: Mollie Greist, Mrs. Riley, Ann Bannan, Harry Riley, Percy Ipalook, Peter Van der Sterre; middle row: Russel and Lesley Cramer, Florence Dakin, Charles Brower, Henry Greist, Fred Hopson; front row: David Greist (head only), Augusta Mueller, Helen Suvlu, Ellen Kanayurak, Harriet Hopson. Reprinted, by permission, from Terza Hopson Collection (#TH102), Inupiat History, Language and Culture Commission, Barrow, Alaska.

There was a terrific storm and it was all we could do to get there. The wind almost took us off our feet and it was snowing so hard we couldn't see any lights at all. Finally got there and after we warmed and rested up we were okay. The men, even Mr. Brower, had "outside" clothes on. Mr. Brower usually wears deerskin pants in winter and moose hide in summer and I've never seen him in real clothes. He sure looked good. We were all dressed up, too. For anyone to come in they'd never think that we were a thousand miles from nowhere.

We had a seven-course dinner, starting with oyster cocktail, and it was some good. After dinner we danced and played pool. Left there at one A.M. The storm had let up and it was beautiful and the moonlight was out. It certainly was the end of a perfect day. We were all dead tired but had had such a good time.

How are you? Hope you had a merry Christmas and that 1924 will be a happy year for you. Wish I could take an aeroplane and come down to see you.

Would like to write more but haven't time as Peter wants the mail over as soon as possible.

January 1924

Dear Folks,

I'd much rather go to sleep than write a letter right now. Andrew's youngest boy, Isaac, has paratyphoid, I guess, and kept me up most of last night. I was out of bed every half hour, so didn't get much sleep. Then, to make matters worse, I had to go to church this morning and Doctor's sermon was worse than awful, so I am sleepier than ever.

Monday, January 14

I knitted some on my sweater but am not getting on very fast with it. I don't like to knit. In the afternoon I read some of Mark Twain to the others and I'm reading *The History of Medicine*. I finished it last night (Saturday) and am reading the *Americanization of Edward Bok* now.

I did quite a bit of studying on my Bible course and read some between taking care of Isaac.

Mrs. Greist came over after supper and knitted. She and I could shake hands as the slowest knitters. We have a lot of fun about it. I crocheted some on my centerpiece corners. I keep Isaac in the laundry at night by my door so I don't have far to go to tend to him. He's some.

Tuesday, January 22

Our Delco[31] is out of commission until the boats get here. Isn't that cheerful? I'm glad the light season is coming on, not leaving us. We have about three hours a day now when we can see to write, read, or sew without a light. Each day it's brighter and most of the day we can see to get around without a light, so it could be worse. The sun peeked up at 11:30 but, because of a little hill, we had to get on the table to see it. Everyone acted like a fool. You cannot possibly imagine how good it is to see it. You know we only had one sunny day in October, very few in November and the sun left the twenty-first of November, so it was almost four months since we had really seen it. Lesley was on the table and I helped our old patient, Susie, up so she could see too, and when she did she pounded Lesley on the back and got as excited as we were. We sure seem like we have a few screws loose when anything happens.

February 28, 1924

Dear Miss Knust,

Our mail has to be over at the school house tomorrow night so it looks like I'd better get busy and finish answering letters.

We have a leg ulcer case, a bad paratyphoid, and an inflammatory rheumatism case, besides the two obstetrical ones. Just got rid of a burn case yesterday. The dearest baby girl. Had tea poured on her and was quite badly scalded. We weren't busy for quite a while, but are making up for it now.

Mrs. Greist gave a party over at the manse Tuesday night. She was going to have it on St. Valentine's Day but heard that Mr. Cramer and Miss Wallace[32] were coming up so postponed it. It was a regular Valentine party, though. We had more fun here in the hospital making Valentines. We cut out funny things from magazines and made rhymes to go with them. Each of the women got three Valentines, the men each got five. You'd never guess what the main dish of the dinner was. Swan, and gee, it was good. Someone told Mrs. Greist that swans live to be one thousand years old and, since this bird weighed over seventeen pounds with the feathers off and insides out, she decided it must be at least one hundred, so started to roast it early in the morning. It was done in no time, so she heated it again for the dinner and it was perfectly delicious. As tender as could be and not a bit gamey. We had all sorts of good things besides that, but that was the best. After dinner we each got a tiny bow and arrow and shot at a heart; I made the booby prize. I'd hit two miles over the heart every time. The bow and arrow are Eskimo made and are like big ones.

It was a nasty, windy, cold night and no moon. I had to come over to see to Lesley and carried some ice cream over for her. The wind had blown a lot of new drifts and I had a terrible time getting over since I had no light. Then to make matters worse, I had discarded my heavy underwear for the occasion and had thin bloomers and silk stockings on. I did have my high boots on, but my knees were exposed and I 'most froze them. Going back I fell three times and was soaked to my waist; the snow was wet. Never again. When I go out in the dark on a stormy night with less clothes on than I ought to have, I'm going to wear my fur bearing pants and take a light. The batteries for my flash had hard usage this year and are worn out. I'm glad the light season is coming. We have over twelve hours of daylight now.

I thought I'd get a lot of writing done today, but Mrs. Riley[33] came this afternoon and tonight I have to go to Bible class at the manse. Doctor is having a Bible course for the English-speaking Natives, so I go, too. Helen says I'm getting "just like Eskimo." I suppose I am. I don't mind the dark or cold and can find my way around no matter how stormy it is.

The other night we were to the manse and had caribou steaks. They are better than reindeer, and that's saying a lot. Doctor Greist is having a wonderful time lately making ice cream. They go out this year and have an excess of sugar and milk, so Doctor is using it up. He makes delicious ice cream, and we get some about once a week, sometimes more often. I'm hoping he'll serve some after class tonight. You see, I still like to eat.

We are all wondering if the naval planes will stop at Barrow on their polar flight. We all hope so, at any rate. Mr. Hopson, here, has never seen an aeroplane. The last time he was in the States was 1904. He's a funny old scout.

Heaps and heaps of love and then some,
Gussie

May 24, 1924
Dearest Folks,

This is letter number six but it's a special edition about Rasmussen.[34]

He came over to call on us last night. Peter and Mr. Hansen were invited to the manse so we had him to ourselves. Both Peter and Mr. Hansen said that he had been away from "whites" so long that he was very shy and embarrassed, especially around women. We found him anything but that.

He came over at eight and stayed until after midnight. He is a medium-sized man, rather dark and thin. At times his profile looks like Captain Amundsen's. He speaks broken English but does very well and makes himself understood. He's jolly and very witty.

June 6, 1924

Dear Miss Knust,

The calendar says it is the sixth of June, but it would take a lot of imagination to imagine it was if one didn't have a calendar. It's twenty-three above zero and about a sixty-mile-an-hour gale blowing. Yesterday it was thirty-three above and quite a wind. We have had some wonderful warm days, though, so we can't kick. But it does seem queer to have it so cold and windy in June. Last year it was much warmer this time of the year. Most of the snow has melted and made the place very sloppy, but if this cold keeps up the rest of the snow will stay until July. The drifts are still about three feet high. The tundra and beach are showing in spots. The snow birds, black birds (not like our black birds, but that's what the Natives call them) and lemmings are around and ducks have been going north for weeks, so even though we don't realize it, summer has come.

Your letters of September 26 and December 22 both arrived here March 26. Our mail service was all balled up this year. The only mail we are sure of when it leaves the States is the early May mail. That comes up on the boats. The other winter mails depend on weather and ice conditions, so one can't say when to send letters from the States to get here at a certain time. I've told my folks to write p.r.n. and send the letters along. They will eventually get here, if the mail driver gets through.

We have had a most exciting and interesting time. Mr. Rasmussen, the Danish ethnologist and explorer, has been here. He stayed ten days as Peter's guest. He was over here

quite a few times and we certainly learned a lot from him.
A Mr. Hansen, who went east on the *Lady Kindersley* last
fall (I met him then), came back with him. Two Greenland
Eskimos were with him, too. Mr. Rasmussen was born in
Greenland and has been exploring for the last twenty-four
years. The way they had their dogs hitched fan shaped, the
heavy ice sleds, and the clothes made like the costumes in
"Nanook of the North" all excited our and the Natives' curiosity. Mr. Rasmussen left with the two Natives Tuesday evening, but Mr. Hansen is to stay here until the *Bear* goes out
and will take movies of Native life. He is out on the ice now
at the whaling camps. Mr. Rasmussen is just fine and was so
friendly. It didn't seem as if we were visiting with a noted
and famous explorer. One night we had Mr. Hansen, Peter,
and a Mr. Andrews[35] (from Kivilina) here to dinner and had
just gotten started when a whale was caught. We all piled
out, left dinner, dishes and everything and went by dog team
to the camp about five miles down the coast and about a mile
out on the ice. We didn't get back until eleven and since Miss
Dakin and I got back ahead of the others, we warmed up
the supper or dinner, whichever you want to call it, washed
up the dishes and reset the table. Mr. Rasmussen had gotten
home while we were out to the camp so he came over with
us. He sat in the kitchen and watched us clean up and helped
when he could. When the rest came over he ate with us and
we had more fun than enough. Wouldn't you like to have
been here, too?

June 8

I was saying this morning "what is so rare as a day in June."
One would have to go a long way to find one rarer than today.
It's 31 above zero, snowing, and the wind is blowing about
an eighty-mile-an-hour gale. It's blowing so hard that all the
snow is drifting in the cracks around my window. I have the

outside window up. I needed a snow shovel to get out of bed this morning.

Monday Doctor brought my gun over to me. He said there was something the matter with me because I hadn't come over for it before. He showed me how to clean and put it together and then I went out to try it on a stick. I'm not a half bad shot, considering I haven't ever had any experience. I was busy most of the morning cleaning up Anna's toys and the room they had. After lunch I went over to the station and got some black canvas for a gun cover, took my gun over to Nellie, and in about an hour she sent the case back.

After lunch Mr. Rasmussen came over with his two Natives to say good-bye. We all took pictures of him. I haven't finished my film yet, but everybody else has good pictures, so I guess I have. Everybody was lined up with cameras and Mr. Hansen had the movie camera out. They had the one ice sled packed up, just loaded with stuff. They started out with eleven dogs for the movie camera to get the start. They stopped about a hundred yards away and came back for two more dogs and to say good-bye. Then they went off full speed. It certainly looks pretty to see the dogs hitched fan shaped and to see the Native swing the long whip back and forth. I wonder if the pictures will be shown in New York and if you'll see them. I'll be in them because I was right near the sled, and again I was running toward a dog when Mr. Hansen was cranking. I have no cap on, my green sweater and a very short skirt, so in case you do see the picture you will recognize me.

Thursday morning before office hours I went up to the graveyard for dirt. That's the only place we can get dirt here. I needed a boat and nonskid shoes. It was awful. The depressions in the tundra had ice covered with about six inches of water; then there were places where perfectly good looking snow was covered with icy water, and the high places were mostly mounds of slippery clay. Going to the graveyard was bad enough, but coming back with about ten pounds of dirt wasn't so nice. It took some careful balancing to hit the least deep and slippery spots.

I went to the beach to get sand to mix with dirt, then I mixed it with manure. I had a wonderfully messy time playing in dirt. Miss Bannan planted some head lettuce seeds in the box. She has had such good luck with the few other lettuce plants that she planted some more. We each had one lettuce leaf on our salad last Saturday and last night we had lettuce sandwiches. The parsley is growing fine, too.

Mrs. Greist says that the aeroplanes are coming the twenty-first of June. I wonder. All our Natives are wild, getting ready for Nelegetuk.[36] Helen had made Percy a bright yellow snow shirt trimmed with red. Big fat Susie, Nick's wife, is going to have a blue sateen one; she is going to be immense in it. When I showed Helen the gloves, rather the mittens Alfred made for me, the first thing she said was "new mittens for Nelegetuk." I hadn't even thought of it.

I fooled around watching the boys fix up the wind break and the skin and by eleven they were tossing in the skin [see Figure 4.9]. Miss Dakin and Miss Bannan and the folks from the school came over, too. Doctor was so peeved because they had Nelegetuk. He says it is a heathen practice and a million other things against it. It was warm and the sun shining made it just great. I helped toss folks in the skin. It's rather hot work. I went up twice; everybody yelled the way I came down. Most folks land on their feet, or side, but if I didn't land standing up I'd dive down. Mr. Hansen took movies of me. I hope you see them.

We had a good supper and were just going to start to play pool while the Natives were eating and then would have to go to prayer meeting. Then a note came for me to come home and give Agnes an anaesthetic. Doctor was wild; he said he knew something would happen, he was sure of it, and that anyone who indulged in such foolish play deserved to get hurt. He had no sympathy for them, etc., etc., etc. Then he asked if I went in the skin. I said of course I had. I got some look. Agnes broke her leg in three places, Doctor says.

Doctor's fussing and Agnes breaking her leg had no effect on the people at all. Thursday even the old men and women went up in the skin. I went up three times. The last time I sprained my ankle and have been limping around since. I'm wearing my high civilized shoes and have it bandaged and it's getting along fine. In fact, I think I'll be able to go out hunting tomorrow if it's halfway clear out. The people sure had one good time. About 5:30 Bobby Brower was fooling in the skin with a seal poke and fell and broke his arm. I happened to be right there so I had the boys put him on a small sled and carry him to the hospital. Doctor was fit to be tied. He sent a note to some Native to have the skin taken down immediately. He raved on to Mr. Brower, but Mr. Brower said it wasn't anything to have Bobby's arm broken; he might have done it playing ball. That's what we all say. I had to give Bobby an anaesthetic to have his arm set. He went home Friday. Mrs. Riley was here to supper and we went down to watch the dancing. The fog had come up and it was nasty and cold. My foot hurt so much that I came home and Miss Dakin went down. Doctor tried to stop the dancing but it didn't work; they danced until one o'clock.

June 29, 1924

I have a child named for me. Poor kid. Bernice at Wainwright has named her new baby Augusta Mueller. Here's her letter:

> Ha, ha. I was so much glad when I heard that Barrow people caught many whale. People here didn't caught whale.
> Maybe I will not write long ones because Mr. Grouse is so much hurry. I name my baby your name, because I love you

much and remember you all the time, so I name her. I send
you one pair seal skin. Close with love, Mrs. Bernice."

The Natives have caught five small whales. I've been out
to the camps twice. Once all but the head was cut up and the
second time everything was cut up. The snow and ice for one
hundred yards around is bloody and all the Natives are the
most gory-looking things. They just cut and go into that meat
feet first. It's a wonderful sight. A whale's eye is the smallest
thing compared with the rest of its body. We had whale meat
chopped and fried the other night. It was real good, but a little too rich to eat much. Mr. Hopson pickles the muktuk, the
black skin. It looks like rubber with fat on it. It's very good
eating, so Miss Bannan has pickled some for us. Mr. Hopson
calls the pickle embalming fluid. I don't like polar bear meat.
It's very tough and fishy. We had some a while ago.

I've just been out feeding a lemming corn bread; he likes it
fine. There are a lot of lemmings around the hospital. I have
one that will eat out of my hand when I can find it.

Wednesday night we were over to Riley's playing Mah
Jongg. Miss Dakin, Miss Bannan, and I had water boots on
and Mr. Riley had soles on his house boots that were exceed-
ingly strong. When the room became warm, the smell was
awful. We have all decided if we ever get used to the smell
of seal water boots and Native-cured oogaruk soles that
we won't ever mind any kind of a smell. Mrs. Riley served
deviled ham sandwiches and Limburger cheese and crackers
and the boot smell was so strong we couldn't smell the cheese
at all. We have to wear the things, though, so we make the
best of it. There's some consolation in the fact that everybody
smells the same. Rubber boots are too heavy and too cold.

I think I've typed enough for once. If anything important
happens I'll add it to this.

Much love,
Gussie

July 27, 1924

Thursday night we went to Bible class. Poor Doctor was almost frantic; Big Jim had leaned over him while he was typing and had given him a cootie, free of charge. The thing bit Doctor all over and he was in misery.

All I seem to write about is the boats, but you folks who get mail three or four times a day can't possibly imagine how it is to wait five months to hear from home. Also, you can go to a store and buy anything you want while all our stuff is on the boats. We're, everyone of us, out of photographic supplies. I'm completely out of calico for trade and have been making my own candy for months. I'm getting sick of taffy and fudge and that stuff; I want hard candies and real chocolates. All my *Saturday Evening Posts, Americans* and other magazines will be more than welcome, too.

Yesterday afternoon, Mr. Hansen and I went out on the tundra. It wasn't especially nice out, but he wanted to get some pictures of the pile of skulls up at the river. We walked around taking our time and at a place where we only saw one leg bone, a lot of wood and a piece of skull, we started to dig, hoping to find something worthwhile. I saw, in a little pool, something that looked like a shovel handle. It turned out to be an old spear point holder cut in the shape of a whale. It's carved out of wood and is about a foot long and four inches across. The men don't use them now; they were supposed to have some sort of a superstitious value. I think they are called fetishes, I'm not sure. Mr. Rasmussen has my book with a picture of one in it. It's quite a curio so I gave it to Mr. Hansen for the museum in Copenhagen. I only saw a few snipes and didn't get any of them. It got horribly foggy and once we stopped until Mr. Hansen made and lit a cigarette. We had been heading toward the buildings before we stopped, when we started we couldn't see anything for the fog, and when the fog lifted again we were walking right away from them. We had a good laugh over it. One surely can lose the way out on the tundra.

I danced continually from about 9:45 until 11:30. The captain had heavy rubber boots on, but I had a waltz with him, too, and he sure is some dancer. I was the only one he danced with. The first mate and crew of the *Teddy* is a rotten dancer, but I got along better with him than Miss Bannan did. I'm getting so I can do any kind of fancy dancing with Peter. When we'd dance we'd have the floor. It was great sport. Peter and I danced four foxtrots, a waltz, and one-step and a two-step without a stop between. Mr. Hansen would have another record on before we got our breath. Then we had coffee and Mr. Hansen and I had one more dance before we went home.

July 30, 1924

We are all fit to be tied. The wind blew the ice out beyond the ridge before the shore ice is out so there sets the *Arctic* again with our mail on her and we folks here just dying to get it. If the captain would spend a little extra money we'd get it because Natives would carry the sacks ashore over the ice. Yesterday the *Nanook* got in; her name last year was *Otilla Fiord*. I went aboard her over the ice, went with two Natives. She was only about a mile from shore but the ice was so broken up the way we went we had to retrace our steps so often that it took us an hour and a half to get to her. She was about two miles down the coast, so I had a little exercise jumping over cracks, etc.

We hear that the *Arctic,* which usually has the bulk of our mail, has very little because the *Bear* was disabled in the Bering Sea and couldn't get to Nome to leave the early mail for the *Arctic*. The *Boxer* may or may not bring it up, nothing is sure, and we are on pins and needles. We hear so many conflicting rumors that we don't know what to believe. All

we want now is our mail off the *Arctic* to see how much we're
getting. The Greists are all packed but still don't know if they
are to be relieved, so they're in a worse pickle than we are.

I got a lot of phalaropes and snipes with my shotgun but
wouldn't shoot song birds, so Mr. Andrews was out of luck.
I only shot birds we could eat.

I had an apple yesterday and it was the best tasting thing
I've eaten. I've wanted one for eight months or more. Today
I had the first orange in four months. You can't imagine how
good they taste.

Sure would like to see you; expect to soon be reading a letter from you, if we ever get it ashore.

Much love,

Gussie

August 19, 1924

I talked a long time to Mr. Lopp.[37] He says he will see that I
get a position with the bureau any time I want it in Alaska.

Mr. Lopp sure is funny. He's trying to make a match with
Peter and me and it isn't working worth a cent. Peter and
I get a lot of fun out of it when "Grandfather Lopp" isn't
around. I stayed there until nearly four and then we went
out taking pictures. We walked about four miles, I guess.
I got a few good pictures. Peter took a dozen; I don't know
how his are. One of Peter and me is good. I had jumped Peter
for something and as we had just been talking about a queer
married couple who are in the bureau service, called Clarence
and Mabel, Mr. Lopp began calling me Mabel and just as
we sat for the picture he said to Peter, "Now, Clarence, look
pleasant." We both laughed and he snapped the picture.

Wednesday Rhoda came in and said she wanted medicine
for Alice, a five- or six-year-old youngster. They had been
inland and after a long hard effort, we got out of her that
Alice ached all over, had fever, was nauseated, had been

sick a long time, had a stomach ache, was short of breath
and weak. Doctor sent her right home and told her to bring
the child to the hospital. You never saw a more pitiful sight.
The poor little thing was all skin and bones. She is so sick
and has a temperature of over 102 all the time. Her arms and
legs are like sticks, but she has an enormous pot belly. She
was so nice and chubby when she left Barrow a couple of
months ago. Now she looks like she has TB more than anything else. She is always so hot, too. I sleep in the room with
her and with two blankets and my bathrobe I'm cold and
all she has over her is a little thin quilt. Even then, she cries
agnokserunga, "I'm too hot." All day long she says *illoahser-
unga,* "I'm all right." Poor little thing. She is far from all right
but always smiles and says she is.

September 28, 1924

Just didn't feel like writing last week so have two weeks
news to write. We're all furious at the *Baychimo* folks. A
smallpox case has broken out in the village. Roy's youngest,
little Elizabeth, about two years old. Thursday it was wild
here. Wednesday night Doctor, instead of preaching, talked
smallpox to these Natives and he must have talked plenty
because usually, when they are told to be here at a certain
hour, any time within three hours of the time is all right as
far as they are concerned. But Wednesday night Doctor told
them to get here at 8:30 and they sure did. The hall was black
with them. I never thought there were that many Natives
in Barrow except at Christmas. There were 230 vaccinated,
some had been done Wednesday at Roy's and some, I think 3,
were done Thursday. It was fun. Entire families would go in
at once, and anyone who tells you that Eskimos have small
families, refer them to me.

We had a good laugh about the sixty vaccines. They held
out like the five loaves. Doctor would make one do for about
six. But everyone is vaccinated.

We're getting quite civilized up here. Friday morning
Eunice came in with a sore throat and it's diphtheria. Roy's
baby is getting over smallpox all right. Now we need some
diphtheria to keep us in touch with outside diseases. Doctor
gave her ten thousand units of antitoxin and it's wonderful
how she has improved. The membrane is almost all gone.

October 10, 1924

Dearest Miss Knust,

I wonder if you've read of all our disasters up here. The
Liebes and Co. boat hung around on the ice for ten days,
changing her position for safety p.r.n., and then she was
crushed about three miles down the coast. Luckily, she was
only about a mile off shore and the ice held her up so that
no lives were lost and a good bit of the cargo was saved. A
skin boat was fitted out and sent to the eastward to have
the traders at Barter Island and Demarcation Point come to
Barrow with their small boats for supplies. Tom Gordon,
the Demarcation Point trader, chartered the *Duxbury* that
had wintered in up there to come down for the things. They
loaded up with some things that had been saved from the
Arctic. Two days ago we learned that the *Duxbury* had gotten
caught in the ice off Pt. Tangent, less than a fifth of the way
to Demarcation Point. We are wondering what those poor
people will do. They will freight some of the stuff by dog
team, but that's an unsatisfactory way. All this station's supplies will have to be freighted up from Wainwright. They are
going to start down tomorrow.

The *Lady Kindersley,* a British ship, was abandoned and the
Boxer, our Department of Education boat, rescued the crew.
She drifted for nearly a month before the crew abandoned
her.

A British ship, the *Baychimo,* came up to aid the *Kindersley*
but got here too late. The *Boxer* had already taken the crew
off. The *Baychimo* was given orders to look for the *Kindersley*

and save some of the cargo, if possible. Nine days after she left here she came back with a smallpox case aboard. Dr. Greist went out to vaccinate the crew. Our Natives had been aboard of her when she first came up and the case was developing then. Result: we have two honest-to-goodness cases and two suspects. They're all isolated in their igloos. Everyone in the village was vaccinated, but there were very few "takes."

A diphtheria case developed, too. We don't know what or who is responsible for that. Fortunately, we have plenty of fresh antitoxin. The case came out of quarantine today. No new ones have developed.

The *Bear* was disabled in the Bering Sea so it didn't get here at all. It seems too bad. It was to be Captain Cochran's last trip and we did want to see him.

The dearest 7 ¾ pound girl was born at 7:10 last night. She's as sweet as can be but sure has one awful pair of lungs.

It gets to ten below zero nights now and there's plenty of snow and ice. We had very little open water this year. All the captains say it's the worst year that has ever been known. The ice was so near all the time that just a slight shift in the wind would bring it in. That's what happened to the *Kindersley*. The wind changed and the fog came in, and the ice came in so fast she couldn't get her engines started before she was caught fast.

The sun is just setting at 4:20 P.M. and the colors of the sky are gorgeous. I wish you were here to see them. You wouldn't be cold up here; it's plenty warm indoors and outdoors we bundle in reindeer clothes. I'm not as cold here as I've been many a time in New York.

Doctor had orders to stay in. There was no one to relieve him. That means he and Miss Dakin both go out next year. I wonder if the board will get someone to relieve her or if I'll be left alone. Poor Mrs. Greist. She had her heart set on going out; they were all packed.

Peter has two little monkeys and the Greists have a kitten. How are those for Arctic animals? The monkeys are full of mischief and Peter's house is a mess from them.

Just think, two years from now I'll likely be home. I send in my last want list this November. It hardly seems possible. It will be hard to leave these Natives knowing that I will never come back. They are dear people and one grows to love them.

I'm glad you like the pictures. One thing I was tickled to get by dog team from Wainwright and that was three gross of photographic paper. I had sent an order down with Rasmussen's photographer, Mr. Hansen, and Lomens put the stuff aboard the Liebes & Co. boat that got as far as Wainwright. Now I can print to my heart's content. My supply was getting rather low. They sent four-by-six paper and I can use one sheet for two prints in most cases.

Please write and tell me about your trip. I'll see you in about two years.

December 22, 1924

Dear Miss Knust,

Thursday I spent most of the day stuffing Aunt Jemima rag dolls with reindeer hair. I did thirty-six of them and it was some job, I'll tell you. I was covered with reindeer hair from my head to my toes. I took them to the manse and Mrs. Greist, to get them out of her way, put them upstairs and they all burned up.

Doctor went to Wainwright right after Thanksgiving and Friday morning, December 19th, the manse burned down. The fire started in the attic, either the Greist's Native boy Isaac or the cat started it. Before Mrs. G. could get water upstairs it was beyond her. We saw the flame and dashed over. There were terrible fumes of some kind, Doctor thinks brimstone[38] from old-fashioned matches, so nothing could be saved from upstairs. The Natives were bricks, they worked and went into the house when it was most dangerous. All the food, all Doctor's medical books, all their clothes, David's new suits that were made for him to go out in, Mrs. Greist's jewelry, all their papers and family photographs, in fact everything personal, was lost. The mission furniture that was downstairs was saved.

December 30, 1924

This letter was sadly neglected. I have only one more day to write so have to get busy. Doctor got back the twenty-first and we were busy trying to get them settled in their new home. They have quite a nice place that used to be a store in the whaling days. It has three nice rooms and they are very cozy.

As all the mission Christmas things were burned up we had decided to dispense with Santa Claus at the church entertainment. Peter had both Santa and his wife at school (I'll enclose a picture), and we thought that would be enough.

Tuesday night when we went in the church to decorate there was a steady stream of Natives bringing gifts of all kinds. We reconsidered and had Long John for Santa. Wednesday afternoon was the church entertainment. We all had the best time. The kids had their pieces down pat and Long John as Santa was a scream. The Natives have been very fortunate trapping this year so far; over six hundred fox skins have been turned in to the trading post and Native store. They were very good to Doctor and gave him all kinds of things, even a sack of flour. They gave each other everything under the sun. Deer skins, snowshoes, hard bread, crackers, flour, sugar, and all other kinds of food stuffs. Calico of all kinds, wood for snowshoes, whalebone, fox skins and even a piece of driftwood. It was a piece of pitch, so was very valuable. It was great sport to watch them give them out. Of course, they weren't wrapped like Christmas presents, but just in newspaper or anything else, and tied up any old way, but securely. One little thing I received was sewed in a sack, wrapped in newspaper, tied with sinew, and had a piece of cardboard box with my name on for a tag.

This year has been an exceptionally fine one. We have had very cold weather but it has been clear and it's quite light every day now for about an hour. Yesterday I went out at 2 P.M. The sky was dark and the moon and stars were up, but all along the horizon were the most gorgeous colors. I wish you could be here for a year and see all the wonderful things. Saturday night, when we came home from Riley's, the sky was just one mass of stars; they seem so near and so very bright. The northern lights were brilliant as could be, too.

Much love,
Gussie

January 18, 1925
Dear Folks,
Thursday night Doctor had Bible class at the school house. Gee, it was cold. Right near the stove it was hotter than blazes, but my feet were like ice. I put my ahtega on the floor and used it as a sort of bag to put my feet in. Doctor was very much interested in his subject, and went deep into scientific details for Peter's special benefit; the poor Natives had no idea what he was talking about. Even Roy couldn't interpret for him. Miss Bannan and I settled down expecting to have to listen for a couple of hours when in came Jeanette with a note. Doctor read it and gave it to me. It was from Mrs. Greist saying that Rhoda was going to have a baby and she had sent her to the hospital. At least she had told Philip to have her taken there. A few minutes afterwards, I'd gotten my ahtega on so that I could help get ready for her. Philip came in and said the baby was born at home, but everything wasn't all right and they wanted Doctor to come to the igloo. If there is

anything that makes Doctor sore it's to have to go to the igloo
to see a patient, and he just raved. He asked me to go with
him, and when we got halfway there one of the girls came out
and said that Rhoda was all right and we needn't come, but
Doctor was on his way and there was no stopping him. When
we got there all was over but the shouting. The house was
full of people: an old woman, Nora (Shirley's mother), Carrie,
Beth, Verna, Dorothy, and a little boy (all kids), Beth's father,
and Philip. Rhoda was lying on the floor on some old blankets and all the mess was in evidence showing that the whole
crew had been there through the performance. Nora was on
the sleeping shelf with the baby. All the poor little thing had
on was a tiny piece of torn blanket, not enough to cover it.
It was a fat, chubby, homely little girl. Rhoda didn't want to
come to the hospital but Doctor insisted. She had no skins to
sleep on and it was so cold. I put the baby under my *ahtega*
and we left Roy to supervise the transporting of Rhoda. The
igloo was a "drop in" affair and I had some job getting out.
The baby seemed to have quite a bit of mucus still in her and
I was afraid to put her on my back for fear she'd choke, and
then, too, she hadn't enough of a piece of blanket to cover
her, and fur is hard to clean, so I thought the safest way was
to put her in the front of my ahtega and hold her there with
one hand. Roy fastened a belt on me and it was some job to
climb out of that igloo with only one hand free and holding
a baby. If anyone but Doctor had been behind me he'd have
given me a boost, but that would have been beyond Doctor's
dignity, so I had to help myself as best I could. Rhoda and
the baby got through their experience in fine shape; the babe
yelled continually until today. Rhoda has milk for her now so
she is quiet. She weighed 8 $\frac{1}{4}$ lbs., but is so homely. Doctor
says he'll let Rhoda go home in five days if everything is
okay.

January 24, 1925

We saw the sun the very first day that we were supposed to, the twenty-first. I sent a note over to Peter as soon as I saw it saying, "Once again it doesn't pay to argue with a woman." The nineteenth and twentieth, the sky was gorgeous and we could see the refraction of the sun; it looked like a fire way out on the tundra. Monday I went over to the store and told Mr. Hopson that we could almost see the sun. He began to spout then and was too funny. Said, "You folks think just because there are a lot of white people here and you want to see the sun that to please you it's going to come two days ahead of time. The earth is going to move faster to please you." I laughed and laughed, and then Mr. Riley came in and said, "Did you see the sun today?" Mr. Hopson nearly exploded. He thinks we're all crazy.

For a while there wasn't anything much to do in the hospital. Now we have Lucy's Rebecca. She is an imp, isn't quite as bad as she was but could stand a lot of improvement. One of Frank and Rebecca's kids is here with suspected typhoid and Roy's Alice with suspected diphtheria. Alfred Hopson's wife was admitted last night "in labor" but after an enema and a dose of salts she feels fine, so unless something starts, she will go home tonight and come back again when there is something doing.

Tuesday Doctor let Rhoda go home. Nora didn't bring much in the way of clothes for her or the baby so I took the baby home under my ahtega. Peter saw me and said I looked like a villager. Someday when the sun really comes back I'm going to borrow a baby and have my picture taken with it on my back. I met old Koocheck and he wanted to know whose baby I had. I said it was mine and then he wanted to know where I got it. That was as much of the Eskimo I understood and all I could answer.

Thursday afternoon I went to Big Roy's house and had more fun than enough. He came over in the morning for medicine, and I've wanted him to make me a medicine man like the one I sold to Mr. Hansen for the Danish Museum. He told Percy he hadn't made that, but had made one of wood and dressed it so I thought I'd go over and get it. One has to crawl into his house through a low snow entrance, then keep stooped over, go through three passageways and three doors before reaching the igloo. I thought I'd never get all the way through. I lost my mitten between two of the doors and since it was pitch dark and I had no light, it took me some time to find it. He has a nice, clean igloo. He showed me a lot of things he was making, some dancing dolls and some ivory. Then he showed me the doll he was making for me, rather had made for me. It was good. I'll bring it home with me. The head and arms move and it's funny. Roy can't talk English and my Eskimo is limited to hospital terms, so we had a puzzling time. I said I'd give him $3 for it, holding up three fingers. He held up five and I said *naga* (no). Then he held up three fingers and motioned as though to cut one in half. I said "yes" to that and to make it more sure, he took out a small round piece of wood and a half a piece. He said "dollar," put the whole piece down three times and the half down once: $3.50. I wrote out an order for him, after a lot of talking with my hands, etc. Then he showed me a piece of whalebone he would make the other medicine man out of as soon as it dried out. I enjoyed my visit there immensely and he seems to like to have me. I stopped in Riley's and then came home and developed a film. I'm going to print tomorrow if nothing happens. Doctor didn't have Bible class on account of his cold, so I wrote letters.

We've been reading in clippings that Amundsen is going to try again for the flight across the Pole; also that Lt. Omdal is coming with him. My, it will be good to see him again. I wonder if we'll scan the horizon in vain again for the planes. This is the third time, so he really ought to come.

Talk about busy. I feel like I had been put into a barrel and rolled around. Doctor came over right from church. He examined Willie, ordered about six things for him. I had to go to the attic for vaccine, thaw it out, and get other things. Willie had to have the bed pan; Fred woke up and wanted the pot, so did Eben;[39] Rebecca didn't bother crying for it but got herself into an awful smelly mess and I had to clean her. I was trying to get dinner and really didn't know if I was afoot or horseback. Willie sure is a sick chap, but the vaccine will do him lots of good. Eben yells just like a dog howls, puts his head back and yowls. I could have cheerfully choked him. His temperature has been normal for three days now so Doctor said he could go home tomorrow. Just as Doctor was leaving, Eben set up his howl and I told Doctor that he does that from about 4 A.M. until 7 so he said, "let him go home tonight." They will take good care of him at home and he'll get good food, so there is no need to worry. I, for one, shall be glad to get a full night's sleep again; I haven't since he arrived. It's a case of getting up about every hour and then from four on, listening to him cry.

February 21, 1925

Dear Miss Knust,

We're all glad this week is over; it has been terrible. Doctor was sick so all services were called off last Sunday. I woke up Sunday morning planning the day for quiet reading and writing. We just sat down to breakfast when in came Bruce with his wife in labor. As sick as Dr. Greist was, he came up and delivered her of a seven pound five ounce boy. Doctor had been very sick the week before and we had been busy with flu and pneumonia cases. Doctor had hiccoughs for seventy-two hours and we were very much worried. Mrs.

Greist, Peter, and Miss Dakin were all sick, but Miss Bannan and I didn't get it until Saturday. Monday Doctor came to the hospital again, but he looked dreadful; he went home and hiccoughed again. Mrs. Greist was very sick, too, and I went down and gave both of them vaccines. We all took the influenza-pneumonia vaccine. Mine affected my stomach. For two days I couldn't eat a thing, and having to work hard all day (our beds were all full) and be up at night, too, wasn't the best thing for it. Tuesday Miss Dakin was quite sick but since both Doctor and Mrs. Greist were sick in bed, she made rounds through the village, giving vaccine and medicine where needed. Most of the Natives were sick, but we couldn't take them all in the hospital. Everything was wild. There is an insane boy in the village, too, who has to have morphine each night. Some of the nights when I felt so rotten (it seemed weeks, but it was only four days) I could have cried when he resisted and we had to use force to quiet him. The flu has been here since February 4 but it didn't get so bad until the beginning of this week. Now everyone seems better. I'm feeling like myself again. We're hoping and praying that we have seen the last of it.

There are three kids in the hospital who don't seem to get well. Patsy with rheumatism, he just about lives here. His ankle was swollen when he came; that went down and so did his temperature so we let him up. Two days later his knee swelled like a balloon and his temperature went up to 102.6. Doctor has put him on strepto-staphylo vaccine. Fred, a five-year-old, came in with a temperature and some intestinal trouble. He got the flu, then his kidneys began to back up. He's the most mournful creature you ever saw, and he doesn't seem to get well. Another discouraging proposition is sixteen-month-old Rebecca Aitkan. She was here in November; she had some intestinal trouble that finally cleared up but Lucy, her mother, didn't give her the food we told her to and the little thing became sick again. Her disposition this time is much better than last, but caring for her is so discouraging; she seems to get better for a day or so then will run a temperature of 102 or more and lose every bit of ground she's gained. Yesterday she refused to eat, would only drink milk. This morning after breakfast she began to vomit and no matter what medicine Doctor ordered it came up. Poor little thing looked like she'd died and been left too long in a warm room. Finally Doctor fixed some powders that stayed down and she seems a little better this afternoon. It just seems, though, as if she'll never get well. When she was here the first time she had such an ugly disposition we were glad to get rid of her; but this time she has been more like a real baby and laughs and plays when she feels well.

The sun is back for almost eight hours a day now and the daylight is wonderful. The boys are flying kites, too; it seems so funny to see youngsters flying kites when the temperature is about forty below zero and the ground is covered with snow. Some of the kites are star shaped; all are made of cloth or seal intestine.

We sure were glad when the news finally reached us January 27 that Coolidge was in. He'd have gotten nine votes up here if we could have voted. Miss Dakin and I are anxious for the next mail to hear who the governor of New York is. The presidential news came from the West Coast, no letters reached here from New York dated later than the morning of November 4. Just think, when this letter reaches you I'll be thinking, "well, next year at this time I'll be planning my packing." I like it here but how I do want to see all my home folks and you, too.

My child Rebecca (she calls me Mama) is crying for me; poor youngster is too fretty for anything today. I'll be glad when 6:30 comes and I can make her go to sleep for the night. I'm sort of tired of hearing her cry.

February 1925

Thursday it was quieter than usual. Miss Dakin was the sickest of the white folks, but she won't let anyone do anything. She's as bad as Doctor: no one can do anything right but her. All my fur boots needed mending, so after lunch I went to Nellie's. Bert was home and he had Nellie get a chair for me. I sat there and we talked about all kinds of things. Little Harry came in and sat on my lap; he's all well now. Bert was making a harness for his dogs. He cuts gunny sacks into strips and then sews about four thicknesses inside white drilling; it makes a fine strong harness. I had a very nice time talking to him. Max was there and he would say something in Eskimo that Bert would interpret. While we were talking, Nellie fixed the boot I needed most. It was like going to a shoemakers at home and waiting for the work to be finished. It seemed funny. Bert, Max, and I were sitting on chairs and Nellie was sitting of the floor working on my boot. I guess Bert is the only Native who has three chairs; he has the nicest house and it's always so nice and clean.

It's only a week until the mail goes out and then no more for about six months. There are so many letters I want to get out just because of that, but that blamed flu knocked all my planning sideways.

Yesterday morning Rebecca seemed much worse. She had balked at taking her food all day Friday, but yesterday she did more than balk. She vomited all over everything and she looked like she was going to die any minute; she had a high temperature and a rotten pulse. Doctor ordered all kinds of medicine but it came up as fast as it went down. Then at last he made up a powder that seemed to settle her a little, but I had to go very easy on the food proposition. She was so cross and fretty all day and wouldn't go to sleep. She messed herself every little while, too, but was too sick for me to punish her for it. She cried and yelled and got on all our nerves in general. She had me up p.r.n. (as often as necessary) last night, too, and again at 6 A.M. This morning I spanked her, though she was better but just cussed. She had been so cute, too, but certainly has an ornery streak when she wants to be bad.

Thought as long as today was Sunday the Doctor wouldn't show up, but he's here. Just as I calmly sit down he calls me. At breakfast this morning I got sat on because I passed the remark that we had gotten further through our meal than the previous week without being disturbed. I don't think there are any babies due for a little while. Amakuk went home yesterday and Jennie goes tomorrow. That will leave us with Patsy, Fred, and Rebecca. It seems as though they will be here when the boats get here this summer. I've given up hoping that Rebecca might get well; she has lost all she gained and four ounces more, only weighs twenty-two pounds and six ounces and is seventeen months old. Jennie has an awfully nice baby this time; her other baby seemed like a half-wit when it was born. It has grown up all right, but this baby is normal and a sweet little thing. They have named him Edward. Yesterday we only had two office cases and one today. We all hope we have seen the last of the flu for a couple of years. Doctor was toting Rebecca around and then he landed here with me; she won't sit by me but wants to sit on my lap, so I am typing with her on my lap. It's quite an art and one only a two-fingered typist can master. Poor little kid, she hasn't vomited today yet, but when I show her a cracker (she usually loves them) she just shakes her head and pushes it away.

February 28, 1925

The mail closes tonight so I have to get busy and finish this up. The wind is still blowing from the northeast but not as hard as it did. My room is far from weatherproof and when the wind was blowing its hardest it kept me busy cleaning the snow out of the corner of my room. Miss Bannan says I don't appreciate indoor sport. She says that it isn't everyone who could shovel snow indoors. You just bet, though, when Miss Dakin goes out I take another room for next winter. This room is too much like outdoors. If no one comes to take her place, I'll take her room; otherwise, I'll take the white patient's room. We don't have a patient in there but once in a dog's age. Haven't had anyone since Lesley left a year ago.

Last night we went over to Peter's again. We didn't think Mr. Hopson would be out in the wind, but it didn't bother him. We beat Peter and Miss Bannan three games. Thursday night hardly anyone turned up for Bible class so Doctor called it off. The latest is that he is going to Pt. Hope with Willard. He wants Bert to take him. Bert is to furnish fifteen dogs and Doctor has agreed to pay him ten dollars a day. Doctor expects to be gone about a month so Bert will make quite a nice sum of money. If Doctor doesn't get it back from the government as he expects to, it will cost the board a little something, though. They sure will fuss. We'll be glad to have Doctor gone for over a month all right.

Rebecca is getting well again and gaining. I hope she keeps it up this time. She plays all day long in her crib, but she doesn't want to eat. I have to punish her every single time she eats. She gets a mouth full and spits it all over everything, then she yells bloody murder.

Peter, Miss Bannan, and I went home with Mrs. Riley. Her house was like an icebox. Miss Bannan and I got wood and Peter coal and got the fire started, then we began to dance with all our fur clothes on. Peter had his big boots and he looked like he was going both ways. He got warmed up first and took his cap off. The room was still so cold that the steam rose from his head. It was the funniest sight you ever saw. We had more fun dancing. I said we couldn't get called for dancing too close together because all our furs kept us about five inches apart. I'd love to have had a movie machine to get a picture of it. Peter had left all his new records there so we danced to "The Cat's Whiskers," "Yes, We Have No Bananas," "The March of the Wooden Soldiers," and a few other ones. They're all good dances, though. We didn't get home again till nearly one. Imagine roaming around in the Arctic regions, with no light but the stars and northern lights, at midnight with the mercury at thirty-nine below. We were very warm and comfortable and hated to go indoors.

I started to read the *Able McLaughlan*'s aloud to Miss Dakin and Miss Bannan Monday. We finished it last night. It sure is good. I'm reading Mark Twain's *Following the Equator* to myself. Mr. Riley has gotten a bunch of Dumas out of their boxes so I will have enough reading matter if none comes up in the mail.

Miss Dakin has been getting the *Daily News* and we are all wondering what is going to happen. She read the last one last night and doesn't expect any more. We are all excited to know how Walt gets back from the camp, if Skeezix[40] is stolen again, or what happens. We're most interested in Walt and Smitty. I hope we get some third-class mail this time. Last mail they left out the magazines and sent darned old parcel post that could have just as well stayed in Kotzebue.

March 8, 1925

I do wish some of you could come up here just for a church service. Really, it's as good as a circus. The last time I went it was so cold downstairs that Miss Bannan and I went up in the gallery and found that the seats were so much more comfortable. So today, although it wasn't cold, we went up. It was hotter than Dutch love and I shed my ahtega right away. The man, an old Native who had charge of the fires, sure was a faithful soul. He didn't let those stoves alone more than ten minutes at a time. He'd be fine to have there on a freezing cold day; he kept a red-hot fire going and most of the congregation kept their ahtegas on and panted. Doctor preached way over their heads for almost two hours. I watched the kids most of the time. They are lots of fun. Little Molly would talk, laugh, and clap for her tiny brother's benefit and make him yell for glee. Elizabeth yelled out of pure cussedness. Every two minutes someone was taking a little kid outdoors, then in they'd come and out would go someone else. George and May were kept occupied with their three youngest, Curtis, Carol, and Luther. Eben Hopson was making life interesting for everyone around him. The middle of the church looked for all the world like an ant hill. One mother would be rocking back and forth with her babe on her back, another would be going sideways, a third would look for all the world like a chicken flapping its wings, sort of punching the baby to quiet it. If I forget when I get home, remind me to give you an exhibition of the various ways to quiet a babe while it's on your back. It's a wonderful show at any rate. It was nasty and snowy out this morning but this afternoon it's lovely and clear. Poor little Rebecca was running around so much this morning that right after lunch she fell asleep in my arms as I picked her up to fix her crib for her nap.

March 14, 1925

Latest news is that Doctor will start for Pt. Hope the eighteenth; one never knows, though, just what he will do.

Monday I felt like printing, so started. We only had our usual three patients. Right after lunch Doctor sent a note over for a nurse to go to Isabelle's and bring things for a newborn baby. He wanted me but Miss Dakin went. There must have been some fuss because both came back as mad as wet hens. I continued to print and all of a sudden Doctor came in. We usually keep Rebecca in the operating room but I was printing in there so had her in the office. Doctor didn't say what he wanted, but he did want the kid out of the office. I got her out and continued to print. After a little he said, "You know Isabelle is coming to the hospital?" Then I got peeved and started to hustle to get a bed ready when in Miss Dakin came with the baby and a crowd with Isabelle. It seems that Isabelle was eating her lunch and didn't feel very good so went to lie down on the bed when the baby arrived. They had nothing ready so Doctor was sent for and, as usual, he ordered her to the hospital. It's a cunning little six-pound girl. They've named her May.

Tuesday afternoon I went over to Riley's. Mr. Riley was lying on the bed looking as sick as could be. Mrs. Riley was sewing so I sat and talked to him. We talked about everything under the sun, railroads in particular. We talked of the food service, speed, and everything, then he told of a trip he took in southern Alaska. It took them nine hours to go seventeen miles. They started with two passenger coaches, a diner, a baggage car, and an ore car, besides the engine. They ended up with a snow plow, three engines, and the two passenger trains. It must have been some trip.

March 21, 1925

Patsy, French, and Rebecca are all outdoors. It's pretty cold, about thirty below, but the sun is shining. I go in and out without a coat, tending to the kids. I have to wear mittens, though, to keep my fingers from freezing when I put Patsy's chair out.

April 19, 1925

It doesn't get all dark at all now. About midnight it's like twilight at home and the Natives are playing ball all night. Two nights last week they played until 3 A.M. I had Percy open my outside window and then I opened my inside one a little, but the noise of the entire village playing ball was rather disturbing. This side of the village plays the station. Even women and kids with babies on their backs play. The entire village stays there to yell and cheer, even the tiny youngsters. We have to stand the noise until whaling starts. The dogs aren't working now and they howl all night long, too. I'll miss the malamute chorus when I leave Alaska.

Yesterday my child was fretty all day long. Poor kiddie, she still runs a high temperature and doesn't get well at all. We thought to give her cod liver oil. She didn't know what it was and took it in her mouth. Then, wow! She got mad and spit it out and yelled and yelled. I don't think she forgave me for it all day. She'd give me the worst looks and for three hours after she got the taste of it she tried to vomit. She fussed and fussed and yelled and cried until I thought she never would be quiet. She's awfully cute at times, though.

April 26, 1925

Spring has come to Barrow. Last Sunday night, right after supper, I happened to glance out of the window and saw something moving near the building. It was a snow bird and make believe he didn't look good. He was so plump, white, and cocky. I yelled and everyone came to the window and oohed and aahed for quite a while. They have come back much sooner this year than other years I've been here. Now all day long we hear them chirping and singing and it's the sweetest sound you can imagine, especially when we haven't heard it for eight months. It's been very warm. Yesterday I went way past the school house with thin boots and only a sweater over me. Then when I came back my baby was crying, so I sat outdoors with her and read for over an hour; still only had my sweater on. I've ruined a pair of fur boot soles so far, so now am wearing *oogaruk*-soled ones until Lucy gets my water boots oiled up. They leak and the only thing to keep them from it is to have them soaked in seal oil, and then one isn't welcome company in a gathering of white people. The snow is melting fast and it's daylight all the time now. In two weeks we'll have twenty-four-hour sun.

I think my baby is getting well now. She is on the gain again and eats anything but mush and rice. I started her in on vegetables, broth, stew, and even blood from the deer meat, and her temperature has come down and she is getting on fine. She is the cutest little thing, but she sure can be as bad as they make them. When she doesn't get her way, which is quite often during the day, she just yells her head off, and she has the meanest yell.

Old Amakuk, an old paralyzed Native, is in with the worst swollen arm I ever saw. He came in one day and it was only swollen from the wrist to the elbow. Miss Dakin put a poultice on it and let him go home. The next day it was swollen clear to the shoulder, about three times its natural size. She has put all kinds of poultices on it without any result, but last night she tried ichthyol ointment and that seems to be doing the trick. Poor old fellow. He doesn't like to stay in the hospital worth a cent and hates like the dickens to keep the bandage on his arm. He takes it off whenever opportunity offers. The other day when Miss Dakin was sick I told Percy to tell him that he'd die if he didn't leave the bandage on, but in no time it was off, so maybe he'd just as leave die.

Miss Dakin was sick all day Tuesday. I tended to Amakuk as well as Rebecca and sure was some busy. Andrew and family and Steve and Eunice all left for the east with a bunch of the Natives who had come down. Edwardson had no flour and only four pounds of sugar when those Natives left, and they say the people haven't been getting seals and are hungry. All the teams took grub up. The wreck surely affected the stations to the east.

June 17, 1925

Dearest Miss Knust,

Three years ago today I left home. It doesn't seem that long, yet looking ahead just one year seems a long while. Next year at this time I'll be planning my trip home. I am hoping to go out by way of the Mackenzie River, that is east from here, by a trading ship to Herschel Island, then by a small boat to Shingle Point at the mouth of the Mackenzie and by river boat to Edmonton. It would be a wonderful trip and interesting, but as yet I don't know if connections can be made. Paul Steen, a young fellow, a trapper who was wrecked here last year, expects to go to Herschel on one of the ships and will write and let me know.

We have been more than busy. At present we have nine in-patients and one who stays all day but goes home at night. In the last six weeks we have had seven operations and, with a full house, operations certainly do make us hustle some. Dr. Greist had gone to Pt. Hope with a crazy boy who was proving too much to be left at large. We had no way of keeping him under guard. When Doctor came back things started. A woman had come down from the east with her husband and family and the night she arrived, she aborted. Since it was her third abortion after eight children she decided something should be done. So Doctor did a curettage and found her torn, so he did a perineorraphy, too [see Glossary]. A woman was brought up from Wainwright in bad shape; she was torn clear through the rectum and hadn't walked for over six months since she had had the flu. Doctor operated on her and she's crawling around some now. She has been sick so long it's hard to make her believe she is going to get all well. Then one of our Natives had been complaining for months with a headache that started after she bumped her head on a nail or something. At last Doctor decided to make an incision and see just what was the matter. There was plenty. Two

depressions, softening of the skull itself, and a brain abscess.
I thought when I started the anaesthetic it would only last
a few minutes, but it lasted two and a half hours. She goes
home this week; she was operated on two weeks ago. Daisy,
a Pt. Hope woman, came up when Doctor did; she has had a
TB knee for years and lately it broke down. When she arrived here she had four evil-smelling sinuses. Doctor put off
amputating the leg until her general condition improved. It
was amputated a week ago. Afterwards, Doctor cut into the
knee and all the bones were infected. Gosh, what a mess. The
stump is septic but is getting along nicely now. Yesterday we
had a herniotomy case and there are two other P.O. [post-op-
erative] cases wandering around the hospital. One is a man
from Wainwright who had a couple of discharging sinuses
on his chest for over a year; he fell on a sled. The other is an
old half-witted fellow from Pt. Barrow who had a badly infected arm. It swelled up from the finger tips to the shoulder.
He gave no history of a cut of any kind so we didn't know
where or how the infection started. But after much poultic-
ing it opened in four places and drained quarts of pus. Then
it wouldn't heal so Doctor opened it under general anaesthetic. He sure did cut it, from above the elbow to the wrist.
Poor old Amakuk hasn't good sense and he decides to take
the bandage off whenever he wishes. It's a wonder it hasn't
become reinfected, but it's really doing wonderfully well in
spite of all the damage he did. One of our men, Timothy, has
had an infected finger for a long time, but since he didn't
want to miss whaling, he put tobacco on the finger and let
it go. He comes every day for hot baths and poultices, but
Doctor thinks the finger will have to come off.

June 19, 1925

Sixteen whales were caught this year. Tuesday afternoon
I quit writing to go to the Nelegetuk on the station side of

the village. Five boats got together and had their Nelegetuk
there. I was tired from the morning's work so I didn't stay
very long. I just watched the skin tossing for a while. In the
evening Miss Dakin went over. Paul had come back with me
in the afternoon and stayed to supper and then hung around
for a while in the evening. He's a nice chap and we all like
him very much. Yesterday our side of the village had their
Nelegetuk. Four boats were in on it. They had a better day
than the station crowd, although it got very cold and foggy
in the evening. We had all our patients there except the P.O.
hernia and the leg case. Daisy's husband stayed at the hospital and tended to her and Owen, the hernia case, so both
Miss Dakin and I were out most of the afternoon. Paul and
I came back to the hospital a few times, he to get warm and
I just to see that everything was all right. The men all went to
Peter's for supper and Miss Bannan, Miss Dakin, and I went
to the manse. We had brant and it sure was good. I have three
ahtega but the patients had them on so all I had to wear was
two sweaters. I was plenty warm as long as the skin was up
because I helped toss [see Figures 4.9 and 4.10], but when the
dancing started I got quite cold so I came home about nine,
sent Lenny home, fixed up the patients for the night, and
was just going to bed when Paul came in, so I stayed up for a
while longer. Today I feel quite a few muscles I forgot I had.
Skin tossing is lots of fun but it nearly takes one's arms out.

We have had the most wonderful weather. The season is
about two weeks ahead of time and the tundra around the
hospital is drier than I've ever seen it. We all hope that it
means an early breakup and that the boats get here soon.
There ought to be three new boats this year. We know that
the Liebes will send up a new one in place of the *Arctic*. The
Hudson Bay people will likely send a ship up in place of the
Kindersley, and although we hope the old cutter *Bear* will

4.9. Skin toss during Whale Feast. Reprinted with permission from Anchorage Museum of History and Art, Eide Album (#B70-25-266), Anchorage, Alaska.

4.10. Augusta Mueller and Helen Suvlu at Whale Feast— "all I had to wear was two sweaters." Reprinted with permission from Terza Hopson Collection (#TH059), Inupiat History, Language and Culture Commission, Barrow, Alaska.

come (there is a rumor that it will), some sort of a cutter will come up.

We're still waiting for Captain Amundsen and wondering if the flight has been postponed again.

July 18, 1925

Miss Dakin had gotten a skull on the tundra to take home for someone and it had some stuff stuck to it. She didn't want to take it home that way and yet didn't want to clean it herself, so I scrubbed it for her. I shut the office door and had a great old time getting it clean.

Thursday morning there was hardly any wind so I went out in my kayak and took a picture of the reflections of the station from the middle of the lagoon. After lunch it began to blow like the dickens, and the lagoon was as rough as could be. I wanted to go to the station to take a piece of cake to Mr. Hopson and get my boots from Mrs. Riley, but the creek was too high and the current too swift to make crossing safe with even high boots, so I took my kayak. The wind almost blew me over, but I landed all right. The wind was against me coming back and I had quite a time. Then, just as I got to the small creek between the lagoons, the water was about a foot higher than usual. I tried to get through a narrow deep cut but a sudden extra strong wind came up and it tipped me right over. It began to rain like everything, too, and I got soaked and then some. It's a wonder I didn't tip before I did. Paul is trying to make me sell my kayak, but nothing doing. I'll want it after he goes because then I'll have to go out by myself. He's afraid I'll tip in deep water, lose my head, and drown. But I'd be able to get out of it even if I did tip in deep water. I'm not afraid at any rate. Paul is a dear and I sure do like him, but he doesn't know that the best way to make me want to do a thing is to say that it's not safe or not to do it.

4.12 Dr. Albert and Mrs. Newhall at Barrow. Reprinted, with permission, Alaska and Polar Regions Archives, Elmer. E. Rasmuson Library, University of Alaska Fairbanks, Yukon Presbytery (#04-C).

We went out for a walk after supper. For the first time it has cleared up for us. We stayed out for about three hours.

As we finished I looked out of the kitchen window (about 10:30) and there was the *Nanuk* almost here. Gosh, it was a surprise. Paul and Hopson hurried to the beach and I came home. Then Miss Dakin, Miss Bannan, and I went down to the beach and Paul came for us in a canoe to take us out to her. We went aboard and got the news of the day, that Amundsen had started and hadn't made the trip; that China was fighting herself; that Japan and California had an earthquake; that the Newhalls[41] [see Figure 4.12] were to relieve Doctor and that they were on the *Charles D. Brower;* that Mr. Brower, his two boys, and Miss Wallace were also on the *C.D.B.;* and I don't know what all. We absorbed all the news and asked for more.

We hung around and hung around and no one came ashore on our side of the village. Then the mail came in and there were nearly seventy sacks, I think. Talk about excitement. We got our letters and began to read them but didn't have much chance because the Newhalls arrived. Mr. Brower came over; he looks fine after his year outside. Peter had to go right after dinner but the Newhalls had a lot to talk about and Paul stayed a while. But I read my letters while Paul was here. Miss Wallace had been over in the afternoon. She had a dress on to her knees and says it's the style. I'm glad I'm not going out because I'd sure not be in style if I had to go back to knee-length dresses.

Dr. and Mrs. Newhall are lovely. He is the jolliest man imaginable and kept us in hysterics all during the dinner. He's always telling something funny. Both are very stout and both are short. They were in charge of the Jessie Lee Home in Unalaska.

The *Baychimo* came in Sunday morning. The *C.D.B.* had been unloading all night so there were only a handful of

people in church. Dr. Newhall preached and it was good to
hear him. Not one of the few natives went to sleep. He came
over to Junior in the afternoon and played the organ for my
eighteen kids. Mr. Alex Smith, a surveyor, was here to dinner. Three men are here for survey work on the oil fields.
They went east on the *Brower*. There are four men due here
before the boats go; Fitzgerald is one of the men who was
here last year. Paul came over Sunday night to say good-bye.
Gee, I'm going to miss him as soon as things quiet down. He
certainly was a mighty good scout to me.

July 29, 1925

Dear Evy,

The boxes all arrived okay. Thanks muchly. Aren't you
glad they're the last? So glad you liked the fur. About the
money. The board does not send us money to go out with,
for some reason unknown to us. That's why I wanted regular
money to get at least as far as Nome on. The board refunds
the money all right but they don't send it up to us. A money
order for that amount is no good because the P.O. very seldom has that much cash. Miss Dakin's brother sent her three
hundred dollars in a registered letter and it got here okay.
Only it has to be put in a very strong envelope to insure its
safety.

Someone in the board sent one of the letters I wrote there
to a magazine and I got a check for $7.50 for it. That makes
$12 I've gotten so far. Guess I'll be a writer. Peter and Jim
were teasing me about Paul last night and said I'd be a good
trapper's assistant.

I got nearly one hundred letters on the two boats. Can you
see the fun I'm going to have answering them. I have a lot
of printing I want to get done, too; all of Peter's negatives,
because he wants us to send them out on the November mail.
The Cleveland church sent up a dandy Victrola, a portable

one, and four dozen records. Someone in Canastota, New York, sent me *Everyland* and the *Junior Endeavor World* for my kids. I sure did get a bunch of things.

August 31, 1925

Dear Folks,

Yesterday it was three years since I hit Barrow. It doesn't seem that long. Next year at this time I'll be on my way home. Gee, it will be good to see all of you. Don't forget to have roast pork, mashed potatoes, and applesauce for my first dinner. I'll telegraph when I expect to hit New York.

October 3, 1925

Dear Folks,

We sure did get the surprise of our lives yesterday morning when we woke up and saw the *Baychimo* sitting out in our front yard. The school time is thirty-five minutes[42] ahead of ours and, although we keep the hall clock at our old time, we have to get up by the school time so Ada can get her work done and get to school on time. Result is that we're all balled up most of the time. Yesterday morning I woke up at six by my watch and had to figure out what time I had to get up. At twenty-five after I was deciding to haul out when I heard Mrs. Newhall yell "Miss Bannan!" and expected to hear her say it's time to get up by school time, when she came out with "the *Baychimo* is out here!"

No sign of the lost Pt. Barrow folks was seen by the *Baychimo*. Everyone thinks they are lost for good. Mr. Larson sure did run into hard luck up here. First losing one of the party to the east, Mr. Scarboro, then losing the schooner, then all his stuff, and now last, himself. It's too bad. He's a fine man and the Natives he was with are good trappers and hunters. Of course they may turn up yet, but no one expects them to. Poor old Joshua died some time Wednesday morning in his tent. He died happy at any rate. He was home. He likely would have lived longer in the hospital, but he was so unhappy; he didn't like our food nor anything else.

Yesterday Doctor had nine school kids come here to have their teeth fixed. About all I did all morning was wait on him, hold kids' heads while he pulled teeth and hold cotton rolls in the mouths while he filled teeth. He pulled eight and filled more than that.

I caught a louse the other day in my head and don't want any more for a while. They seem to like me. I have a family every once in so often.

Tomorrow Doctor is going to have communion. The men asked if they couldn't have clean cloths to wipe off the glasses between folks. We were quite surprised and delighted to know that they are thinking that much about cleanliness. We have over sixty medicine glasses so I hit on the idea of using them for individual glasses, so that's what they are going to do. We have no tray for them so will use large pie plates. Who says necessity isn't the mother of invention?

October 14, 1925

Dear Miss Knust,

I've just come in from taking pictures; wanted to get the relatives of our children who are at Sitka so I could send them out on this mail. I had to go way to the end of the village and, since the snow is up to my knees in most places and there are no trails as yet, it was some job walking. It has snowed hard for two or three days and the snow had drifted quite high around the buildings.

I think the first missionaries originated the Christmas tree made of sticks. This year the church that is supporting me sent up two six-foot artificial trees and we are going to use them at church. The people of that church have been more than good to me. They sent up a 250-pound box of toys, games, dolls, and things for my own use, besides the two trees. A wealthy woman, the owner of the Taylor and Son store in Cleveland, pays the freight.

This was a very early season. All the boats got in and out safely. The first boat came in July 25 and we all went aboard of her and asked poor Mrs. Pederson a million questions. We also had apples and oranges. The mail boat, the *Brower*, got in the next day and the *Boxer*, *Bear*, *Holmes*, and *Baychimo* all came in very early. The new captain of the *Bear* is very nice. We were so glad to see the old *Bear* come up again. All the papers said she'd made her last trip, but Captain Colville thinks she will be up again in 1926. Miss Dakin and the Greists went out on her. The new missionaries, Dr. and Mrs. Newhall from Unalaska, came up on the *Brower* so they were here when the others left. No one came to take Miss Dakin's place, but Mrs. Newhall is taking Miss Bannan's work and Miss Bannan helps me when necessary. She doesn't know beans about nursing, but I have taught her how to take T.P.R.'s [temperature, pulse, respiration] and she can bathe patients and make beds. But when we have a very sick patient I have to do the staying up nights.

Have had a little boy here for a month; he goes home today. He had a bad conjunctivitis and something the matter with his hip so he couldn't walk. They had him in a tent way on the other side of the village so didn't bring him for quite a while. Once he got here he improved rapidly. The only case we'll have left is Hester, who has been here a week. She poured gasoline on the fire and burned both buttocks, one leg from the knee to the hip, both arms and quite a few burns on her back and abdomen. It's a wonder she didn't burn all up. She ran out of the house and Paul, a Pt. Barrow Native, saw her and threw her down and himself on top of her. She is a husky twelve-year-old and has been a brick through it all. She never yelled once and only cries a little when I put the first coat of Pyroseptine[43] on it. Dr. Newhall has been a missionary in Unalaska for twenty-seven years and, although he'd read of the paraffin dressings for burns, he'd never used it nor seen it used. We'd used a lot of it in the Met and I told him how good it was. He is not a bit like Dr. Greist, who was always on his dignity and afraid that a nurse might question his ability. Dr. Newhall is willing to try anything once—and best of all, the Pyroseptine is doing all and more than I claimed for it. Dr. Newhall says he never saw a burn heal as quickly as this one is. Of course, she doesn't smell any too sweet. I almost give up my breakfast when I dress the leg, which is one big third degree burn and as gooey as a burn can be. But it's all healing in from the edges. Doctor looks in when I'm doing the dressing but gets out after the first few smells and says, "My, but I'm glad I have a graduate nurse here."

I can sing in Eskimo. Of course just hymns, but it's something. The Doxology is my specialty:

Jehovah *nalsuniluksput*
Aitchoktoa igatigut
Nalatuktoanisiu
Angun, Ergnek, Ilit kusek.

And the chorus of "We Shall See the King Some Day":

Tautukniagikput omealik (elyane)	"We shall see the king"
Tautukniagikput elyane	"We shall see some day"
Attautchemmuklutig	"Gathered round the throne"
Kokokpagnit inyugne	"He shall call his own"
Tautukniagikput omealik	

I can sing both of those now without a paper in front of me. It's lots of fun.

Much love,

October 17, 1925

Life just seemed to be one job after another this morning. As soon as I got up I took Clara's and Hester's temperature, then gave Clara medicine and Hester water to wash with, tightened Clara's binder and then had breakfast. After breakfast Miss Bannan washed and combed Clara and made her bed while I bathed the baby. Then I had to dress Hester's burns and that always takes about an hour. I wish you could see how rapidly those burns are healing up. It was ten o'clock before I got all the regular work done. Miss Bannan went to church and Clara and Hester wanted me at intervals until it was time for the baby to nurse and then it was dinner to get ready. So now it's almost one o'clock. I hope things stay quieted down because I would like to get a few notes written to go down to Wainwright with Dr. Newhall tomorrow.

That girl who was admitted last Sunday afternoon didn't have a hemorrhage until ten at night. She lost about a pint of blood, then a half hour later she had another and another at four in the morning. I thought surely she would die before I could give her a hypo each time, but she seemed to get over them and didn't hemorrhage all day Monday. I slept down in her room and just as I was getting ready to go to bed she had another hemorrhage. I gave her a hypo and another at one. She seemed as well as usual then, but at two thirty I heard a noise and she was having the worst hemorrhage. She didn't move at all but the blood poured from her mouth and before I could get to her she was dead. I straightened her out and went to my own bed but didn't sleep. I guess all that blood upset me. I hope I never have to see another like it. The poor old mother is blind and she took it awfully hard. Eskimos usually are very quiet and reconciled to death, but she made quite a time. Jane was a dear youngster and a lot of help at home, I think. Both boys are crippled; that whole family is TB.

October 25, 1925

Our Delco is still out of fix, so we are getting our Christmas
packages done up while we still have some daylight. Have all
the children up to four years done. Friday night I made out
a list of all the people in Barrow and Pt. Barrow. We had a
good many of them from last year, but new ones have come
into the village and old ones have left so the list changes each
year. Each baby got an outing flannel dress, a cake of soap,
a wash cloth, and a toy. Each boy over two got a suit or cap
and gloves, a book, a toy, and a ball. Each girl over two to
four got a doll, a dress, a book, and a ball. Everything is so
nice and new, too. The mission boxes were lovely this year.
We have all kinds of balls, dolls, ties, ribbons, handkerchiefs,
gloves, and stockings that came up. I pressed and cleaned
over sixty neckties the other day. They look pretty decent.
Other years they got them without pressing. People send up
old ties of all kinds.

Thanksgiving 1925

Thursday we all go to the school to dinner. Just think, next
year I'll be home and maybe have turkey. Our oranges are all
gone so we have to do without fresh fruit until summer and I
said this morning, "Just think, next year at this time I'll have
all the apples, oranges, grapes, and bananas I want and won't
have to think about doing without them." Miss Bannan told
me to shut up and I kept right on, "pork, real applesauce,
cow's milk that isn't canned, fresh cranberry sauce." They
were ready to throw me out. I'll miss a lot of things that we
have up here, but, gee, I'll be glad to get home.

The health of the village has been very good. We have had
many outpatients, two thousand, but since the boats came,
very few sick enough to stay in the hospital. Babies were
born in the hospital and two in the igloos since the first of
August. The last baby was the dearest little boy, as good as

gold. His mother, Helen, helped in the hospital over three years and she takes very good care of her baby. She says he only cries when she carries him on her back Eskimo fashion, and then she bathes him every morning and only feeds him every three hours instead of any time he cries, like the other Eskimos do. All the mothers in the village keep their babies so much cleaner than they used to.

Wednesday, November 25, the teachers had a program for Thanksgiving and the children did very well. They love to memorize and are not a bit self conscious. They were all dressed up in clean clothes, but I doubt very much if our children would call them dress-up clothes. Some of the boys had overalls on and some khaki trousers much too large for them, hitched up with men's suspenders. One little round-faced kiddie had on a black satin dress that her mother had made of the lining of a coat that came up in a mission box. It had sparkling buttons all down the front and make believe she didn't think she was the most dressed-up little one there. One poor little shaver had a pair of torn pants, an undershirt and a man's vest on, yet his chest was out as far as anyone's and he was as pleased as punch to be in the front row in everything.

Dr. Newhall had Thanksgiving services in the morning and Miss Bannan and I went. A lot of the Natives had come in from their trapping camps so that the church was pretty well filled. In the afternoon the Eskimos had their meeting and feast. They had frozen seal, walrus and deer meat, muktuk, frozen fish, tea biscuits, and Eskimo ice cream. They ate all afternoon, but this year we had no tummyache cases reported the next day. They have much to be thankful for this year. The trapping season was very good. They caught more whales than they have for years, and the sealing, walrus hunting, and fishing have all been exceptionally good. They are all well fed, which accounts for the little sickness in the village. This trapping season has started in pretty good, too.

December 5, 1925

Sunday the wind blew a gale and we had given up hopes of the mail for another day and went to bed early, disgusted. But Mr. Sylvester[44] brought it over at about ten. Mr. Brower had sent it over with the boys, but there was no light here so they took it to the school house. We were all excited and read until about midnight. I got thirty-some letters and a couple of packages. One was a box of candy that Paul had given to someone on the *Brower* to leave here, and he forgot and took it to Nome where he mailed it and a letter for me and one for Miss Bannan from him. Peter sent a Christmas present from Nome.

A little Newhall arrived yesterday morning at 2:25. He only weighs five pounds ten ounces and looks just like Doctor. I have been pretty busy and haven't been in the mood for letter writing. I'm going to make thirty-two carbon copies of the Thanksgiving and Christmas doings and just write notes with them instead of letters. I'll be home to tell you all kinds of things, so my letters won't be much from the first of the year on.

December 13, 1925

Nothing much has happened since last week. The baby wasn't doing very well and I was up quite a lot nights and there is no chance of getting any sleep during the day, so I didn't go out nor do anything much but care for Mrs. Newhall and Warren Blake. He lost ten ounces in four days and hasn't gained it yet. We have put him on bottled milk, Eagle Brand condensed, and hope he weighs more than five pounds tomorrow. He sleeps all day long and we can hardly make him eat. Mrs. N. is up and around today so she will care for him nights now. I still bathe him. His head was injured when he was born and I'll likely bathe him until that gets well. He is so tiny, looks like a plucked chicken.

Old Amakuk's arm is all well and he hadn't been around for over a week when he breezed in the other day. His shoulder hurt and he had a cough (he wanted some candy). The old fellow has quite a sweet tooth. His shirt was a sight so I gave him a clean one. His hair is almost to his shoulders so Doctor cut it, then shaved him, put cold cream, talcum, and bay rum on him, and I wish you could have seen Amakuk admire himself in front of the mirror and dance around. Since then, though, Doctor has been scratching and I bet he got cooties because Amakuk had them in his head.

December 20, 1925

Five more days until Christmas. The blamed kids have the Christmas itch, I think, and I can't do a single thing with them. They are full of the old Nick and we're so busy that they get on our nerves. Big Roy, Mrs. Brower's brother, was brought in from the trapping camp Monday. He is paralyzed on his entire left side and is quite a care. He seems to be getting some power back in his foot but his hand is still helpless. It's a wonder he didn't freeze to death. He was found in his tent with his clothes half off. His head, face, and one toe were frozen, but all seem to be getting well.

Big Roy is the hungriest thing. He wants to eat all the time and gets away with all kinds of grub when I do feed him. I hope no one else gets sick until after Christmas. We are planning to have Helen and Lee come here Christmas day so we can all go the station. That is, if Warren is well enough to be taken over. I told Mrs. Newhall that I would take him under my ahtega.

Hester went home today. I bet she was glad to go. Her leg has a small spot that isn't quite healed but we wanted to get rid of her for Christmas and she can come each day for her dressing. They have a nice clean igloo and she'll get decent food at home.

December 20, 1925

Dear Miss Knust,

I wonder if you have your Christmas shopping done yet? Gosh, it will seem good next year to go wandering through the stores again. The other night when I was over to the store they had the toys and things out, and it looked like quite a display to an old sourdough like me. Honestly, I'll need a guardian and handcuffs when I get back to the States. Miss Wallace, Mr. Hopson, and I became childish and had more fun racing the mechanical toys and blowing up balloons, playing with a big ball, and acting foolish in general.

My child Rebecca was sick again, just a case of malnutrition. Her father is a lazy half-breed and they don't have enough food. As soon as we gave Lucy stewed fruit and crackers for Rebecca she began to get well without staying in the hospital. She sure is a cunning little thing, but as bad as she can be. Now she has the rosiest cheeks and is too sweet for words when she comes to visit us. Her mother expects a baby in January and that will likely cure Rebecca. All these kids are ornery until the next one arrives. Then they settle down and take life as it comes.

I want to wash my locks and then go over to the station and have Miss Wallace give me a haircut for Christmas. Today is our darkest day. It's snowing and windy so I'll have a job to get there, but I need the haircut.

I'll be seeing you in less than a year and it sure will seem good.

Christmas 1925

Friday morning I got up at six instead of seven o'clock and got the paralyzed man fixed up before breakfast. We ate breakfast by the light of two red and two green candles with the tree in the center of the table. It was lovely. After prayers, the girls did their dishes in a hurry and we did up our work as quickly as possible. Miss Bannan fed the man and I bathed the baby while Mrs. Newhall kept the girls going. Then we all went out to the hall tree and Dr. Newhall was Santa and gave out the presents. Then we all went to the dining room and had the most exciting time of all. My friends certainly were more than good to me. I have so many lovely new things that I'll be all dressed up when I get outside. At four we went to the station and had dinner and a good time to end up a perfectly glorious Christmas—my last one in Barrow.

January 1926

Dear Folks,

I'm really beginning to feel like a human again. For a few days after New Year's I was too tired to move. Warren turned over a new leaf New Year's day and began to eat so we were happy about that. I just made one New Year's resolution, that is to get outdoors every day, if only for half an hour, and I've kept it up so far. I doll up in my fur pants, lined ahtega, wristlets, mittens, and fur boots, then I don't care how cold or windy it is.

January 31, 1926

Life is one thing after another up here. It's the end of January and no sign of the mail. We have been looking for it since the twenty-seventh and are just about ready to chew each other's ears off when mail is mentioned. We have had one wind storm after another and even though the men have fifteen dogs on the mail team I guess they can't make any headway against this head wind. The sun, too, has failed us. We've only seen it one day and that day it was windy as the dickens. Today it's trying to snow and has come up, but it looks very pale with the snow and wind blowing a regular curtain in front of it. Also, we have a crazy man in the village. He was brought down from the eastward. He heard voices and noises, threatened to kill his wife and beat up his blind son, so they brought him down and have him under guard in Kivilik's house and are to have a trial tomorrow and then send him down the coast with Ned to Pt. Hope. Mr. Brower tried to get us to take him, but this isn't a nut house and Doctor sent a note to Mr. Brower saying he was referring the insane case to the U.S. government and since Mr. Brower is the judge and commissioner up here he had to care for him.

We have a sick little boy here. He was brought down from inland. First they said he had eaten a lot of black skin and was taken sick then. Then when he screamed for his mother they said he was not to be left alone since he had been "very scared." He didn't appear scared when he yelled, just cussed. Yesterday Doctor had Nita, his mother, here with Peter's wife and from her story, that man from the eastward isn't the only crazy one in the village. They had a camp away from Nita's and she put some fish heads in a skillet and when she turned around for a minute and looked back the fish heads were gone and she saw "little men" in the flames. There was no dog nor person in the room with her. Then she went outdoors and when she started back in the house she couldn't breathe, saw black spots that looked like the little men before her eyes, and fainted. They hustled to Nita's camp and told the story in Clarence's presence and scared the kid. Martha says she hears voices, etc., too, when no one else does. Things are getting interesting in Barrow.

All we can think and talk about is mail. It's an awful state to get in. There'll be more than two nuts in the village if it doesn't get in pretty soon.

I've been sleeping at the other end of the house since Clarence was brought in. I slept in the little room until Lucy ran a temperature. Then we had to move Carrie there and I used the dining room couch in the hall next to the kid. Clarence raised a fuss when he first came, but has improved a lot and is a real good youngster. We had a lot of fun before Carrie went home with May yesterday. I'd bathe Wesley, then as soon as I'd finish, Miss Bannan would bathe May and by that time Warren was awake and Mrs. Newhall would bathe him. We had a regular baby hospital. Warren seems to be holding his own and looks better, but he sure is a weak little tike. He doesn't weigh six pounds and is almost two months old.

Yesterday afternoon in all the blow, Mrs. Sylvester and I walked to the end of the village. Going down it was all right, but coming back the wind was in our faces and she almost froze hers; it got white. Mine seems to be toughened and I don't get nearly as cold as I used to.

February 4, 1926

Dear Miss Knust,

As you can see by the enclosure, you should have gotten a letter on the summer mail, but it came back to me instead.

We were nearly frantic, waiting for the mail. It should have come in the twenty-ninth at the very latest and didn't get in until last night. We were all going around in circles, couldn't think of a thing but the mail. It's an awful feeling.

I started home about 4:30. It was pitch dark and I had no flashlight with me so stumbled over drifts, etc.; as I neared the hospital I heard a team going along the beach, but I'd done enough stumbling and had been disappointed so many times thinking teams were the mail that I didn't even tell the folks I'd heard the team. In a few minutes John Aitken arrived and said the mail was in. We didn't get it until nearly six but were too excited to eat. I ate one hotcake, a piece of cake, and a dish of applesauce.

The patient who had her leg cut off last spring sent me a lovely pair of fur boots. They're the prettiest I've seen.

We have been very busy this past month. We had three babies, two in the wee hours of the morning. How I hate to get out of a warm bed at 1 A.M. and sit around in a cool, if not cold, house waiting for a babe to arrive. The last one, an 8 $\frac{3}{4}$ pound boy, was born at 8:43 A.M. He was born with a caul so should be brilliant. Doctor said I didn't look natural, that I should have had my pajamas and bathrobe on with my hair standing in all directions.

Glad to know you heard Captain Amundsen.[45] We're quite excited now over two telegrams Mr. Brower got. They come by mail from Kotzebue, so are over a month old, but a Captain Wilkins,[46] who was Stefansson's photographer, wired and said he would be here in an airplane the end of this month. We can hardly wait.

All my thoughts and plans now are of HOME. I hope to get home in October some time. Mr. Brower has offered to take me to the eastward first on the Liebes and Co. ship so I'll see more of Alaska. That depends on the weather and ice conditions, though. I'm sure going to bring my outfit out, smelly boots and all. My fur pants are rather moth-eaten looking, but they'll do.

I've been very well and happy as per usual. Hope to see you as soon as I get back. So glad you're happy at the Nurses Club. Sure will come to visit you.

Afterword

D R. NEWHALL DIED SUDDENLY of pneumonia in February
1929, thus Dr. and Mrs. Greist were returned to Barrow
in August of the same year.[47] They remained until 1936 when
the hospital was transferred to the Alaska Medical Service of
the Bureau of Indian Affairs. Mildred Keaton (chapter 7) was
the receiving agent for the BIA.[48]

Early in 1937 the Barrow hospital burned. All patients and
staff got out unharmed.[49] The eight-bed makeshift hospital
that followed the fire consisted of a small frame building, a
sod igloo, and a tent. It was replaced by a fifteen-bed hospital
in February 1939. The Alaska Native Health Service replaced
this 1939 facility with a new twelve-bed, two-million-dollar
facility that opened its doors April 12, 1966.[50] It is a single-
story wood frame structure erected on wood pilings. The
Barrow service unit has five village-built clinics within its
boundary, staffed by community health aides.[51]

Ownership changed again in 1996 when the Barrow hospital was transferred to the Arctic Slope Native Association.[52]
With the discovery of oil in Prudhoe Bay, new challenges
faced the Inupiat of the North Slope. The dominant lifestyle
of the United States was thrust upon them suddenly and
forcefully. Against overwhelming odds and opposition, and
without special training in business or government, the
North Slope Borough government, the Arctic Slope Regional
Corporation, and the ANSCA village corporations were created and survived. The first mayor defined the borough's primary goal as providing its resident population with the same
basic services enjoyed by other Americans. This goal was a
difficult challenge. Since 1972, the quality of life for North
Slope Borough residents has greatly improved. Barrow in
1993 ranked as the twelfth largest city in Alaska with around
four thousand residents.[53]

Endnotes

1. Augusta Mueller, letters 1922–1926, Alaska Nurses Association Collection, Augusta Mueller file, Series 14-1, Box 37, Folders 609-610, Archives, Elmer E. Rasmuson Library, University of Alaska Fairbanks, Fairbanks. Mueller's letters to her "folks" consist of 181 pages of single-spaced typing. In addition she submitted seventy pages of mostly handwritten letters to "Miss Knust," a nurse friend. Ruth Benson of Fairbanks helped Effie Graham in selecting the content for this collection. Priority was given to experiences relating to nursing practice, with samples of other experiences. For example, Mueller gave detailed descriptions of all Christmas menus and only one is given here.

2. Social Security Index.

3. Application Form, filed by Mueller in 1934, for a nursing position in Alaska, preferably with Eskimos. National Archives, U.S. Department of Interior, Office of Indian Affairs, Alaska Section. This application was reviewed by Elinor Gregg and Mueller was considered for employment as a "village nurse." There is no evidence of finalization of the application.

4. Mollie Greist, "Nursing Under the North Star," unpublished manuscript (no date), 93. Alaska Nurses Association Collection, Series 13-2, Box 29, File 477. Archives, Elmer E. Rasmuson Library, University of Alaska Fairbanks, Fairbanks. This manuscript is a corroboration document supporting Mueller's letters. Mollie Greist, a nurse as well as the wife of Dr. Henry W. Greist, was at various times a teacher in the school, a weather observer, and founder of the Mother's Club. This social group promoted the health of both mothers and children.

5. Ibid., 224.

6. Hudson Stuck, *A Winter Circuit of Our Arctic Coast* (New York: Charles Scribner's Sons, 1920), 210.

7. Stuck, *Winter Circuit,* 209.

8. M. Greist, "Nursing," 56–60.

9. For more information on the Brower family and the whaling/trading establishment at Barrow, see Margaret B. Blackman, *Sadie Brower Neakok: An Inupiaq Woman* (Seattle: University of Washington Press, 1989). This is a biography, with autobiographical elements, of Charles Brower's daughter Sadie. The latter was a child during Mueller's residence in Barrow and provides another perspective of this time, as well as corroboration of many details.

10. Augusta Mueller to Catherine Gair. Letter 8 April 1956.

11. Augusta Mueller to Catherine Gair. Letter 17 March 1956.

12. Augusta Mueller to Catherine Gair. Letters 9 February 1956, 26 February 1956, 8 April 1956, 17 March 1963, and 2 May 1963. Augusta Mueller file, Series 14-1, Box 37, Folder 609, Alaska Nurses Association Collection, Archives, Elmer E. Rasmuson Library, University of Alaska Fairbanks.

13. Mueller's writing is full of references to sea vessels important to the life of Barrow in the days before air travel. In addition to the Coast Guard Cutter *Bear* (see William Bixby, *Track of the Bear,* New York: David McKay, 1965),

there was the *Boxer,* a Bureau of Indian Affairs Department of Education service ship that delivered personnel and supplies. The *Boxer* was "formerly a barkentine rigged naval training ship, had an overall length of 120 feet—converted to a diesel auxiliary schooner" as noted by Edward L. Keithahn in *Eskimo Adventure* (New York: Bonanza Books, 1963), 4. The *C.S. Holmes* was "a big schooner, which carried freight, coal, and groceries, operating with both sails and engine" (M. Greist, "Nursing," 88). The *Herman* was an "old whaler of 325 tons with a 250 horsepower diesel" (Carl Loman, *Fifty Years in Alaska,* New York: David Mckay, 1954, 161).

In her letters, Mueller details problems and interactions among these and other ships during the ice problems of late summer 1924. They include the *Letty,* the *Teddy Bear,* the *Fox,* the *Arctic* (which sank), the *Nanuk,* and especially the *Lady Kindersley,* a Canadian ship that was almost lost and the *Baychimo,* the rescuer. The latter ship was caught in the ice in the late 1920s and remained a derelict floating in a chunk of ice for many years (M. Greist, "Nursing," 142).

14. Jim Allen, whaler and trader from Wainwright, Alaska (M. Greist, "Nursing," 73–74). He and his family had a close relationship with the Brower family (Blackman, *Sadie Brower Neakok,* 94–95).

15. Florence Dakin, a missionary nurse already in Barrow, was the head nurse of this small hospital. The Greists' initial contacts with Dakin had been confrontational (M. Greist, "Nursing," 57, 62).

16. Helen Suvlu, a nursing aide and general assistant. She was still working at the hospital when Elinor Gregg, supervisor of nurses for the BIA, visited in 1936. Gregg said, "The doctor had left, and an epidemic of diphtheria was being managed by a good sort of Native practical nurse. She devoted many hours of work, but naturally her judgment was limited." Elinor Gregg, *The Indians and the Nurse* (Norman, OK: University of Oklahoma Press, 1965), 161. M. Greist states, "Helen came down with TB the second year after we left Barrow and died in a tent on the beach without the care of a nurse or a doctor" (M. Greist, "Nursing," 159–160). Greist spells Helen's last name as "Surber."

17. Mueller was an amateur photographer.

18. Jim and Helen Nichols were teachers in Barrow from 1921 to 1923. Their child is Betty (M. Greist, "Nursing," 66).

19. Roald Amundsen, polar explorer, made several visits to Barrow during Mueller's tenure. This was in preparation for a polar flight. Lieutenant Oskar Omdahl is his pilot. Robert Stevens details Amundsen's polar air attempts and successes in *Alaska Aviation History,* Volume I (DesMoines, WA: Polynyas Press, 1990), 108–120, 302–317. Amundsen had a cabin in Wainwright so travel to Barrow was not that difficult.

20. *Ahtega:* an outer garment, a parka.

21. Fred Hopson, a colleague of Brower. During Mueller's time he was the general cook for the Browers and a storekeeper (Blackman, *Sadie Brower Neakok*, 60–63).
22. *Oogaruk:* bearded seal, also spelled *Ugruk.*
23. Russel and Lesley Cramer were in Wainwright, Russel as a teacher. They arrived in 1922, possibly on the same ship as Mueller. In her full manuscript Mueller refers to Lesley often, particularly in the winter and spring of 1924 when Lesley had gone to Barrow for delivery and spent several months there. The Cramers' photographs were donated to the Historic Photograph Archives of the North Slope Borough, Inupiat History, Language, and Culture Commission, Barrow, Alaska.
24. Reference to the old whaling (also called refuge) station, which was the Brower business establishment. In Mueller's day it was a store and also a dining area where Hopson cooked for the family (Blackman, *Sadie Brower Neakok,* 33–34, 48).
25. Primus stove: small alcohol burner.
26. This is probably Percy Ipalook, who became a Presbyterian minister, serving Wainwright, Wales, and Gamble ("Percy Ipalook Makes First Visit Here from Wales," *Jessen's Weekly* [Fairbanks, AK], 23 April 1948, 2).
27. Peter Van der Sterre, teacher 1923–1925, was also in charge of the mail and reported the status of the reindeer herd (M. Greist, "Nursing," 90, 95, 98; Knud Rasmussen, *Across Arctic America,* [New York: G. P. Putman's Sons, 1927], 308).
28. The Greist son, David, is approximately five years old at this time. His mother describes him as three years old on arrival in 1921 (M. Greist, "Nursing," 61).
29. Ann Bannan was a Presbyterian missionary who filled all kinds of needs (M. Greist, "Nursing," 152–153). During 1922–1925 she was the hospital housekeeper.
30. Harry Riley, clerk employed by Brower (Blackman, *Sadie Brower Neakok,* 80).
31. Delco: electric power plant operated by gasoline or diesel fuel.
32. Edna Wallace, friend of Mr. Brower. Sadie Brower Neakok addresses this as a problem to their family (Blackman, *Sadie Brower Neakok,* 46–47).
33. Mrs. Riley, wife of Harry (see note 30).
34. Knud Rasmussen, Danish ethnologist from Greenland. Hansen is his photographer. This visit to Barrow is described in his book *Across Arctic America.* Also see M. Greist, "Nursing," 98.
35. Clarence LeRoy Andrews, 1862–1948, naturalist and photographer. He traveled in and out of Alaska, beginning in 1892, and published two Barrow-related articles in *Nature,* "Migratory Birds" (February 1936) and another on nesting (March 1945). Barrow residents collected specimens for him.
36. Feast held at the end of whaling, correctly called "*nalukataq.*" Whaling is still an important season in Barrow (Blackman, *Sadie Brower Neakok,* 203–216).

37. W. Thomas Lopp, education officer for the Department of Interior, Alaska Region, who hired government field nurses at this time. In the 1920s, his office was in Seattle and he visited Alaska school sites during the summer (Jeanne Engerman, "Letters from Cape Prince of Wales," *Alaska Journal* [Autumn 1984]: 41).

38. Brimstone: sulfur.

39. Eben Hopson also appears as a distracting toddler in church. He became an important Eskimo political leader. Mueller reported in a letter to C. Gair, 17 March 1963, that she had seen him on national television. As state senator, he assisted Sadie Neakok with a game violation problem (Blackman, *Sadie Brower Neakok,* 180–184).

40. Walt and Skeezix, characters in the enduring and popular comic strip, "Gasoline Alley."

41. Dr. Albert Newhall, a missionary at Unalaska for many years. Mt. Newhall near Unalaska may be named after him ("Unalaska/Dutch Harbor," *Alaska Geographic* 18, no. 4). His first wife, Agnes, died in 1919. The Mrs. Newhall in Barrow is his second wife.

42. Timepieces were synchronized once a year when ships arrived. In the intervening months there apparently were discrepancies, which became rigid, between the mission and educational staff on the matter of the correct time.

43. Pyroseptine: one of the paraffin methods of dressing burns (Bertha Harmer, *Textbook of the Principles and Practice of Nursing* [New York: MacMillan, 1925], 617).

44. The Sylvesters arrived in the fall of 1925, he as the replacement teacher for Peter Van der Sterre. Sadie Neakok found him a difficult teacher (Blackman, *Sadie Brower Neakok,* 67).

45. Amundsen traveled from Spitzbergen, Norway, to Teller, Alaska, in the dirigible *Norge* in spring 1926. He did not land in Barrow (Stevens, *Alaska Aviation,* 303–317).

46. Carl Ben Eielson, pioneer Alaska pilot, accompanied Wilkins on this flight. They landed in Barrow in the spring of 1926 while Mueller was still there (G. H. Wilkins, *Flying the Arctic* [New York: G. P. Putnam's Sons, 1928], 49–64).

47. M. Greist, "Nursing," 126.

48. M. Greist, "Nursing," 147–149.

49. Charles Brower, *Fifty Years Below Zero* (New York: Dodd, Mead, 1944), 303.

50. "Alaska Gets Hospital," *Science News* (April 1966) 89: 290.

51. Phillip Nice and Walter Johnson, *The Alaska Health Aide Program: A Tradition of Helping Ourselves* (Alaska: Authors, 1998). Community health aides are individuals from Alaska villages who provide health care to people in their own villages. They possess basic skills to function in a restricted manner as health care providers in rural Alaska and are able to deliver episodic care and selected health surveillance activities.

I Have Traveled Over Eleven Thousand Miles: Stella Louisa Fuller

Delano Red Cross Nurse, Alaska Peninsula, Aleutians, and Kenai Peninsula, 1922–1924

STELLA FULLER LED A colorful and checkered career. She sought—and found—adventure and challenge. She served as a pioneer industrial nurse, a public health nurse, a teacher of nurses, a wartime nurse, and as a Delano Red Cross nurse.

Stella Fuller was born April 26, 1878, in Lawrence, Wisconsin, the second of two children of Loyal M. and Alice Clark Fuller.[1] She grew up on a farm and graduated from "common" school in April 1894. From 1895 to 1903, she taught in rural schools in Brown County, Wisconsin. She graduated from Milwaukee County Hospital School of Nursing in Wauwatosa, Wisconsin, in 1907. She graduated without having a high-school diploma, which was not a requirement at the time. For the next few years she worked as a private duty nurse, hospital nurse, and for the Visiting Nurse Association. She is credited with being the first hospital social worker in the state of Wisconsin. In 1916, she joined the staff of the Wisconsin Anti-Tuberculosis Association (WATA) to encourage the employment of public health nurses. She left WATA to become a Red Cross nurse in France toward the end of World War I.[2] After the war Stella Fuller chose to continue work in public health nursing with the Red Cross.

The American Red Cross Nursing Service was organized in 1909, and the Town and Country Nursing Service (Public Health Nursing) was established by 1913.[3] Then came World War I and the withdrawal of many rural nurses for war service, crippling this peacetime activity. The cessation of the war on November 11, 1918, left thousands in active Red Cross chapters eager to expend their zeal and enthusiasm for public service. Of the many projects and plans for continuing service that were considered at the time, public health nursing seemed by far the most promising.[4]

Jane A. Delano was national director of the American Red Cross Nursing Service until her death in France in 1919. In her will, Delano created a substantial fund as a perpetual memorial to her parents, with the provision that the income be used for the maintenance of public health nursing services in needy locations. The nurses were to be known as

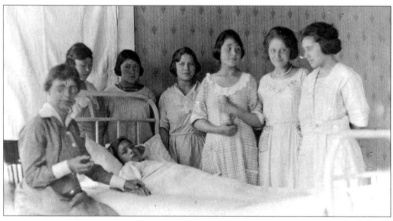

5.1. Stella Fuller with home nursing students. Reprinted with permission from Neville Public Museum (#5712.26 3250-174/ 2056), Brown County, Green Bay, Wisconsin.

"Delano Red Cross Nurses."[5] These nurses were required to be in perfect health and have no unfavorable family history. To avoid the emergency of being called home in the midst of their service, they had to give assurance that no member of their families was dependent upon them. They had to be an enrolled Red Cross nurse with at least two years of public health nursing experience and possess good education and training and if possible some teaching experience. Preference was given to nurses between the ages of thirty and fifty.[6]

Stella Fuller met these requirements, and on June 14, 1922, the Delano Red Cross Nursing committee voted to appoint her as the first Delano nurse and asked her to accept an assignment to Alaska.[7] Stella's appointment was based upon the survey of a vast medically underserved area of Alaska by Agnes Holland and upon a request for nursing services by Dr. J. H. Romig, an influential medical missionary and pioneer. Seward was the headquarters town.[8]

Following her Alaska experience, Fuller returned to Kenosha, Wisconsin. Here she was employed as a public health nurse by the Kenosha Health Department, and for a short time she was director of nursing of the Kenosha Hospital. In 1937, she became a writer for the New York Life Insurance Company with headquarters in Green Bay, Wisconsin. She spent her retirement years in Green Bay, where she was very active in church work at the St. Paul Methodist Church. She maintained her own apartment until a stroke forced her to enter a nursing home. Stella Fuller died August 14, 1966, at eighty-eight years of age at St. Mary's Hospital in Green Bay and was buried at Lawrence, Wisconsin.[9]

Stella Fuller's account of her Alaska experience as a Delano Red Cross nurse is derived from letters and monthly reports to Clara Noyes, chairperson of the Delano National Committee, and from letters to Mary Cole, public health nursing director, Pacific Area.[10]

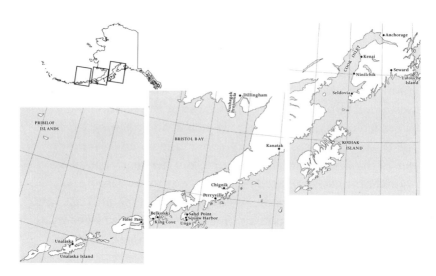

5.2. The Starr. *Reprinted with permission from Anchorage Museum of History and Art (#B90-3-12), Anchorage, Alaska.*

Letters and Reports Written by Stella L. Fuller 1922–1924

Letter to Miss Mary Cole, Seward, October 17, 1922

Dear Miss Cole:

I have just returned from my trip to Unalaska, the last town or settlement in the very large territory selected as my district. I was on the boat for two weeks in the worst weather the steamer *Starr* has ever experienced. The *Starr* [see Figure 5.2] is seaworthy but that is the best we can say about her—she rolls, nosedives, bucks, and shakes like a thing of evil disposition. The waves came over the hatches and down the ventilators, dishes crashed, and the poor victims of "mal de mer" clutched the sides of their berths in agony and awful fear of being thrown out. One woman was thrown on the floor and got a fearful bump. Of course the portholes had to be closed so the air was not very good. I could tell you a lot more about the peculiar habits of the *Starr,* but this will give you an idea of what it means to be a passenger. Fortunately, I am a good sailor, and got along very well.

I visited most of the towns, although we arrived at many in the night! Nearly everyone in town gets up to meet the mail boat, so it wasn't so bad—excepting the places where there was no harbor. There are several settlements where the passengers and cargo have to lightered in small boats.

In Unga we were put off in the lifeboats, in the rain, and carried ashore by sturdy seamen in hip boots. Such are the ways of Alaskans in the Peninsula towns.

About ten days ago, the second mate became very ill—temperature 103, partial stupor, and other alarming symptoms. After three days we were able to call a doctor at Unalaska, who said he thought the man had eaten something which did not agree with him. He advised me to give him more cathartics and said he thought he would soon be well. The man got worse rather than better and I began to give him nursing care for typhoid fever. It was a good guess—three days later Dr. Chase, one of the territorial health officers, came on the ship and verified the "diagnosis." We brought him in last night and this morning he was taken to the hospital in La Touche, a place about six hours east of here. He was in deep coma so we did not get him here any too soon. I had a great time trying to give enemata and sponge baths with the *Starr* performing stunts as described above. My arms and back are black and blue from falling against doors and other projections, but I am not complaining. It was a great experience.

We also had a case of trachoma—a little child being taken to the Children's Orthopedic Hospital in Seattle. Dr. Chase had seen her and made the diagnosis. Her mother had sent linen—towels and bedding—with her, so it was not hard to keep her from infecting others.

There were two Native girls on their way to the Indian school in Oregon who gave me a good deal of worry—they were young and ignorant of the ways of men. I tried to chaperone them but could do nothing with them. Something should be done to provide protection to the Natives who are sent long distances to the "outside."

I am going to remain in Seward for a month to get settled in my little three room and bath and to get my office and work organized. The office in the Legion building does not seem just what we want so an effort is being made to provide a really nice place which will be in keeping with the dignity of the work we want to do. Everything is hopeful, although it is going to take some time to get started. We want to make this a model chapter and to lay the foundation for a lasting program. You will remember the great distances and the difficult methods of communication, and make some allowances. Because of these drawbacks, we can never hope to have the branches represented at our chapter meetings and can get letters to them only once a month, but we will do our best to keep them interested.

Seward looked like a metropolis after the salteries and canneries to the westward, and the people down at the wharf looked like relatives. They are really fine to me. I am going to a real dinner tonight, and to a party given by the Eastern Stars on Monday. You will be amused when I tell you that the good ladies have even provided a man to take me! I shall tell him we will consider it a contribution to the Red Cross!

We will have a meeting of our Red Cross Thursday and will let you know what we plan to do. I think we will have to limit the work to places east of Chignik during the winter months and I have an idea that we should concentrate on antituberculosis for the entire three years. The conditions are pitiful among the Natives—no clinics, no sanatoria, no doctors to speak of, and no educational program. Please send me everything you can find—literature, slides, films.

I am enclosing an expense account covering the return trip. We hope to get free transportation on the *Starr* or a rate. Won't it be fine if we can get it? There is so much to do that we hardly know where to begin. One of the first things we hope to do is the sending of the monthly report to the division.

Please remember that the mail boat is the great excitement up here and we all look for letters from our friends and from those who expect us to keep smiling.

Narrative Report
Written at Unga, November 28, 1922

The month of November has been the biggest Red Cross month in Alaska since the days of the war. The old-time spirit of giving and of serving has come to life again, many who had thought there was no further need for the Red Cross have become active volunteers, and there is a splendid feeling of friendly cooperation among the children as well as the adult population.

On the morning our roll call[11] was to begin, a call came from Lake Kenai, a place fifty miles "inside" asking for help for a woman who had broken her leg. We had an obstetric case needing immediate attention and several newborn babies, so it was impossible for Dr. Baughman, our only physician, to be away. Our train runs north only twice each week but it happened to be "train day" so I traveled comfortably for twenty-three miles on the government railroad, transferred to an open motor boat for four hours in crossing Lake Kenai, and walked a few miles to the cabin in the mountains where the woman had suffered, without attention, for twenty-four hours. Several sourdoughs and a college man or two were standing about, waiting to be directed, and they were fine assistants in helping to put on splints, prepare lunch for the patient, and transport her to the landing where she could cross the lake. We put her on a cot and the men carried her over the mountain trail to the landing where Dunc Little, an old timer, had an Alaska mulligan of moose meat, hot coffee and raspberries of his own canning waiting for us all. Night had come on before we placed the patient in a motorboat, covered it with a canvas top, and took her safely to Mile 23.

In the morning, Mrs. Jackson, world traveler and used to the best of everything, was hoisted into a box car and sent to tunnel where her husband got a special train to take her the rest of the way to the Anchorage hospital. I was compelled to remain at the roadhouse with the men for two days out. I never received more courtesy from any folks anywhere! The ranges of snowy mountains, as far as the eye could see, the brilliant sunsets on Lake Kenai, and the tales of fishing, hunting, and trapping, the hardships of the prospector's life, the quaint humor, and the Alaskan habit of abusing one's best friends to their faces were more entertaining than shopping on Fifth Avenue or Michigan Boulevard.

Several other nursing cases were visited for several days— mostly maternity cases and infant welfare work. Maternity work in Seward includes assistance during birth.

I sailed on the steamer *Starr* for Unga on Sunday, November 19, and arrived on Sunday evening, November 26. Miss Clark and Miss Simonson, teachers in the territorial school, met the boat and welcomed me to their little "teacherage" connected with the school on the hill overlooking the rock-bound bay. When told that Dr. R. E. Davis was a passenger on the *Starr*, bound for the Pribilof Islands in the Bering Sea, they immediately sent a message to the ship waiting a mile out at sea while the cargo was being lightered in. The doctor was glad to come over to examine the school children and any others the teachers had in mind. It was dark, but at the ringing of the school bell, all the kiddies and some of the parents came trooping up the hill to see what "dear teacher" wanted. All the pupils were given a thorough examination excepting the examination of the eyes. The doctor expected to do them on the following morning, but a heavy storm drove the ship out to sea and he could not return to land. The greater part of the food supplies for which the people had been waiting for six weeks had to be landed at Squaw Harbor where there was less danger of the *Starr* being dashed on the rocks. When the wind subsides the cargo will be brought round in small boats.

P.S. The storm still rages and the people of the village are concerned for the safety of the *Starr*. We can see her being buffeted about in the bay not far from the surfswept rocks. The coast of Alaska is a dangerous one to navigate and these hardy Scandinavian seamen are brave men.

Seward, December 29, 1922

I arrived at Unga on November 26 and left on December 25. The results of the examination of the school children by Dr. R. E. Davis were reported in November. The month of December was spent in following up the school work, giving health talks, teaching Home Hygiene and Care of the Sick, and First Aid, conducting a Little Mother's League, and assisting the school teachers in arranging a health program for the evening of the roll call day.

It was the first health program ever given in Unga. The interest was keen. The parents sat in silence while their sons and daughters applied head bandages, transported injured playmates, changed beds, served breakfast trays, etc. At the close of the exercises, Mr. Frank Brown, manager of the Apollo mine for thirty-five years, spoke to his neighbors about the Red Cross. He announced that Mr. Bob West and Mr. Larsen, men at Port Moller in the Bering Sea, had sent a radio, contributing $20 each to the Unga roll call. This was a great encouragement to the people present. In a very short time about $116 had been given.

Unga is a small island of volcanic origin, located in southwest Alaska. It is a part of the chain of islands that makes the Alaska Peninsula. The village of Unga is in the southern part of the island—its treeless mountains and hills overlook an enclosed bay that contains many storm-swept rocks and reefs.

Only small fishing boats can reach the docks. Ships of larger size, such as the mail boat *Starr*, must anchor in the bay, away from the dangerous rocks. The mail, cargo, and passengers are lightered by the ship's lifeboats and by the fishermen who go out in dories. Sometimes, the sea runs so high that the freight has to be left at Sand Point, another settlement on the island. The Alaska Codfish Company maintains a radio station which is a great convenience.

There is no doctor or dentist or nurse on the island. The U.S. cutters stop at Unga very seldom and the doctors have given service only in acute cases.

A hospital somewhere in the center of the peninsula would be a great blessing to these people. There should be clinics and follow-up work. I can do little except to teach the people personal and community hygiene, home nursing, and some of the principles of first aid.

My next visit should be made in the spring and a dental or tonsil clinic arranged, if it is possible to secure a dentist or a surgeon.

On my return to Seward from Unga I went ashore at Kanatak, the new oil town of Alaska. I wished especially to see Dr. Silverberg, who directed the recent roll call and sent $76 to the headquarters of the chapter at Seward. Dr. Silverberg is employed by the Associated Oil Co. He has been in Kanatak only a few months. No field representative visited him and the Delano Nurse was not able to go ashore with the roll call material because of the difficulties in landing. Considering these facts, we are very grateful to the doctor and others for their interest in the Red Cross. He was not in the village at the time of my visit. Most of his time was spent at the seepage, seventeen miles back from the beach.

Dr. Pollard, the dentist from Kodiak, was in town and we discussed the possibility of his going to Unga to do some of the dental work which is so badly needed there. It may not be advisable for a dentist to visit Unga before spring when the fishing begins.

Chief Roth Kalmakoff [see Figure 5.3], a Native who was educated at Wood Island, took me to visit the merchants and several families of his tribe. The Native population is about fifty-four. Half of these are school children who have no school. Requests have been sent to Mr. Lopp to provide a teacher as soon as possible. There are also several white children of school age.

Kanatak is a typical boomtown:[12] violations of the Eighteenth Amendment[13] are common and gambling is practiced. There is no marshal, nor commissioner. There is a small Russian church with services for the Natives when a priest is

5.3. *Chief Kalmakoff with wife and visitor, 1922. Chief Kalmakoff (l), wife (r), and Haddie (c), a village visitor. The chief supported Stella Fuller's efforts to start a school in Kanatak. Reprinted with permission from Anchorage Museum of History and Art (B65-18-182), Anchorage, Alaska.*

able to come. The white people are very much interested in the Indians and have already done much for them. I expect to visit Kanatak for several days while the *Starr* is on the way to Unalaska and return. If possible, this will be done before spring.

We arrived in Seward December 29. The remaining days were spent in going over a large supply of mail that had accumulated during my six weeks' absence.

Narrative Report
Seward, February 22, 1923

On February 10 I sailed for La Touche, the only eastern branch in our chapter. The entire population, three hundred to four hundred, is employed in the copper mine of the Kennecott Copper Corporation. There is a splendid hospital there and considerable welfare work is being done by the mine owners. I met with the three members of our executive committee and we came to the conclusion that it would not be necessary for the Delano Nurse to make regular visits to La Touche. The mine doctor will examine the school children using the American Red Cross cards and will report the results to the chapter. The Juniors are active and are preparing an Alaska exhibit to be sent to the museum at Washington, D.C. We hope to get some subscribers to the *Courier* and have been promised cooperation in the next roll call.

While in La Touche, I injured my back riding on a toboggan. The hospital doctor and nurses cared for me in the hospital for several days and the members of the committee were very kind.

On Friday I returned to Seward on a Nome freighter. My little home looked very good to me. A better place to rest a hurt back could not be found anywhere. It is roomy and comfortable. My breakfast window opens on a glorious panorama that is a daily feast to the soul. As I begin my grapefruit, the first rays of our eight o'clock sun strike the top of Sheep Mountain. When I finish my breakfast food the slanting bars of gold have reached Nameless Peak, and when I have eaten my toast and emptied my coffee cup, the whole range shines in the light of day.

On February 24 I sailed for Kodiak, settled by Russia when Washington was president, to remain about a month.

Comment from Kodiak [Excerpts]
March 9, 1923

In Kodiak and on Wood Island there is a telephone system, electric lights, and running water.

The housewives are clean in many ways but they have little knowledge of sanitation. They will line their walls and ceilings with oilcloth, which they wash regularly, cover their floors with white sail cloth and the cleanest of hand-made rugs, insist on the whole family taking a Russian bath, but the idea of spreading disease through using utensils, coughing, and careless living does not occur to them. The rules of the Greek Russian Church force them to kiss a cross which the priest holds. The helpless tubercular patients are carried up to perform this act of devotion and the others follow and kiss the same cross.

The school children are bright and are able to learn to a certain age or grade, and after that it is difficult or impossible for them to go on. They are musical and love to dance.

April Report
Seward, April 1923

The following is my narrative report for April 1923. The first week was spent in Seward doing office work and planning Junior Health Day to be given on May 5. On Sunday, April 8 I sailed on the *Starr* for Kanatak, arriving on Monday afternoon.

There is no school at Kanatak although there are about twenty-five children of school age. I asked for the use of an empty building and conducted a school for Natives, young and old, for one week [see Figure 5.5]. I got to know them more intimately than would have been possible in any other way. Very few speak English; they are not sure of their ages, nor of their names. We had no equipment, but we made some charts on the backs of old calendars and got along fairly well. They seemed interested in the lessons on personal hygiene. The old chief visited the school every day and insisted on the best cooperation. The adults who attended were anxious to learn. They would drop in at odd times during the day and ask to be taught the simplest lessons in reading and arithmetic. One man wanted very much to learn to do long division. We are hoping that Mr. Lopp, director of education for the Natives, may establish a school next year.

On Wednesday, April 18, I sailed on the *Starr* from Kanatak for Chignik, a cannery village six hundred miles west of Seward. Arrived at 3 A.M. the next morning. There was no place to live or to work at the place where we docked so I went with the new school teacher in a gas boat ten miles up the river to the cannery operated by the Alaska Packers Association. There were several oil prospectors and two traveling dentists in the party, and we had an amusing time trying "to rustle grub" (an Alaska saying), but we managed to get along. The neighbors helped us to clean the teacherage and school opened the following Monday, the day I was to return on the gas boat to meet the *Starr*. The teacher and one of the dentists assisted me in the physical inspection of the children. The tide was going out and we had to hurry and I came back up the bay where I had to wait until the twenty-sixth because the mail boat was behind her schedule. The cannery folks kept me and I visited the half dozen Native families who live at the head of the bay; some of them had

5.4. *Stella Fuller in bidarka at Kanatak. Stella is the second from the left. Reprinted with permission from Neville Public Museum (#5667.3 3250-174/2056), Brown County, Green Bay, Wisconsin.*

5.5. *Stella Fuller at school she initiated. Stella Fuller (R), with Kanatak students, village chief at her right. Reprinted, with permission, Neville Public Museum of Brown County, Green Bay, Wisconsin.*

tuberculosis. One woman was dying with it but there is little chance for any of them. The cannery crew has a physician who comes up each summer to look after the employees; they have little interest in the Indians. There is no one at Chignik in the winter except the cannery watchman. The Natives go into the hills to trap.

I arrived in Seward on Sunday evening, April 29. A prenatal case—wife of a naval man to the westward—was at my house and will remain a week before going on to the Government Hospital in Anchorage. The last day of the month was spent in trying to further the plans for the Junior Program.

May Report
Seward, Alaska, May 31, 1923

The following is my narrative report for May 1923: From the first to the thirteenth I was in Seward. While there, I directed a junior health week; we had a health program, a health exhibit, and a clean-up campaign; the children earned about thirty-five dollars to be added to their service fund for next year. I gave two demonstrations in first aid, one before the Woman's Club and one for the high school; wrote several notices for the *Gateway*, attended our chapter meeting, wrote monthly reports, got out five hundred tuberculosis charts to be distributed throughout the chapter territory, and entertained a prenatal case at my home; she was en route to the Government Hospital in Anchorage.

On Sunday, May 13, I sailed on the *Starr* for Nushagak and other Bristol Bay ports. From Seward to Unalaska, I made shore visits, checking up on former work and making new contacts with the people. At Unga I made a short talk on our hope for a traveling clinic and visited a patient who was very much in need of a curettage. A radio message was sent to the U.S. Revenue Cutter *Algonquin*; the ship came to Unga and

the doctor performed the operation with success. I was very
sorry to find that the women and girls who had taken the
class in home hygiene and care of the sick were not giving
the woman nursing care; they considered that, inasmuch as
she had brought the illness on herself, she did not deserve
the care they knew how to give!

Several villages west of Unga have recently suffered an
epidemic resembling flu. Fortunately, the U.S. Revenue Cutter
Haida was near and the doctor took charge of the situation,
remaining at one place for eight days. The epidemic started
at King Cove on March 17; it was brought by a man on the
Str. *Katherine D,* owned by the Pacific American Fisheries.
Seventeen Natives from Belkofsky went to work at the cannery at King Cove; they became ill at once, and on March
26 two dories full of sick men were sent back to Belkofsky,
a distance of thirteen miles. The priest at Belkofsky, Father
Dimitro Hotovitsky, carried eight men from the beach to their
homes. By the first of April the whole village of 141 people
were ill with fever, and many were delirious. The worst patients were moved to an empty house. By the middle of April
eleven persons had died. The U.S. Bureau of Education gave
coal, meat, drugs, surgical supplies, and $150 for the relief of
the sick. The priest and four small boys about twelve years
old made soup, gave nursing care, dug graves, and buried the
dead. The U.S. Cutter *Haida* came to Belkofsky on April 27
but the epidemic had spent itself by that time. The cannery
boat brought a dead body from King Cove on April 8 and
deposited it on the beach; the priest protested and the sailors
buried it. Three persons died at King Cove and eight at False
Pass. I had heard of the sickness but could not reach the villages until the regular monthly trip of the mail boat.

Mr. Dan Sutherland, Alaska delegate to Congress, and Mr.
Al Chamberlain, senator from the third district, were passengers on the *Starr* from Seward to Nushagak; we had several

conferences regarding the need for medical assistance along the peninsula. They were both very much interested and promised to do all that they could to interest members of the legislature and congress.

We arrived in Dillingham, which is across the bay from Nushagak, on May 23. The U.S. Bureau of Education maintains an orphanage and a hospital for the children who were orphaned during the terrible epidemic of flu in 1918; the institution is also open to anyone in the district. Dr. Drtina is in charge of these and came down the bay about ten miles to meet the boat. After talking with him for an hour I saw that there was little use of my staying in the Bristol Bay settlements for a month; the villages are far apart and are sparsely populated. The doctor invited me to visit them for a month but agreed that I could do little work there. After making a hurried call at the hospital I returned to the ship and came back to Unalaska where my time could be more profitably spent.

I was on the ship for thirteen days during the month and 2,011 miles, according to the way the *Starr* sails.

[The next report is an excerpt from a news story entitled "Surgery on the Aleutian Islands."[14]]

To one accustomed to doing public health nursing in a community where there are doctors, hospitals, dispensaries, clinics, and nurses, a sudden transfer to a district lacking all these is rather upsetting and a bit discouraging at times. To a nurse used to city and county nursing, where there is street car or auto transportation, and where it is possible to reach home every night, it is somewhat of an adventure to charter a gas boat to make a call, or to travel for a week on a steamer before reaching one's destination. To a badger, used to busy cities and towns, fertile prairie lands, rich with fields of grain and corn, great forests and wooded hills, it is difficult to become used to a sea coast stretching over a thousand miles, lined with treeless volcanic mountains: majestic and grand, but not like home.

For ten months, I had traveled on the steamer *Starr,* a rebuilt halibut boat, visiting the villages, calling in the homes of the people, trying to learn their medical needs, and doing any public health nursing that was possible under the conditions.

The August mail boat is called the "School Ma'am's Special." There were teachers aboard for Unalaska and Bristol Bay points. A few seasick passengers needed my care, but there was plenty of time for fun and for making cocoa down in the galley at night. At False Pass, where the *Starr* took oil, we met Dr. Nevius and discussed our plans for the clinic. His ship, the *Pioneer,* went with us to Unalaska, reaching there first, since the mail boat had to stop several places en route.

There seemed little more that I could do in False Pass; the September mail boat was not due for some time so I decided to try to get to Unga, one of the villages farther east, by gas boat. We started on Sunday, a beautiful day. By the time we reached Belkofsky, we were in a raging gale and storm bound for a time. It was not a hardship to be there, however. The priest's wife is charming and his children are happy, bright-eyed little folks. We met the government teacher and attended a dance at the schoolhouse. Father "Hot-whiskey," as he is called by the fishermen, wished us to return to False Pass with a woman who needed the doctor's attention.

When the wind had moderated and we could get out to the launch in a dory—there is no dock at Belkofsky—we headed for False Pass with the patient. When we reached King Cove the sea was decidedly "lumpy," and we were wind-bound for two days. The wind was blowing at such a terrific rate when we landed that we had to crouch down on the dock, for fear of being blown into the bay. We had a nice time in King Cove in spite of the constant rain and the howling wind. The patient and I found places to sleep ashore, and the "skipper" of the gas boat was an able cook. We made delicious duck mulligan and the finest corn bread. I was allowed to provide a dessert which seemed to be appreciated, especially by the Eskimo boy, Sammie, who shipped as a sailor.

In the meantime, one of the engineers on the *Pioneer* was seriously ill with appendicitis, and the ship was searching for me to help with the operation. Captain Lukens finally came into King Cove and I was taken aboard and brought to False Pass, arriving the next morning. We were ready to operate the same afternoon. The man's appendix had ruptured and at first his condition was critical, but he made a splendid recovery. I nursed him until the *Starr* returned and we did one more tonsil case.

The traveling clinic we have asked the government to provide has not materialized but the help already given by the different government services operating in Alaska demonstrates the need of it. The conditions are similar to those in Labrador, where Dr. Grenfell[15] is doing such remarkable work. Like him, we need money, ships, doctors, and nurses.

Cook Inlet Villages
July 1923

The following is my report for July 1923: I took my vacation from the first to the twenty-fifth of July. On the twenty-fifth, I closed the Red Cross office in Seward and moved the records and supplies to my rooms, since we have used it very little during the past ten months. Most of my time is spent in the branches.

On July 26, I sailed on the *Admiral Evans* for Seldovia, arriving at midnight. The following day I went in a gas boat to Ninilchik, a Russian village on Cook Inlet. The day was beautiful—the inlet, usually so rough and wild, was like a mill pond. The men were very kind and made every effort to provide comforts lacking on a fish boat. One man but recently released from a year in jail was especially kind—insisting on lending his pillow because it was cleaner than the one in the bunk.

The population of Ninilchik is about one hundred; there are log cabins, a Russian church, a school, a store, and a dance hall. The people have cows, chickens, and gardens and there is free firewood, beach coal, clams, and all kinds of fish. There are many beautiful wild flowers and berries in abundance on the hills. There is no doctor, dentist, or nurse.

I visited all the homes, had a public meeting in the schoolhouse, where I explained the work of the Red Cross in war and in peace, inspected the babies and the school children, and conferred with the parents. Home visits were made again relative to defects found in the inspection.

Brief Annual Report
September 30, 1923

The following is my narrative report for our first fiscal year— October 1, 1922, to September 30, 1923:

I have traveled over eleven thousand miles and visited most of the settlements in the district assigned—the Alaska Peninsula, which is about one thousand miles long. My transportation expense has amounted to $503.05, about forty dollars per month.

The scarcity of doctors and the lack of hospitals has made any definite program impossible. I have just gone on from day to day, not knowing what the next would bring. I am anxious to do some prenatal and infant welfare work and am sorry that I have not been able to teach more classes in home hygiene and care of the sick.

This first year has been harder than any that will follow. I know most of the villages now and the people know a little about my plans. The twelve months have been happy ones—

the Alaska people have been very nice to me with only one exception. (This person has moved out of my territory.) So far as I know there have been no serious mistakes in my work, and we are looking forward to better and bigger things next year.

It if pleases the committee, I should like to spend two months outside next fall, taking my 1924 and 1925 vacations at once. I suggest this because of the great distance and the expense of a trip outside.

Miss Cole has been a great help to me and I wish to thank the Delano Committee for the letters and supplies that have been sent.

Seward, November 1923

The month was a very busy one owing to my activities in the Seventh Roll Call and the conducting of four classes in home hygiene each week in my apartment.

The result of our membership week was truly surprising. No one really knows the population of Seward but it may be six hundred—not more. When I tell you that we raised nearly $650 in this little town alone, you will realize that it was a real war time roll call!

Letter to Mary Cole, Pacific Division
Seward, December 8, 1923

In regard to my visiting the chapters in [southeast] Alaska, I hope you will not think me obstinate when I say that I think it would take me from my district—the territory in which I hope to establish some sort of lasting health program before the fall of 1925. We have just had a most amazing roll call and it is my desire that they be given more service, not less. You are right in saying that my work cannot be very constructive until the government does something to supply medical and hospital care, but the government is doing something—a doctor has just been sent to Unalaska—and the government ships did a lot this summer.

Suppose we compromise—if you wish, I will gladly undertake to keep the Anchorage and Fairbanks chapters interested in a Red Cross program. They are nearer and I could do it while working in Seward. May I suggest that a supervisor be sent to visit the nurses in southeast Alaska—perhaps someone from Seattle. She could make the trip as quickly and at about the same expense that I could from here.

May I say a word, too, about sending a nurse to do teaching work? The people have said a great many things against the idea—just the other day a man from Anchorage said Miss Holland's[16] work had done more to kill Red Cross interest in Alaska than anything he knew. They liked her personally, but they did not think it was a wise expenditure of funds. They understood she was getting a very high salary, they knew she lived in a hotel, etc.

Please forgive me if I seem to be throwing cold water on your scheme and if my letter gives you the impression that I do not appreciate your wanting me to do it; I do appreciate it, but since we have raised nearly $1,400—more than that, the exact sum to date is $1,440.76—I cannot do less than visit the chapter territory, even if I have to teach school, as I expect to do at Kanatak.

Mailed from Seward
February 24, 1924

I left Seward for Kodiak on December 26 and arrived the following day. I remained until Saturday, January 5, when I sailed for Kanatak on the freighter *La Touche*; the *La Touche* was making the trip for the steamer *Starr,* which was being repaired after her accident in December.

I visited the Baptist Mission on Wood Island, made an effort to secure services of a dentist from Seward, discussed the possibility of our having a tonsil clinic next summer, and spent the greater part of three days with a patient who had a strangulated hernia. She died—there was no one to operate.

I arrived at Kanatak on Sunday evening, January 6. Going ashore after the ship drops her anchor at Kanatak is always exciting. The weather is always bad—the wind comes across from the Bering Sea. This time there was a rope ladder transfer from the high freighter to a tug that bobbed far below. Then, when we had come nearer land, a scramble from the gas boat to a dory [see Figure 5.6] while the waves dashed over, and lastly, a ride on the shoulders of a longshoreman who had just been released from jail in Kodiak for bootlegging! I ventured the opinion that 130 pounds was too much for him; he said he was "a little soft from being inside so long."

I spent two days at the home of one of our committee, storm bound. The tide had separated his home from the Indian village. On the ninth I was carried across the water on a man's back again and spent the day cleaning up an old cabin. The four weeks I lived in it were the most miserable of my year and a half in Alaska. But it is past now so I'll not bother you with the details.

The teachers in Kodiak had given me some old schoolbooks. For the second time, I attempted to teach school in Kanatak. We got up another petition to the director of Indian Schools and hope that Mr. Lopp will at least visit the village this year. Some of the white folks are selling liquor to the Natives; this is especially wrong at Kanatak, because there are three Indians there who have committed murder.

There were a number of nursing cases—two maternities, a severe case of eye infection, a broken arm, an injured leg, a patient who was threatened with pneumonia, etc. The doctor at the seepage, seventeen miles over the mountains, sent advice by carrier. If a nurse or teacher were with the Natives all of the time, they would soon learn to make layettes and to understand the need of proper care when their babies are born.

I left Kanatak on the first day of the month, after waiting on the beach for three days in an effort to get out to the *Starr*, anchored half a mile at sea. The storms at Kanatak are beyond my powers of description. I'll not attempt the impossible. This little incident may help you to understand how the wind and the cold may try men's souls. The radio man from the ship had come ashore to attend to some business, never thinking that he would be holding up the sailing for three days. He was so disgusted that he wired his resignation as soon as he did get back to the boat! When we finally crawled up the ice-covered *Starr* and the angry captain had put out to sea, we found that the fighting winds would not allow us to proceed, so we anchored for four days more. We knew that there were some people and some horses at Wide

5.6. *The* Starr *at Kanatak. Transport to shore required lightering. Reprinted with permission from Anchorage Museum of History and Art (#B65-18-168), Anchorage, Alaska.*

Bay, desperately in need of food. Each day the captain would try to move forward. We would try to round the cape to get into Wide Bay, but the gale was too strong, the ship would not respond to the wheel, the icy spray soon covered us with several inches of ice, the ship would begin to list, and back we would fly to shelter. We were short of oil, water, and ballast for such a trip; we lost an anchor, etc. We had to abandon the hope of reaching Wide Bay and we skipped several other places where we encountered fields of ice.

The schoolteacher, Mrs. Tait at Perryville, should have taken the previous boat to the westward. It was nearly time for her to be confined. I decided to get off at Perryville if she did not board the ship. It was night when we reached there. She came out in an open boat with her husband and little girl. It was very cold. She climbed up the rope ladder and over the ice-covered decks. Having been in the far north for a year she knew that an ice-covered ship is dangerous. She came into my arms weeping with nervous fright, but we—her husband and I—soon had her as calm as usual and he said goodbye to her and returned to shore with the Natives. The captain put off at Perryville the passengers who had expected to stop at Wide Bay. We picked them up on the return trip.

The whole trip to Unalaska was one of horrors. Mrs. Tait announced herself in labor about the time we struck a sand bar (the captain had been keeping close in to avoid the awful wind) and for two hours we waited for the stork and wondered how we could possibly deliver the patient safely. The Russian priest was on, but he was too seasick to be useful, so I planned to appoint the second mate as first assistant if we needed one. However, it was a case of false pains. We got her safely to Unalaska and she gave birth to a nice baby boy.

I returned to Seward on the same boat and will remain here until I have regained my strength and enthusiasm for the ocean. This was the first time that I was ever frightened, the first time I ever forgot the ethics of the sea and asked foolish questions of anyone who would listen to me.

We made Wide Bay on the return trip and picked up the people. They had not been hungry, but eight horses had died of starvation. Some passengers had to be landed at the nearest place we could reach to their homes.

I am doing the usual school and district nursing, keeping up the chapter organization, and planning our junior program to be given on the twenty-eighth of March.

Letter to Mary Cole [Excerpt]
Seward, February 19, 1924

A few days ago I wrote you a note saying that I would be willing to visit the nurses in southeastern Alaska, but since that time I have had a letter from Miss Fox saying that the Delano Committee had approved my final decision. This means that I will not be going to Juneau, Ketchikan, and Wrangell. I am sorry, since you were so anxious to have me do it, but my better judgement tells me that I must not undertake more than I can do. Our chairman was against my doing it but is willing to have me go to Anchorage and Fairbanks. I sincerely hope that I may be able to inspire and encourage the workers there. I will be sending my narrative report in a few days and will help Mr. Urach to get out the 1040s, which are so long overdue.

Many thanks for your sympathy concerning my swollen face. I believe it is all right now, although it is still sensitive to cold. I wish I could have a long talk with you and am anxiously looking forward to my visit to the States in the fall.

Letter to Elizabeth Fox, National Division
Public Health Nursing Service, Washington, D.C.
February 19, 1924

Some time ago I wrote Miss Noyes concerning many problems that have come up in the work here. Perhaps the letter was read in your meeting of January 26, but since you have not replied to it I conclude that you want me to use my own judgement. It is very difficult to secure advice from such long distance. Sometimes the conditions are much changed before you have time to reply to my letters. For instance, one of the members of our committee wished me to find out whether it would not be a good thing to conduct a sale of Red Cross clothing since we had so much on hand. It would have been wrong. We have needed the things and are now making good use of them.

We appreciate Dr. Meeks' interest in our chapter work and feel sure that she will be a help in getting the attention of the Bureau of Education. I hope, however, that any doctors who are assigned to this territory will be capable of doing major surgery.

I will be sending my narrative reports, which are long overdue, by this week's mail. With many thanks for the helpful letters that come from headquarters.

Letter to Mary Cole, Pacific Division
March 5, 1924

I have discussed the employment of a public health nurse by and for Seward with the officers of the chapter. They think it could be done early in the fall—before the roll call, providing that we could get a properly qualified woman who would fit into this little community at one hundred and fifty dollars per month. They could never pay more—that should be understood at the outset, but you know how small this place is. If she did no traveling it would be a very easy job.

Of course they will want a paragon—committees always do. There are one or two points that must be given serious thought, however. She must be optimistic and deaf to gossip and I would suggest that she be young enough not to have gray hair—mine is getting whiter with each passing day. But I am talking too fast and too soon. We have not completed our reorganization yet—you may not approve—the branches may not—the manager may not, etc.

If all these plans do go through it might be nice to ask the Delano Committee to let me spend my third year in Anchorage and Fairbanks. We will hear from our branches in a week or two and will forward petition and further information. In the meantime, we will be glad to have any advice that the division can offer.

An afterthought: I may be able to get Anchorage and Fairbanks to employ a nurse together—six months in each place? If I do, what becomes of *me*?

Letter to Clara Noyes [Excerpt]
San Francisco, California, March 28, 1924

I wired you today that I am planning to go to the St. Francis Hospital next Tuesday, April 1, for an antrum operation and some dental surgery. I expect to be there about a week. My return to work will depend upon the results of the operation, of course, but the surgeons do not expect any complications. It is not advisable to do all that I have to have done at once, that is, reconstruction work which the dentist thinks may be done in six months or, perhaps, not at all.

My return ticket from San Francisco to Seattle is good until May 31, but I hope to be back in Seward long before that.

You have my letter stating that Seward Chapter is ready to try to take over the Nursing Service, and Miss Cole has a perfectly splendid applicant who will be ready to report for duty in Seward about June 1. Her contrast to the Delano nurse is so favorable that I shall be only a dim memory in a short time.

Now the question arises, what is to be done with Stella Fuller? Does the Delano Committee still consider her a Delano nurse? Does the committee want her to remain in Alaska until the three-year period is finished? The only other chapters that might possibly be given the services of a Delano nurse are Fairbanks and Anchorage, and they are not the types of towns or localities that Miss Delano had in mind.

Miss Cole, as you know, would like to have me remain in Alaska to help to hold the ground we have gained, but if that does not seem wise, she wishes me to remain somewhere in the Pacific Division, and I am willing to do so.

If the Seward Chapter takes over the Nursing Service in June, do you not think I should return to start the work and to pack my things, even if I do not remain in Alaska?

Miss Cole and I are taking it for granted, from Washington letters referring to the Delano budget, that my traveling expenses were to be paid in case I found it necessary to come Outside. This is very fortunate for me because I am having my first experience in paying big sums of money to the doctors, and I assure you they are big.

After eighteen months of interesting work, which I thought was going to last three years, it is upsetting to find myself, like Mr. Micawber, again "waiting for something interesting to turn up." Perhaps the fact that I may be having to find another position will make it possible for me to attend the Nurses' Convention in Detroit. I would like that.

Miss Cole and I will be waiting to hear from you.

March Report
San Francisco, California, March 29, 1924

The first two weeks of the month were spent in nursing two patients, planning a junior program to be given on March 29, arranging a joint meeting of the chapter and the Chamber of Commerce, looking up underweight children, arranging for delivery of maternity cases from Kenai Lake, sterilizing and demonstrating preparation for maternity work for interested volunteers, and having many conferences with members of the executive committee concerning the possibility of the chapter taking over the nursing service now financed by the Delano Fund.

Although there has been no official action on the part of the chapter, each officer has agreed that the service should be put on an independent financial basis. They are grateful for the service that has been given them and are eager to show their appreciation.

The rent money for my apartment in Seward is paid until April 30. I will be glad to have you send me directions as to my future work soon so that I shall not have to pay the rent for May, if you do not wish me to return to pack my things and wait for the chapter nurse who will probably arrive in June. I have written to Seward that my return will depend on the Delano Committee.

Letter to Jenny Wren
Unga, Alaska, June 22, 1924

I don't think I owe you a letter, do I? But this is the longest Sabbath Day in the memory of man, and I am justified in telling my troubles to my friends.

You perhaps knew that I went to San Francisco this spring for an antrum operation? Result of some Alaskan dentistry. Miserable experience, but I am O.K. again, except that I am minus much jaw and several teeth. Fortunately, these defects do not show on the surface so my beautiful (?) face is still unmarred.

Just now, I am in Unga, a fishing village of two hundred souls on a treeless island where the honk of a motor or the rattle of a wagon are unknown. Likewise, the jazz of the movie house and dance hall. We have no church, no doctor, no dentist, no summer weather, no summer clothes, no summer pleasures, unless you include walking by the sea. But it is too much with us. We wish we could see a grain field. The scenery is wonderful in a wild, hopeless sort of way. It would be, without trees, you know.

Am hoping to get some kiddies to the government doctor twelve hours west of here for tonsillectomy and adenoidectomy (T&A) operations. Have asked the Cutter Service to send a dentist but the answer was not encouraging. Eventually, the little mail boat will appear off Wild Keley's Rock where the white water always roars, and I will take my seasick way to another village with similar opportunities. The work is too limited to be successful. When I get much discouraged, I scrub my cabin floor, fry some fresh cod, and carry great quantities of water from the spring in the valley. I am sure the work I have done all told could have been accomplished in six months or less, in a smaller, better populated district. I have not the courage to try to make this clear to the Delano Committee, though I think the people here know it.

July Report
Seward, Alaska, August 12, 1924

From July 5 to July 17, I made visits to homes in Unga and for a week nursed a young Native boy who had a very high fever. He made a good recovery.

From July 17 to 26 there was little to do in Unga. On the twenty-sixth, en route to King Cove, I again visited the Natives at Squaw Harbor. I went to King Cove, expecting to help Dr. Nevius, USS *Pioneer*, with a surgical case. The patient went with me from Unga. On our arrival in King Cove we had a conference with the doctor and the captain of his ship and decided to return to Unga with the patient, via Ikutan, on the cannery tender *Redwood*. We came to this conclusion when we learned that Captain Lukens could spare Dr. Nevius to do the tonsil cases in Unga. There were no good quarters for surgical work at King Cove. At Ikutan we picked up two more patients, members of a family in which we had done surgical work last year. From July 28 to 31 we were all on the cannery boat, en route to Squaw Harbor, from where we expected to take a gas boat for Unga and begin work on the ten or twelve cases waiting to be operated. I had sent a radio to branch chairman; he had had a house arranged— extra lights, etc.—and we were to begin work the day we arrived.

During our entire time on the *Redwood*, the captain and Dr. Nevius (and for a part of the time the doctor from the cannery at King Cove) had been drinking. When we reached Squaw Harbor on the morning of the thirty-first, the first aid man asked our help regarding a child who had been burned the night before. I visited the child and approved the treat-ment, but asked the first aid man to go aboard the *Redwood* for Dr. Nevius, who I had not seen since we had left Ikutan. The man tried for several hours to get the doctor to come ashore but was unsuccessful. During that time, the gas boat from Unga with the branch member had arrived and was waiting to know what I was going to do. I consulted four or five men and we decided that I could not go on with work of such importance under the conditions. (We had no trained helpers and would have done work without the usual aid found in hospitals.)

I did not wish to give the reason for a sudden departure, and finally told them I had received a message making it necessary for me to go to Seward and we would have to post-pone the work. There was a boat on which the Ikutan cases could return in the evening. They also had relatives in Squaw Harbor and Unga. The other patient, a bone case about sev-enteen years old and able to be around, had friends in Unga. I made no explanation to the doctor. In fact I did not see him at all. He went in another gas boat that was going to Unga and took all his instruments with him. The boat was run by a man who was also drinking and they had a passenger, a merchant from Unga, who was in the same condition. I do not know what the doctor did in Unga, since we have had no means of communicating with our branch folks.

Since there was no place for me to stay in Squaw Harbor, I decided to remain aboard the *Redwood* and go, if necessary, to southeast Alaska where I could get transportation to Seward. The officials of the cannery who were on the boat were very kind and helpful. When we had been out an hour or so they learned by radio that the mail boat *Starr* was still at Sand Point and would wait for me if I could reach there in a reasonable time. Shortly after, we sighted a fish boat. I was transferred to it and in two hours was on the *Starr* with my friends. I found that more violations of the Volstead Act was the reason for the delay at Sand Point, but we got away and arrived in Seward on August 4, in time to meet Miss Taake, the field representative from the Pacific Division office.

Letter to Clara Noyes
Seward, Alaska, September 15, 1924

I have your letter of August 19 advising me to resign my work with the Seward Chapter. With it was a letter from Miss Ledyard saying that Mr. Hunt thought I should remain until December 1 because the chapter needs my help in conducting the eighth roll call. I am accordingly giving the acting chairman, Mr. Ralph Reed, my resignation today and am enclosing a copy to you. Another copy is being sent to the division office.

Mrs. Jessie Ellsworth has very kindly offered to act as roll call chairman, but since she has had no experience in this line of Red Cross work, she needs a great deal of help. I am mailing letters bearing her signature to all the branches today, enclosing an article written with the help of Miss Pickett. We often refer to her splendid little book.

I will try to visit Kodiak and Seldovia before December 1. Indeed, I would like to make a trip to every branch and shake the hand of everyone along the coast. I would like to thank them personally for their great kindness to me during the last two years. I am sorry that I have not been allowed to finish the three year's assignment. I see now that I took the matter too seriously and perhaps wrote too many letters to the division office and to you. However, I am sure that the committee and the division office see the matter much more clearly than I can see it and are justified in advising me to resign. Many of the missionaries who are sent up here have hung on, from a mistaken sense of duty, long after their period of usefulness has passed. I should not care to do that.

May I suggest that, in the event that another Delano nurse is sent up, that more, many more, letters of the kind that Miss Cole knows how to write be sent to her? Your illness in the spring and Miss Fox's trips to Europe were a hardship to me. I heard nothing from the committee for months. Please do not think I am criticizing the splendid committee people who have had my interests so much at heart and who have been so generous with expense money and supplies. I am being frank in the matter because I am thinking of the great help the committee and the division director can be to the nurse who works in Alaska.

Mail after November 15 should be sent to me in care of the Calhoun Hotel, Seattle, and marked "Hold."

Please extend my heartiest thanks to your committee for giving me the great opportunity which has been mine. I hope that Miss Delano—if she could know all about it—would not be entirely displeased.

Annual Report—Year End, October 1, 1924

To Miss Noyes

October 2, 1924

The following is my narrative report for the year ending October 1, 1924. October and November 1923 were spent in Seward; I conducted four classes in Home Hygiene and Care of the Sick each week in my apartment and did the usual school and district work with considerable direction of the seventh roll call. Our collections amounted to about $1,500—the largest return since the War.

The day after Christmas, 1923, I left Seward for Kodiak and remained until January 5. While there I inspected the school children, made forty-seven home calls, encouraged monthly weighing of pupils, made an effort to secure a dentist from Seward, visited Wood Island Mission, talked with the branch committee, etc.

On January 5 I sailed for Kanatak on a freighter. The *Starr* had been on the rocks in December and was still out of commission. The weather was terrible and my whole stay in Kanatak was rather uncomfortable. I did all the nursing work I found to do among the Natives and had one to two calls to the few white people there, taught school in an old saloon, and sent another petition to the U.S. Bureau of Education asking for a teacher. This request was granted and this year (1924) there is a school in Kanatak.[17]

I left Kanatak on February 1 in the worst storm Captain Johansen has experienced for years. I was aboard the *Starr* seventeen days. We encountered storms all along the coast; the ship was iced down, we were short of oil, I had a patient who developed pains which indicated a visit from the stork, and we struck a reef but were off in ten minutes. We finally reached Unalaska. I discharged the woman to the doctor at the Methodist mission and returned to Seward.

On November 10 I had had a tooth extracted and had trouble from an infection of the jaw and antrum. It became worse in March and the local dentist advised me to go to the states. I arrived in San Francisco on March 24, was operated on, and had several conferences with the division people concerning the conditions in the Seward Chapter. Before leaving my chapter, I had been given to understand that the executive committee might consider taking over the work if the Delano Committee agreed. They were advised to go ahead, but on my return I learned that the Seward Committee had decided that it could not be done. They voted to pay the sum of $100 each month toward the salary and traveling expenses of the Delano nurse, beginning in October. Later word was received from the division that this was not wise, that it would be better to save the money until the chapter could take over.

There had been some discussion, too, relative to a division of the chapter, since the great size of the territory makes any work difficult and inefficient. After careful consideration of this matter it was given up. An attempt was made to secure the assistance of the U.S. Bureau of Education, but this was not carried to a successful conclusion because in the opinion of the division and the Delano Committee, the proper approach had not been made. Mr. B. B. Mozee, the district superintendent for the Alaska Division, however, asked me if I cared to work on the peninsula for the Bureau of Education. This indicates an interest and help will eventually be given, I am sure.

I returned to Seward on May 10, in much better health but perhaps not as strong as I should have been to travel in the Aleutian Islands, where vegetables, fruit, milk, and fresh meat are scarce. I went to Unga and stayed there the entire month of June (I visited La Touche for a week before sailing west). This month marks the beginning of discouragement caused by the difficult conditions in Seward and Unga at this time. The surgical clinic that I planned for Unga had to be abandoned because of the intemperance of the government surgeon.

On my return to Seward, I conferred with Miss Yeteve Taake, F.R. [field representative], from the Pacific Division. She interviewed several Seward folks who had just come back from the west. They gave her a poor account of the district and the chance for work there. Later, the chapter met and nine members voted that the nursing service should go on and requested the continued help of the Delano Fund. Miss Taake recommended that the present nurse should be relieved and someone with greater physical strength and more enthusiasm be sent. The division and the Delano Committee have accepted this recommendation and I will be leaving Seward on November 30, 1924. I am remaining until after the eighth roll call, at the suggestion of the division manager.

Letter to Stella Fuller
November 5, 1924

Miss Stella Fuller
Delano Red Cross Nurse
Seward, Alaska
My dear Miss Fuller:

The National Committee on Red Cross Nursing Service wishes to express its deep appreciation of the fine service you have rendered as a Delano Red Cross nurse in the isolated territory of Alaska. From the reports and records of accomplishment, the committee believes quite firmly that you have not only performed in that community the type of work which interested Miss Delano so vitally, but have through your enthusiasm and devoted service created an influence that will live indefinitely.

It gives the Delano Memorial Red Cross Nurse Committee at National Headquarters, great pleasure to forward this

message for the National Committee, with which it heartily
concurs. With best wishes for your future success wherever
you may go, I am
    Very sincerely yours,
    Chairman, National Committee
    Red Cross Nursing Service
    Chairman, Delano Memorial
    Red Cross Nurse Committee

Afterword

At the time of Fuller's employment, the territory of Alaska
did not have a rudimentary health department to take over
nursing. Begun as a demonstration in an almost unworked
field, many Red Cross chapters by 1923–1924 were passing
out of the pioneer stage. Who should be responsible for the
long haul?[18]

In Alaska, services continued to be fragmented and spo-
radic as the territory of Alaska struggled with overwhelming
needs, tremendous barriers to transportation and communications, and lack of resources and organization to deal with
many of its problems. Although some services of a health
department were established in 1936, it wasn't until July 1,
1945, that an official Department of Health was established.
An "Agreement Between the Territorial Health Department
and the Alaska Native Service on the Unification of Nursing
Services" was negotiated in October 1948, whereby the
Territorial Health Department would assume responsibility
for public health nursing services to all residents of Alaska.[19]

Presently, in the geographic area previously assigned to
Stella Fuller, there are seventeen public health nurses serving Seward, Homer, Kenai, Dillingham, and the Aleutian
Islands.[20] In addition there are community health aides in
every Native village. Alaska Native hospitals in Dillingham

and Anchorage provide tertiary care for the Native population. There are medical clinics with midlevel practitioners
in Unalaska and Sandpoint that serve local residents. Travel
today is largely by air, except for the Kenai Peninsula, which
is connected by road to Anchorage.

Endnotes

1. S. S. Cooper, "Stella Louisa Fuller 1878–1966," in *American Nursing: A Biographical Dictionary,* Vern L. Bullough, Lilli Sentz, and Alice P. Stein, eds., Volume Two, (New York: Garland 1992).
2. Ibid.
3. E. G. Fox, "Twenty Years of Red Cross Public Health Nursing," *The Red Cross Courier* (December 1932): 173.
4. E. H. Cavin, "Twenty-Five Years of Public Health Nursing," *The Red Cross Courier* (July 1937): 15.
5. "Delano Nurses Named to Fill Isolated Posts," *The Red Cross Courier* (August 1922): 1. The terms of the endowment were as follows:
   - It should be ascertained that no funds for the salary of the nurse are available from federal, state, or county sources or from agencies or individuals in the locality.
   - The lack of local funds should not be due to transitory conditions such as crop failure, drought, disasters, etc.
   - The locality should represent an established settlement and not a temporary one, such as might be found in lumber camps or mining towns.
   - It should be possible to make satisfactory living arrangements for the nurses.
   - It should be possible to get about in the locality by one means of transportation or another.
   - It might be well if there were other organized work within reasonable traveling distance, as a settlement, church, school, or other similar undertaking. The nursing service should not be in any way attached to the settlement or school, however.
6. Ibid.
7. Delano Red Cross Nursing Committee letter to Ms. Van de Vrede, American Red Cross, Atlanta, GA, 14 June 1922, RG 509.201, Alaska, Delano Nursing Service, National Archives, Washington, D.C.
8. Agnes Holland, notes on Alaska Chapters to the American Red Cross, 1922, RG 509.201, Alaska, Delano Nursing Service, National Archives, Washington, D. C. In a letter dated May 8, 1922, Agnes Holland to Mr. Arne of the American National Red Cross, San Francisco:

I think the right place [for a Delano nurse] would be the southwestern coast beginning at Kodiak and extending along the islands
there. The inhabitants are far from any hospitals and have neither
doctors nor nurses to help them. Seward is the nearest Red Cross
chapter. Dr. Romig is the current chairman and he has been asking
the government and the Red Cross to send in a public health nurse.
Transportation will be by boat direct from Seward on the Admiral
Line. There are a number of government schools scattered about, also
some missions. Churches are rare and mostly Russian Greek. Living
arrangements not certain.

Seward is a town of about two to three hundred inhabitants.
Fishing, fur trading, and prospecting in the nearby mountains are
the chief industries. There are two churches, a good school, and a
fine hospital. No other organizations except Red Cross, PTA, and
Ladies Church Societies. The Seward branches embrace miles and
miles of territory. Afognak, Akutan, Bethel, Coal Harbor, Cold Bay,
Chignik, Dillingham, Dutch Harbor, Katmai, Kaluk, Kenai, King
Cove, Kodiak, Naknek, Nushagak, Sanak, Sandpoint, Sarechef,
Traveloff Bay, Uyaskak, Unalaska, Unga, Uyak, and Portage Bay with
mostly all Natives of the Aleut tribes. Splendid furs come from the
islands, and prospectors are looking for oil and coal. Fishing is the
main industry. Government schools and Russian missions are found
throughout.

Seward was finally chosen after careful consideration and advice
from Commissioner W. T. Lopp, Bureau of Education; Assistant Red
Cross Manager Arne, Northwest Division; Mrs. Bishop [Ebba Djupe];
and Agnes Holland, PHN (Mary L. Cole letter to Clara Noyes, chairman, Delano Nursing Committee, 30 June 1924, RG 509.201, Alaska,
Delano Nursing Service, National Archives, Washington, D.C.).

9.   Cooper, "Stella Louisa Fuller 1878–1966."
10. Stella L. Fuller, Letters and Field Trip Reports, 1922–1924, RG 509.201,
     Alaska, Delano Nursing Service, National Archives, Washington, D.C.
11. Roll Call: This term was used for a Red Cross fund-raising and membership
     drive. The first one was held in 1917 and they were continued annually until
     World War II. Initially, persons were asked to give one dollar to join the
     American Red Cross. (Letter dated October 23, 2000, from Jean Waldman,
     American Red Cross, to Elfrida Nord.)
12. L. J. Campbell, "Kanatak: From Boomtown to Ghosttown," *Alaska Geographic*
     22, no. 1, (1995). Campbell credits Fuller for her initiation of the school and
     includes a photo of her and her students.
13. Eighteenth Amendment: The Prohibition amendment relating to the purchase
     and sale of alcoholic beverages.
14. Stella L. Fuller, Letters and Field Trip Reports, 1922–1924, RG 509.201,
     Alaska, Delano Nursing Service, National Archives, Washington, D.C.

15. Dr. Wilfred Grenfell (1865–1940) was a medical missionary serving the needs of fishermen and others in the widespread area of Newfoundland and Labrador. His mission established a wide variety of services. *Encyclopedia Americana,* 13 (1997): 481.

16. Reference to needs assessment survey completed by Agnes Holland, Red Cross representative, preceding Fuller's appointment.

17. The village of Kanatak survived until the 1940s, experiencing great variations in population during this time. For example, the teacher arriving in 1926 found the village almost empty (P2010 file, Alaska Region, National Archives, Anchorage, Alaska).

18. Fox, "Twenty Years of Red Cross Public Health Nursing."

19. Alaska Board of Health, Meeting minutes of October 27–29, 1948, unpublished, RG 311-43-986, no. 17. Alaska State Archives, Juneau, Alaska.

20. State of Alaska, section of *Nursing Directory* (Juneau, AK: State of Alaska, 1999).

The Country is Beautiful, Beautiful Now: Gertrude Fergus

Bureau of Education School Nurse
White Mountain, 1926–1927

GERTRUDE FERGUS WAS BORN December 26, 1898, the second of three girls in the W. M. Fergus family of Whitehall, Montana. She attended grammar schools in Whitehall, Missoula, and Billings, graduating from Billings High School in 1916. She first enrolled in the University of Montana St. Patrick's Hospital School of Nursing in 1916, then graduated from the University of Cincinnati School of Nursing and Health in 1921.[1] Her first job was as supervisor, Psychiatric Wards, in Cincinnati General Hospital.

Fergus went to Seattle, Washington, in January 1922 and registered for private duty. Instead, she accepted a position as a county nurse in Clallam Bay near Port Angeles on the Olympic Peninsula. In September 1926, Fergus accepted a nurse position with the Bureau of Education in White Mountain, Alaska.

In 1924, the Bureau of Education had opened an industrial and trade school at White Mountain for Native children, both boys and girls. The White Mountain Industrial School was a combination boarding and day school and consisted of eleven buildings overlooking the Fish River. One of the school's successful programs was herding several thousand reindeer and canning reindeer meat. The school closed its doors in 1947 when the Mt. Edgecumbe School near Sitka was opened.[2]

Gertrude Fergus became the sole health care provider for the school, with the nearest other provider in Nome, about seventy miles away. Her work included the intensive nursing involved with typhoid patients confined to bed. In addition she provided health care to the village and had walk-in visitors to her clinic. She was called upon to do a little of everything, as her letters testify. The responsibility of making medical decisions made her ponder the need to attend medical school.[3]

After one year at White Mountain, Fergus was appointed as nurse at the Tanana Hospital in the interior of Alaska in August 1927.[4] The Bureau of Education had developed a small hospital at the old Fort Gibbon site near Tanana on the Yukon River. Eben W. White, MD, was in charge. During the summer of 1928, she worked as a public health nurse on board the *Martha Angeline*.[5] Fergus resigned from the Bureau of Education on August 22, 1928.[6] Gertrude Fergus married William Percy Baker, M. D., a dedicated country general practitioner of Clallam Bay, in December 1928.[7] She had first become acquainted with Dr. Baker in Clallam Bay in

6.1. Gertrude Fergus, 1921 Graduation photograph, University of Cincinnati School of Nursing and Health. Courtesy of Newsome and Betty Baker, Clallam Bay, Washington.

1922. He had served in southeast Alaska from 1915 to 1918, when he was called into World War I service. The Armistice was signed before he saw duty and he returned to Clallam Bay.[8]

The Bakers became the parents of two sons, Newsom and William. Dr. Baker died in January 1961; until her death in February 1988, Gertrude Fergus Baker kept busy with many projects, all useful and charitable, in addition to managing the only store and gas station in Clallam Bay.[9]

The letters to her family from her year at White Mountain are included here. She sent these to the Alaska Nurses Association in response to their 1956 request. Her Tanana letters were few, and no letters were submitted from her Yukon River assignment.[10]

Letters written by
Gertrude Fergus 1926–1927

Nome, Alaska
September 1, 1926

Dear Family:

Please consider this a letter to all of you and let it go the rounds, for I'm sure I shall have a hard time writing all the details to each one individually.

Two weeks ago this A.M. I was starting from Seattle and fully hoped to have reached White Mountain by this time— but the fates seem "agin me."

Sister will remember introducing me at the dock to a Mr. McGuire who, in turn, introduced me to a Dr. Kittelsen,[11] also going to Nome. The doctor was one of the men who discovered gold at Nome (and has been there most of the time since). He was returning from Mayo's in Rochester where he had had an operation for cancer of the stomach—and because they had given him absolutely no hope, he was hurrying home to die. He invited me to come frequently to his cabin so he could tell me all about the country I was getting into— and I gladly accepted the invitation.

The sea was smooth but a heavy fog lay between us and Vancouver Island, so we had only occasional glimpses of the land. Even this we left behind before noon.

Our passenger list was short so it did not take long for those of us who were not seasick to get acquainted. I'll admit that my head felt a bit "woozy" and my stomach wobbly, but I didn't miss a single meal (although I lost two). Those first days passed uneventfully. We walked miles every day, read some, and slept more. Early Tuesday morning everyone was excited over the appearance of land—a great jagged rocky island. Before noon we were passing along the coast between many small islands—none of which were near enough to be seen well.

However, at about two o'clock we turned to False Pass where a fishing boat came out to meet us for mail and a little freight. As we pulled away from the little harbor I went up on the upper deck to read but suddenly discovered a most wonderful fairy-like peak piercing the low-lying clouds. I could scarcely believe my eyes but watched and watched until the clouds drifted away and a most superb range of mountains came in view. First of all was a little round mountain that looked like a miniature of Mount Rainier. Then came Mt. Isanotsky (the peak I first saw). At first view it looked like a mighty inverted ice-cream cone, so high and so sharp and yet of such even contour was it. From this side we could see three gigantic glaciers reaching from almost the top of the peak down to the very ocean. The shore here is rough and guarded by rocks such as are along the coast at LaPush. As we continued westward the contour changed, and instead of it appearing like a sharp peak it was an immense crater of which the west rim had broken away and spilled forth another glacier much larger than the three on the southern side.

By this time the sun had set but the afterglow was caught by the clouds and reflected on the great fields of snow and ice. And then I discovered the third peak—Shishaldin—trying to peer through the clouds. Its sides were covered with old lava flows and its head was lost in clouds and smoke, for Shishaldin just slumbers. At no time were we able to see all of the mountain, but we were told that it has an even crater rim above which always lies a cloud of smoke.

By the time we had passed the mountains darkness had settled down, and with it a strong wind and "white caps." About 10 P.M. we started through Unimak Pass. Although a full moon was scheduled for us, we were unable to see much. The clouds were low and obstructed most of the view. Oh, yes, I was up to see. In the afternoon Dr. Kittelsen had asked me to stay with him during the nights since he was getting very much weaker. So I was awake when the *Victoria* [see Figure 6.2] left the choppy waters of the pass and turned into the calm waters of the landlocked harbor. But here a stench arose, so that I longed for the open waters and strong wind. We had reached Akutan.

Morning light revealed a tiny harbor among most beautiful hills. In contour they resembled the hills of the oil country of Wyoming—gaunt with deep corrugations made by swift streams. But they were the most beautiful shade of

6.2. The Victoria. *During the 1920s and 1930s, this commercial vessel made trips from Seattle to Nome with stops en route. Reprinted, with permission, the Anchorage Museum of History and Art, French Album (1394-13-1-57).*

green imaginable!! And down through this greenness came tumbling many little waterfalls. The water of the harbor was absolutely still and reflected the hills and clouds and the first bright rays of the morning. And there anchored near us and seeming to float in her own white reflection was the *Algonquin,* the U. S. Coast Guard cutter. She seemed like a bit of home to me for she has often stopped at Port Angeles.

When I was able to leave my patient and get round to the other side of the boat I discovered the "village"—a dock onto which we were unloading our oil barrels, three buildings that looked like saw mills, and eight or ten houses. Near the bow of our ship four dead whales were anchored to a buoy.

After I had watched the dissection of two whales I fled to the refuge of the hills. They were covered with rank grass more than knee high and quantities of wild flowers, mostly fireweed and monk's hood. I have never seen more beautiful monk's hood in any cultivated garden than grew in great profusion all over the hillsides. We gathered an arm full for our dining tables.

We stayed in Akutan about twelve hours and at 2:30 P.M. started on the last lap of our journey. Perhaps it was my imagination, but it seemed to me that the waters of the Bering Sea looked colder than those of the Pacific—and I'm sure the wind was colder. From then on to Nome I really didn't see much, for I slept days and worked nights. About 5 P.M. Friday everyone got mightily excited, for we could see Sledge Island and that was only an hour from Nome. Sometimes the island was almost hidden by the shower of hail that suddenly descended upon us.

I was muchly surprised when we arrived at Nome to see the boat anchor far out in the bay. On account of the "freeze up" it is practically impossible to keep a dock here, and the bay is so shallow that the boat must keep a half mile off shore.

I shall never, never forget that evening. The crowd of ex-
pectant passengers watching the distant shore where heavy
rain clouds broken by one shaft of sunlight lay thick over the
hills, the town with its church towers silhouetted against the
sky and the first lights twinkling in the streets, and the light
tug with its barge struggling out through the heavy surf that
beat the shore.

I must stop now—this has been written in snatches during
the night. I have been kept on for the nights to care for the
doctor who is undoubtedly dying now—as he has been for
days. I must give this to Dr. Schwartz[12] when he comes and
he will take it out on the boat that leaves for Seattle in a few
hours.

More of my story later.

September 4, 1926

Dear Folks:

A sharp hail storm struck us just as we dropped anchor so
that the people from Nome who came out on the lighter to
meet us were drenched. I did not see the actual arrival of the
little tug and lighter, for I was busy in my patient's stateroom
giving him a hypodermic. He had waited for it until he knew
that his wife was on the tug, then he was ready for the stimu-
lant to keep him going until he could reach home.

My first impression was of the little woman in a slicker
and hat followed by a huge man who seemed to fill the whole
room. As soon as possible I left the room and almost immediately met the pleasant little Dr. Schwartz and his wife,
a nurse, who had also come out to meet Dr. Kittelsen, my
patient, and arrange for his move into Nome. All the other
passengers were unloaded from the ship like so much freight,
for the sea was running high and it was impossible to put
out a gangplank. The doctor was carried out on his mattress,
put in a huge box and let down in a freight sling. Then Mrs.

Kittelsen, Dr. and Mrs. Schwartz, and myself went down in the next load. A stretcher had been brought out on the barge. This was placed on two trunks and an Eskimo in oilskins stood at either end of it to steady it as the barge rolled and pitched in the heavy seas.

To me it was wonderfully picturesque—the crowd of passengers huddled together at one end of the barge, the pile of baggage in the center, and beside it the stretcher with the dying man on it, a crying woman kneeling among the baggage, and the two Eskimo standing like guards over them. Once a great wave came near sweeping over the barge and deluging everything. The rain poured steadily and the surf pounded on the shore ahead of us. Only a blinking red light showed us the way to safety into the mouth of the river.

Everyone was silent and anxious as our little tugboat swung into the channel and the barge hesitated on the crest of the great breakers before it plunged down between the two

6.3. Barge at Nome waterfront. Reprinted, with permission from the Anchorage Museum of History and Art, French Album (1394-13-2-02).

great bulkheads and swung into the more peaceful waters of Snake River. On the shore were running figures and anxious calls and an occasional shout: "Hie, there, that you Charlie?" "Got home, did you?"

Finally, the barge was made fast to the piling on the shore [see Figure 6.3] and a gangplank was put out. We waited until all the other passengers had gone ashore before we left the barge. Even the crowd waited to see the doctor. All of Nome was there to pay respects to him.

Mrs. Schwartz had a Ford coupe at the landing and took me directly to Dr. Kittelsen's home. I had only a vague impression of a struggle through a crowd of white-faced people standing in pouring rain, finding our car in a side street, driving over plank paving in very poor repair, down dimly lighted streets between old dilapidated buildings, and coming to a halt in front of an old ramshackle building that bore the sign "Old Stoves for Sale." We went up a long flight of dimly lighted stairs and down a long hall, then into a very pleasant living room with the impression of many windows and lovely flowers.

In a few minutes my patient had arrived and my work began. Dr. Schwartz stayed with us all night. But before quiet settled down on the house I had met all the prominent people of the town.

There was Grant Jackson, the towering man who had come with Mrs. Kittelsen out to the *Victoria* and who had made all the arrangements for the doctor's comfort coming in. There was kindly Judge Lomen[13] and his charming daughter Helen, who offered me the use of their home as mine as long as I might be in Nome. Then came the marshall and attorney and the doctor's partner, and many, many more, all offering help in any way we might need it. At last everyone went home and all was quiet except for the rain beating against the windows and the surf pounding on the beach just beside us.

Night passed quickly and by the time dawn came slipping in at 3:30 the wind and rain had ceased, and I could look out across the grey sea with its many lines of rolling breakers.

Many nights and days have gone by since then. Dr. Schwartz got another nurse for days and I have been sleeping at the Lomen home during the day and working nights. People have been wonderfully kind in taking me for drives out to see the country around here. The hills remind me of northeastern Montana but the sea makes me think of Clallam County, so I surely should not have a chance to get lonely.

Nome itself is old and worn looking. All the houses look dilapidated because they stand on stilts and seem drab. No paint seems to withstand the freezing without losing its gloss. And the freezing and thawing of the ground makes no foundation secure. All the buildings are swayback or tipsy. The streets are narrow as alleys for the most part, and are paved with old planks. A few of them are being graveled at the present time.

Yesterday morning my patient died and last night I had the first real sleep I have had for ten days. I slept fourteen hours! Today we went out to see the arrival of an airplane from Fairbanks; therefore, this letter now. I understand that all mail in the post office will go out with the plane Monday. The price of a trip from Nome to Fairbanks is $1,000. The capacity of the car is four passengers. This time there will be but one, a Colonel Steese of the U.S. Road Commission.

Tomorrow I am invited out to ptarmigan dinner. Doesn't that sound good? Ptarmigan, I am informed, is much like quail, is brown speckled in summer but pure white in winter. I have also enjoyed the wonderful blueberries which grow in such profusion.

I don't know when I shall get to White Mountain, either on the *Donaldson,* a mail boat which leaves here Tuesday for Golovin, or else on the *Boxer,*[14] which is due here from the north any day now. I am hoping the *Boxer* gets here before the Donaldson leaves, since I would much rather go on her.

Since the doctor's death I have been staying with a Mr. and Mrs. Frawley, old, old friends of Mrs. Kittelsen's. They insisted on taking me in until I can get off to White Mountain. Everyone here tells me that I shall like my place very much. So I am eagerly looking forward to that and to getting settled.

Have been living in my suitcase since July first. It will seem good to get into a place of my own again and have things as I want them.

A Mr. and Mrs. Neeley who went up on the *Victoria* are also en route to White Mountain. He will be carpenter in charge of the little sawmill there. She will teach cooking and sewing.

I have seen the Eskimo girl who was the only survivor of the Wrangell Island tragedy[15]—and also the man and dog who were heroes of the "serum race" from Fairbanks to Nome last year.

I have met Dr. Welch and his wife who were on the hospital ship on the Yukon this summer. I have an appointment to talk it all over with Dr. Welch tomorrow. He is a queer, fidgety little man with a shock of white hair that stands up on end all the time, very red sunburned face, a tummy like Santa Claus, only slightly smaller and firmer, and a flow of very expressive and explosive language when needed. Mrs. Welch,[16] a nurse, is tall and dark and rather dictatorial, I imagine. When I saw her she was overcome with grief over Dr. Kittelsen's death, but I had the impression of a rather overbearing personality, under other conditions.

Must stop now. More later.

White Mountain, Alaska
September 16, 1926

Dear Folks:

Please notice that at last I'm here! A week ago Sunday the *Boxer* dropped anchor at Nome and I momentarily expected a summons to go on board her. But a heavy southeast wind piled the surf so high that she had to seek shelter behind Sledge Island some nine miles away, and it was not until Wednesday morning that we were able to get away.

Mr. Wagner and Mr. Range, director of this district of the bureau, were aboard with twenty-five youngsters collected from all the points between Pt. Barrow and Nome. Also, there was a wee teacher from Pt. Barrow. She had been with a married sister, her husband and baby.

I wish you could have seen those Eskimo children that night! We reached Golovin Bay but did not go ashore because of surf and rain. All the children gathered in the hold between decks—there were their bunks covered with reindeer skins. One of the boys played a small box organ and all the others sang—hymns mostly, all the old familiar songs— "Home Sweet Home," "Swanee River," "Kentucky Home," "America," "Aloha," and "It Ain't Goin' to Rain No Mo'." But they sang well and with great spirit. The hold was dark except for one small lamp. The organ stood among barrels and boxes and stacks of hides. On either side were the low bunks, on one of which was a little girl soothing an earache with a bag of hot salt. The boy who played the organ was a hunchback and beside him stood a larger boy who had a cane. There were no unhappy faces, although this was the first time that most of them had ever been outside their own villages.

The following morning the surf had calmed down but the rain poured. After breakfast we were all loaded into the little launch and taken ashore where Mr. and Mrs. McCallister and Mr. Neeley awaited us. I liked them immediately. Mr.

McCallister is head of the school and has been teaching here four years. Mr. Neeley I met on the *Victoria* coming up. He and his wife have charge of the dormitory and he is teacher of the upper grades and the wood work and manual training. The other teachers here are Mr. and Mrs. Burlingame, whom Sister met when the *Boxer* sailed. They do not appeal to me particularly. Mr. B. will teach mechanics and have charge of all repair work; also head of the Boy Scouts. Mrs. B. teaches primary and supervises the laundry.

We really have quite an establishment here—about fifty boarding school pupils. Since the dormitory is not yet completed, the boys sleep in the old bunk house that belonged to the Wild Goose Mining Company some years ago. Mr. Neeley, with the help of two men from the village and some of the larger boys, is building the new wing to the dorm for the boys. Since this is an industrial school, most of our pupils are above twelve and are the best pupils from each of their respective stations. Regular academic work is carried on in the mornings but the afternoons are devoted to industrial work. The girls have cooking and sewing and home nursing, and the boys carpentry, gasoline engines, and training in making Native boats. A Native woman comes in to teach the skin work and all the parkees and mukluks for the pupils will be made right here. Several of the girls are also training to be teachers in the Native schools. They are a bright, happy, willing crowd.

Oh, yes, I forgot to mention in our staff the Native teacher Isaac and his wife; "Ma," the colored cook; and Buster, fifteen-year-old hunchback son of the McCallisters. Most of the village people are away fishing or tending reindeer but in another two or three weeks they will all be home. I celebrated my first night here by officiating at a birth—Gregory Ahsukpum—weight 7 ½ pounds.

You would like my cozy little house. Although it is a consolidation of three, it is good-looking outside and in. The windows are large and plentiful. The porches on the south are all windows so that plenty of light comes in. A long shelf under the windows in my living room holds my little leather library, my candlesticks, pictures of the home folks, and a bouquet of Mrs. Howard's flowers. A hanging basket above is full of wandering Jew. Yesterday Mrs. Neeley and I took some of the girls for a walk through the woods up back of the school, and the trophy I brought home is a beautiful "center-piece" of mosses, lichens, reindeer moss, and some trailing evergreen and red leaves that I have never seen before. They now fill an aluminum pie dish and grace my table.

The house faces south overlooking the river, trees, and hills beyond. From the little ridge just back of our school I can see over to Golovin Bay and Bering Sea—by winter trail nine miles, by boat in summer twenty-five miles. The Fish River meanders everywhere, has dozens of mouths, hides among the scrub willows, and can hardly find its way out again. The whole flat between us and the distant hills is filled with many channels of the winding stream. But it twists and turns so that we can see both sunrise and sunset reflected in it. The timber is small Sitka spruce. We would think of them as ornamental trees "Outside" (as the U.S.A. is known here). But they are a very real addition to the landscape and furnish us fuel and timber. The trees come right down to my little white house and both beautify and protect it. I have already taken pictures of the house and the beautiful views I have from my windows. Some of these long winter evenings when I have nothing else to do I'll try developing and printing. And if they are good I'll send you some prints.

Friday evening—Last night was my night to chaperone the girls to prayer meeting and after that Mrs. Neeley and I took an hour to examine each other's heads. We have been eradicating pediculosis from the heads of our pupils and feared we might have become contaminated—as we were! Therefore, this afternoon has been spent in shampooing our respective (if not respectable) heads. I believe the safest way is to wear a bathing cap while treating others for pediculi.

Monday, September 27, 1926

Everything is going beautifully so far—everybody busy. My mornings are always taken up with my patients and then afternoons I have been varnishing my floors. The plain brown linoleum, like that on your kitchen floor, absorbs every spot until it is varnished. So I have moved everything from my living room and bedroom into the kitchen and have scrubbed and put on two coats of varnish. My hospital room is also in a state of turmoil but should be dry enough to put to rights tomorrow.

Tuesday, October 7, 1926

Dear Home Folks:

There is no telling when this letter will reach you for winter is fast closing in upon us here and we are about to be shut in from the outside world. October first brought the first flurry of snow—just a few dry flakes that did not even reach the ground. But each succeeding night has been colder and each day has brought a little more snow. Tuesday the scow, which has been bringing our freight up from Golovin, made its last trip and our fifty tons of coal are still there. It will all have to be brought by dog team and horse team when the river freezes over. Tuesday was really a memorable day for it brought the first great cakes of pancake ice swirling down the river. It also took our colored cook.

Poor "Ma" had not been very happy here and she felt imposed upon. When she saw the ice come down the river she decided that she would not stay here all winter. So she left with thirty minutes' notice and went down with the scow. Since then Mrs. Reiley, Mrs. Burlingame, and I have been doing the cooking for the fifty of us at the dormitory. It really has not been a terribly hard job for, of necessity, most of the meals come from tin cans. About the only baking is bread, thirty loaves three times a week. Fortunately, "Ma" left a batch just out of the oven so we had bread enough to last until tomorrow.

Tonight I have been down to the wash house for a bath. The two tubs of the village are located in the wash house, fully a block from my house. Whenever sponge baths get too objectionable I hie me down the hill—that is, whenever I can get hot water. All the water is carried from the river and put into huge gas tanks, which are connected to the big heater. The difficulty is that the tanks are iron and my bath sometimes leaves me a saffron yellow. It is grand to have a good soak, even in rusty water, but I do hate to come out and climb the hill in mud and rain. Wonder how I'll like it at fifty below. Guess I'll not take any baths. We save rainwater for drinking, but when that is exhausted we have to boil the river water. It reminds me of the old days in Billings when we had to boil the Yellowstone. I certainly learned water economy then and to good purpose.

The older Eskimos here do not at all approve of bobbed hair. The younger girls who have been away to school are bobbed but greatly against their parents' will. So in that at least I am approved in the village. All the other teachers here are bobbed, and since Mrs. Neeley is a beauty expert, everyone's hair is well trimmed. You should see the style of our dormitory girls.

And speaking of braids, you would laugh at our "Ellis Island." Arriving at White Mountain, the newcomer alights from the boat and climbs a rather steep incline paved with planks up to the platform that runs along in front of the gymnasium, warehouse, and school with the sign "Ellis Island" over the door. This is the famous wash house. Here every child is stripped, bathed, shampooed, and given clean clothing before he climbs on up the hill to my house where his hair is combed with a fine comb and kerosened and vinegared if necessary. Then he is taken to his place in the dormitory. I have regular inspection of the children once a week and this includes head inspection as well. Most of the heads have been infested when they arrive, but we have waged a successful war. Do you remember our war in Billings when we all had itchy heads?

October 14, 1926

The one thing I miss here is the fresh fruits and vegetables of the coast country. Everything comes from cans or it is evaporated. We have had fresh meat, reindeer, ducks, and ptarmigan. So that gives variation to the canned corn beef hash or ham or bacon. We still have eggs and butter from Outside.

These nice afternoons when I have not been too busy with patients I have been taking the girls for short walks across the hills. This whole country is dotted with many little lakes or ponds and most of the rest of it is covered with moss, boot-deep and wet. Last week we found ice an inch and a half thick on some of the ponds in the woods. I always take my camera along and have taken many pictures. Have great fun experimenting with developing and printing. Guess the pictures will reach you eventually with the letters. I've written Sister and she has sent on home.

I miss the great variety of scenery in my dear Clallam County but find things and people very interesting. The Natives here have rather adopted me because I resemble a Miss French who nursed here for two years and whom they all liked very much. Occasionally, they even call me Miss French.

Maggie Kowchie, a rather influential and quite intelligent squaw, is trying to teach me some Eskimo but finds it rather hard work. She is also making me a parkie of the native squirrel skin. Some of the dormitory girls are making my mukluks. So far I have worn rubber boots or oxfords but I'm anxious to get the mukluks for the heavy snow.

My little house is quite a comfort and will be very homey soon. I'm making sofa cushions and a table runner for my big library table. My cushions seem doomed. First of all I was given a bag of down by one of the villagers. I put it on my enclosed porch until I got a ticking for it that wouldn't leak feathers all over everything. One night the porch door blew open and a dog ran off with the bag. The next morning my down was strewn all over our end of the village! I rescued about a third of it, but I could have murdered the dog. Then I sent to Nome for cretonne or some such material in blues and orange—and the package was atrocious. Two pieces I dyed today with diamond dyes, and made them a solid color. I plan to embroider them with yarn and perhaps I'll have some decent pillows yet.

Tuesday, October 20, 1926

It is beautiful here but unfortunately it means we are cut off from Golovin—our only way out and in. The salt water of the bay does not freeze until later so the only way for any mail to get out is for someone to walk the twenty-five miles over the half-frozen tundra to Golovin. Naturally, only letters are carried out.

Tomorrow one of the Eskimos is walking down to go herring fishing in the bay and has promised to carry out letters for us. The *Victoria* is due in Nome tomorrow night and in Golovin about Friday. After that there will be no communication with the outside world until the snow is deep enough for dog team travel from Fairbanks. Everyone here has been burning the midnight oil writing letters by the ream.

I must admit that I have been most too sleepy to do much writing. I am not accustomed to getting up at 6 A.M. every morning as I have been doing lately, and my days and evenings have been more than full with just the ordinary round of work. Last night I was scrubbing my kitchen floor at 11 P.M. And tonight I ironed until 8 P.M. and had a caller after that. My days are so interrupted that I scarcely get any of my housekeeping done until about 4 P.M. I do manage to make my bed and sometimes sweep the floor before people begin to arrive.

Our days continue warm and sunshiny but the thermometer dropped to three above zero last night. No real snow yet. The ground is clear and frozen.

Things are not exactly as pictured at the Seattle office. For instance the "typewriters" promised consist of one Corona privately owned by Mr. McCallister. Someday I may be able to get a portable from Nome. I am purchasing skates from Mr. Pfaffel's store at Golovin and they will be delivered when the travel by dog teams is possible. Mr. Burlingame, our mechanic, is making himself a pair.

I try to keep regular visiting and office hours but the village does not observe them. Old Isaac is my worst customer. He arrives any time from 6:30 A.M. to 10 P.M. He always wants some "cotting to fix 'em"—that is, a pound of cotton to dress the draining TB sinus in the hip. He is our only ivory worker in the village—also the village gossip. All day he tramps up and down the village with his crutch or sits at his bench in the window and calls to everyone who goes by. He always questions me: "How Mrs. Kaoki today? Bad sick? Mrs. Beuben? What matter? Stomach? Cough? You go Ruby Punnikouk? She sick? No? Maybe Jennie? You go see—tell me maybe?" And maybe I don't. The most constantly used phrases in the village are "Maybe" and "I don't know." They never seem positive about anything. Always "Maybe." *Qui anna!* or "Thank you" is an expression not only of thanks, but of pleasure—pleasure at meeting you, pleasure at your leaving, pleasure about something you've said. The old people who do not understand English simply bow and smile whenever they meet you and repeat *Qui Anna! Qui Anna!*—I'm not sure of the spelling but it sounds that way.

Eskimo language is simply many unwritten dialects.[17] Our people from the far North and from the Yukon have difficulty in understanding the village people or those from around Nome. Consequently, with so many teachers around me and no written vocabulary to which I can refer, I am not progressing very fast.

November 1, 1926

Saturday night we had a Hallowe'en party for the youngsters. As a special treat Mr. McAllister brought out a box of apples. The first we had since we came up on the *Victoria*. I never appreciated a Jonathan before! You have no idea how good they tasted. Next winter I am going to have a box of apples and one of oranges sent in before freeze up. It is impossible to buy anything of the kind here.

Mr. Pfaffel at Golovin has a typical little old general store with a bit of everything and not much of anything. He also has a branch store at Council, twenty-five miles above us. However, shopping is a difficult matter. When we heard that a dog team was coming from Golovin we telephoned for skates and various other things. We got skates, one pair of eights and one of nines, all he had in stock. I had ordered ten yards of unbleached muslin and got ten yards of Indian Head,[18] of which I am making butchers aprons.

I sent to Nome some weeks ago for cretonne for sofa pillows. I wish you could see what I got! Two pieces I dipped in dark blue dye so as to have colors that at least tried to harmonize. Guess we will have to order from Sears and Roebuck after this.

We have not yet begun to notice very short days. The sun gets up between 7 and 7:30 over White Mountain and goes down about 4:30. It is dark by 5:15. But it is light fully an hour before we can see the sun. The light on the distant hills across the valley is beautiful and the sunsets are like Montana's gorgeous ones.

Mama, I have thoroughly enjoyed wearing the grey jersey dress. That and my uniforms are the only things I have worn since I came here. Am still wearing the same clothes I wore during the summer in Clallam County except that I've put on heavier stockings. My floors are cold and drafty. Will have weather strips put on the doors.

I've been having lots of fun trying to learn to speak Eskimo. All of my patients help me so I've begun to know the names of the various parts of the human anatomy. Have also been learning to make thread of reindeer sinew. The reindeer is certainly the salvation of these people. They use the skin for mattress, for mukluks, the fawn skins for parkies, the flesh for meat, the bones for the dog food, and the sinew for thread. Not an ounce of it is wasted. I am enclosing one of Mrs. McCallister's pictures of a reindeer and fawn.

This month's report shows 66 patients and 366 treatments by the White Mountain nurse, so you see time hasn't hung heavy on my hands.

The clock says 8:55 and we must turn our electricity off at 9 now. Our gas supply is limited and longer nights are coming, so good night for this time.

November 13, 1926

Golovin is officially our post office, although our mail for White Mountain all comes to Mr. McCallister in a locked mail sack and goes out from here the first and fifteenths of each month, at which time our mail is supposed to be delivered. I say "supposed" to be, for we have to wait for the river to be either completely frozen over or completely free of ice in order to make the trip. Our letters were brought in the first of this month but all the second and third-class mail is still at Golovin since the carriers had to make a detour of fifteen miles in order to get out around the open water of Golovin Bay and Reindeer Slough at the head of the bay. The walking was very difficult over frozen humps of moss in the tundra and through thinly frozen ponds and wet underbrush. It made a trip of almost forty miles up here so we were indeed thankful to get even our letters.

Although our weather has been below freezing most of the time for three weeks, it has not been cold enough to close the river at the riffles nor to freeze the salt water of the shallow bay. You asked how long my contract lasted, for one year only here, then I may have a transfer if I wish or may return to the U.S.A. Now I think I would like a transfer to some other part of Alaska, preferably along the Yukon. I like it here and probably would have a hard time finding quarters as comfortable, people as congenial, and salary as ample, but I would like to see other parts of Alaska and know more about it all. Our requests must be in by April 1 if we wish a transfer, so I have quite a while to decide the matter for myself. I am still hoping to get on the *Martha Angeline,* the hospital boat on the Yukon. However, time will tell.

Have just come back from my rounds of the village [see Figure 6.4] and now at 3:20 must turn on the lights. The sun has set with a rosy glow behind the southern hills and heavy snow clouds are sweeping in from the coast. Already the air is filled with tiny particles of finest snow.

All day the older school boys, under supervision of Mr. Reilly, have been cutting ice and storing it for next summer's use. Our little Fordson tractor is kept busy these days hauling ice, cutting wood, and pulling timbers into place for the uprights of the new shed. It was even used for a hearse at our first funeral. The daughter of a Native judge died at Chinik and was brought here for burial. The best carpenter, Simon Muchpaedebuk, made the grave; the shroud was an old fashioned nightgown with ruffles on sleeves and neck and down the front; the flowers are some paper ones, made by Mrs. Neeley. The casket, a plain box covered with white muslin and put in another box, was placed on a cart behind the tractor, then the judge and his wife, with the tiny son of the dead woman, seated themselves on the casket and the procession started up the long hill to the cemetery.

All of the village inhabitants followed, some walking decorously, some running ahead and turning up a shorter, steeper path to the barren little cemetery high on the hill. Here the services were held with the beautiful words "and there shall be no night there," the only ones I could understand. Four of the village people sang "Sometime we'll understand." I was surprised at the sweetness and harmony of their voices. The little woman who sang alto carried her two-week old baby on her back. She had walked the mile and a half up the hill and thought nothing of it. There was also old blind Iksuk, led by

6.4. Village of White Mountain in 1920s. National Archives, Alaska Region.

his funny little wife, Coymoyuk. He joined in the singing of the hymns heartily and grunted "Eh—eh" occasionally during the short services. Just as the prayer was ended one small overly curious boy fell into the grave and had to be rescued by Simon. The day was cold and windy; the sun had already set but a queer green light lingered over the distant bay and hills and was reflected in the snowy lake and twisting of the river. No tears were shed but everyone seemed to feel like the woman who climbed the hill with me—"Too bad; too bad; we all go sometime; too bad; good woman."

My trip to the village today was a happy one. All my patients are recovering, except the judge's wife. She is an old crone, far advanced in TB, and has been broken by the death of her daughter and the extra burden of caring for the two grandchildren. She is in bed all the time and Lucy, aged sixteen, does the actual work, but the worry and extra confusion is there. Seven people living in one room is enough to make anyone tired.

November 20, 1926

Yesterday the first winter mail from Nome came in by dog team. However, we have had so little cold weather and snow that the rivers are not frozen and the ground is bare in many places so that the travel was very difficult, two days and a half for the trip that is often made in one day. Unfortunately, our mail was carried on down to Golovin, our official post office, and will be brought to us sometime next week. However, I did have a paper sent me from one of the men I met in Nome, but that was the first outside news since papers dated September 8.

I am busy these days caring for a typhoid patient[19] [see Figure 6.5]. Luckily there are not many patients in the village so I can devote all my time to my boy here in the hospital. I am very worried about him. Was up and walking around for two weeks at home and then was brought by dog team about thirty-five miles. Had a temperature of 105 ½ when he arrived.

As usual, I'm sleepy. But my broken sleep doesn't seem to affect my "general health" for I'm getting fat. I'll write more letters when I'm less stupid for sleep.

December 5, 1926

The Eskimo's greatest delicacy is "Eskimo ice cream," made from reindeer suet and seal oil worked together until it is the consistency of ice cream. Into this is mixed flakes of boiled fish (usually tom cod) and sometimes cranberries and salmon berries. It looks delicious but I have been very reluctant to taste it. The smell of the seal oil is enough warning.

Tonight I have the three boys who bring in my wood and water making ice cream for me. They are pretending that the freezer is the tractor and they are having a hard time getting the engine started. You would enjoy hearing their chuckles.

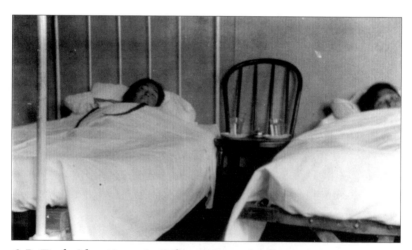

6.5. Typhoid patients in White Mountain dispensary, 1925. Alaska Region, National Archives, P2010, Historical Album, Anchorage, Alaska.

I make ice cream about every third day for my typhoid patient, for whom I have been caring these last three weeks. At last he is beginning to show slight improvement, and I have hopes now of pulling him through. He had been sick at home in Golovin for two weeks but had not gone to bed until he fell to the ground from sheer exhaustion.

Then his father brought him twenty-five miles over a very rough trail. Since then I've been busy day and night. Shall be more than glad when he gets to the point where he is not delirious at night.

However, the work doesn't seem to hurt me any. I weigh 143 pounds instead of 130 as I did most of the time in Port Angeles. My appetite is amazing and I sleep like a trooper (when I get a chance).

Yesterday I had a patient from Council, twenty-five miles northwest. Since he had acute appendicitis the only thing I could do was to apply ice packs and give him morphia and send him on to Nome, two days' trip by dog team. I had been doctoring him by phone for the last ten days, but since he showed no improvement, he decided to risk the trip to Nome. More and more I feel the responsibility of the job here and wish I were an MD. If I can manage to save enough while here I think I shall go back to the University of Cincinnati for my doctor's degree when my two years are finished here. That would mean four more years of school and one of internship before I could even start to practice, and thirty-five is rather late to begin to build up a practice. However, I'm thinking very strongly. Then I should like to go back to Clallam County and establish myself there. Wild dreams? Maybe, but at least I enjoy dreaming.

December 13, 1926

Please pardon all this scribble with pencil, but I've lost my fountain pen (as usual) and I can't use a bottle of ink while

I sit on the edge of a bed. I have acquired another typhoid patient—dear little cuddly girl of three. She demands a great deal of attention and if I am not here beside her, she comes to find me. My boy is improving nicely, has passed the worst of the illness, and as his temperature goes back his appetite comes up. It does my heart good to see him eat. But he is still delirious at night and is so weak he can hardly turn over in bed alone. So between the two of them and my regular village patients I am kept out of mischief.

We had a little measles scare but I guess it is past now. At least the allotted incubation time is over. The evening before Thanksgiving everyone in the village, except my typhoid patient and myself, went to the school program and that night, late, I had a call to see a small boy who had broken out with measles at the program. However, nobody else had contracted it, so here's hoping. The people have been fine about observing the quarantine.

Only two weeks until Christmas. I can hardly realize it, for days speed so very quickly here. Our weather has been clear and crisp, ranging from sixteen degrees below to plus ten. We are indeed fortunate here in our little pocket in the hills, because we are well sheltered from the storms. Nome and Golovin and Council—in fact, most of Seward Peninsula have been in the throes of blizzards while we have had merely cloudy weather with a little snow and very little wind. Tonight the snow is falling in great soft, lazy flakes that heap the ground with a lovely glistening blanket and put Christmas decorations on all the trees.

The big box from home arrived on the last boat and was brought up some three weeks later when the first dog teams could come up, about the middle of November. I opened the box and took out the magazines and some of the toothpaste but the other things have all been carefully left in the box until December 25.

Mrs. Neeley has been more anxious to open it than I. She has been staying from 8:30 to midnight so that I can get that much uninterrupted sleep, and today she did my usual washing of seven sheets and bed gowns, etc. That must be done every day. Often I think of when Clark had typhoid, and more and more I marvel that Mama managed things so none of the rest of us got it. We were all so crowded in that Billings house and there was so much for one person to do. I was too small to appreciate it all then, but I certainly appreciate and admire more and more, now.

My boy has been fed again for the "dozenth" time today, and now he and little Ida Isabella Austin have dropped off to sleep. Guess I'll follow their example while I have a chance— no telling how long it will last.

December 26, 1926

Edward Gregor, my half-breed typhoid patient, still spends most of his time in bed and needs much attention. Little Ida Isabella made a good recovery and went home to her mother the day before Christmas, although she will have to remain in bed at least another week before she is strong enough to be allowed up. Poor Edward hung at death's door for a week before it was decided that he return to his trouble on Earth.

Christmas Eve I took him down to the school program. Four of the dormitory boys put him in my sleeping bag on a sled and pulled it down to the big gymnasium. I wish you could have seen his face as he listened and watched and finally got two Christmas presents and the usual treat. It was well worth all the work I'd put in trying to get him well.

Little Ida with her soft black curls (like the ones on Sister's doll, Lois) her immense black eyes with their fringe of long, long lashes, and the roses in her cheeks was indeed a picture. Also, she was soft and cuddly and liked to be mothered. She called me Mama and as she grew better chattered away to me

in Eskimo which Edward sometimes interpreted. For about
four weeks, I was busy night and day with them. Last night
was the first time in six weeks that I did not get up during
the whole night. The minimum before has been three times
and the maximum was about every fifteen minutes. And you
know my failing for sleep.

Twice Mrs. McCallister and twice Mrs. Neeley came and
stayed until midnight, so that gave me a real chance to catch
up a little. Anyway, I'm gaining—145 pounds, so I guess you
won't have to worry about my ill health.

All Christmas day was filled with one procession of patients and visitors. The village had a big celebration down at
the gym. Early in the fall "city taxes" had been imposed by
the village council to pay for the big treat. A poll tax of one
dollar for each able-bodied man between twenty-one and
fifty and a small property tax on dwelling and gas boats had
supplied funds for a banquet of reindeer meat, boiled, frozen
and fried fish, frozen salmon berries and huckleberries, and
Eskimo sweet potatoes and ice cream, as well as white man's
food. The sweet potatoes are roots of a shrub that grows in
the swampy deltas of the Fish River. The largest ones are not
any larger than your little finger but they are sweet and good,
either raw or cooked.

My gifts to the people here were books purchased in
Nome. I fully expect to enjoy them myself when the owners
have finished with them.

My birthday was busy with the usual routine of patients
in the morning. In the afternoon three small girls came over
from the dormitory to deliver an envelope in which were two
birthday cards from the older girls. After they had delivered
the envelope they sat on the floor and made me sinew thread
and played jacks until the supper bell rang. In the evening I
went down to help Mr. McCallister make out the requisition
for next year's supply of drugs. Monday I cleaned, Tuesday

washed, and today I am drying bedspreads and sheets in my kitchen.

Last night Mr. Hansen came in by dog team to get some treatment for rheumatism. He has a cabin here and has a Native boy to bring wood and water and I go down twice a day to give him a rub. Fortunately, everyone in the village is well and Edward will be going home the last of the week. I shall have time to dispose of the many things I had planned before Christmas.

9 P.M.—Supper was just over when I was met by a small girl with the following note: "Miss Fergus: Miss Sam Alexine is going to have child birth hurry up. At blind man's house."

I have just come from the blind man's house where Grace gave birth to a nine-pound girl. Now all is quiet and peaceful and Edna Absukpum with infant Gregory is there to stay all night with Grace. And I'm home for a good night's sleep.

December 29, 1926

Tomorrow I must take inventory to go in with the requisition. Mr. McCallister and I have been talking of the possibilities of a hospital here. It is really badly needed. With this many villagers (250 now, and more coming) and all the children the government sends here, the responsibility is altogether too much for one nurse. Most fortunately, our measles did not spread and we have had no serious accidents or epidemics. But a hospital is badly needed. I have had to send two appendix cases over the three-day trail to Nome—much of it rough, hard sledding. And now I am sending a man with compound fracture of the ribs. Such things should be cared for right here. And you may be sure that I'd have been thankful for some medical advice with my typhoid cases. Mr. McCallister thinks with our sawmill and home labor he could build a suitable building for $5,000 and use my present quarters for living quarters for a doctor and nurses. Anyway, I am hoping for it strong.

January 17, 1927

Now we get no news via radio except that which is printed in the *Nugget*.[20] There is no radio here and little incentive to have one since there is great difficulty in receiving regularly. I heard a Nome man remark the other day, "There are two things in Alaska to teach a man to swear—a dog team and a radio. You never know how either is going to act." He had just bought a fine set and for the first five or six weeks programs came in splendidly: Los Angeles, San Francisco, Australia, Japan, and Vancouver. And he about decided that the people who complained simply didn't know how to operate one. Then suddenly the programs stopped, and for six weeks he had not been able to get one single thing. Another disadvantage up here is the difference in time. Stations on the Pacific Coast begin broadcasting at 3:00 or 4:00 P.M. our time, and "sign off" at 9 P.M. or earlier. Those in Australia and Japan do not begin until after midnight, so we are out of luck, rather. The Nome paper comes regularly once a week but seldom has much news in it to interest us, since we know little of local interest around Nome.

So far as I can learn Fairbanks is the up and coming town of Alaska. All others are retrogressing. Of course, the work with the bureau does give an opportunity to save money because there is no opportunity to spend. Personally, I would like to get another station in some other section of the country. I would like to see the people, customs, etc. of the Arctic, but I'm lonely for the mountains. So I have to decide whether it will be the Arctic or Aleutians next year. Our applications for transfer should be in the Seattle office by April 15. Not much time left in which to decide.

Last Thursday, January 6, I had a telephone call late in the evening asking me if I would go to Elim, twenty-six miles east of Golovin, to see the missionary who was sick there. Naturally, I agreed to go and the Native who had brought the message as far as Golovin said that he would come for me early in the morning. I worked most of the night getting my curtains (which were soaking) washed and dried, my house put in order, and my bag packed. But during the night a warm wind swept in from the southeast, changing the snow to rain and melting the ice so that by morning, travel in any direction was absolutely impossible. Golovin Bay was covered with overflow from the streams. The snow was too deep and soft and wet to allow teams to go around the bay, over the hills. So I waited until Sunday morning when we had enough of a freeze to form a slight crust on the snow.

Julius, the Eskimo, arrived about noon and while he was feeding himself and his dogs I dressed—put on long underwear, corduroy knickers, red flannel shirt, heavy sweater, double squirrel parkie lined with squirrel and covered with an outside parkie of drill, reindeer boots that came above my knees, and dogskin mittens over my green knitted ones. Then I climbed into my nice down sleeping bag and was wrapped up in a dogskin robe and lashed to the sled. A slight wind was blowing, but I was warm as could be, although my eyelashes froze to the wolf ruff on my parkie. How I wish I could describe to you all of the fun and beauty of that trip.

Just as we drove up to the dog barn of the roadhouse, another team came in from the opposite direction and we had one grand fight. (I was still lashed to the sled.) But the drivers and Mr. Dexter came to the rescue and before long peace and order were established.

The driver of the other team proved to be Mr. Rydeen, manager for Lomen Reindeer Company and newly elected superintendent of the territorial schools. He was just returning to Nome from a round-trip visit to all the reindeer camps on the Seward Peninsula. We spent a very pleasant evening together visiting Mr. Pfaffle, the storekeeper. I had met Mrs. Rydeen while in Nome.

Early Monday morning my driver packed me in the sled
and we started out across the ice of the windswept outer
bay—six miles of ice marked by a straight row of trees set in
the ice every fifty feet—then up McKinley Creek and up-up-
up-up over McKinley Hill—the trail now marked every thirty
feet, the stakes making me think of a fence through the hills
from Geyser to the Merrimack Ranch. Straight across the hills
to lead up over the barren tops and down through tiny willow thickets in little ravines, then up over more hills. Far to
the north we could see great herds of reindeer moving slowly
along. The snow was deep and drifted so that we could not
see the tracks made by Mr. Rydeen the night before. A slight
crust had formed but broke through at every step, cutting
the dogs' feet and making travel doubly difficult. Seventeen
miles from Golovin we came to a great divide and looked out
upon a blue and gold world. The sun had already dropped
below the horizon but the afterglow lit up like tiny gold vol-
canoes the hundreds of conical peaks to the west, north, and
east of us, while far to the south the blue water of Norton
Sound gleamed around the edges of great gold and white ice
cakes. Immediately before us was Walla Walla Mountain, a
great white cone with a lovely forest reaching from the shore
halfway up its steep sides.

We rapidly dropped down the eastern side of the divide,
down through the timber, and finally out to the shore where
we found the Walla Walla Shelter Cabin, a stout log building
about twelve by twenty with built-in bunks filled with grass;
a small cook stove made from a gasoline tank; a rude table
with white enamel cups turned over upon it; a stack of dry
wood in one corner, an axe and saw hanging on the wall, and
a sign: "Please help keep this cabin clean. Always leave wood
and shavings." We stopped long enough to get a drink for
ourselves and dogs from the little creek running by the rear
of the cabin. I inquisitively inspected the fish cache and dog
barn and then climbed back into my sleeping bag.

The trail now led out across the ice along the shore—probably one hundred yards or more from the beach. The snow was soft since no wind had packed it, and the dogs were very weary. I napped a little and watched the coast and thought how much it resembles the coast from Neah Bay to Clallam Bay (if that could be frozen and snow covered). Once more the stars and moon lighted us on our journey. Finally, after almost nine hours of steady travel, we rounded a headland and saw the lights of Elim on the cliffs above us.

Like White Mountain, Elim is built on a high bank in the timber. We drove right up to a big log house with a hip roof and were welcomed by two big boys who came out to hold the dogs and help unpack me. Mrs. Ost,[21] the missionary's wife, came to the door with a light, and soon I was inside a big homey kitchen and surrounded by wide eyed, pink cheeked, tow-headed children. Mr. Ost himself lay in the big bedroom adjoining the kitchen, and as soon as I had removed a few layers of my clothing I went in to see him. He is enormous, big of head and chest and hand and heart. He is noted in all this country for his hardihood on the trail and his capacity for work. But this had proved too much for him, and his heart had demanded a rest. However, he was still running the village from his bed. That evening various of the Natives came in to sit beside him and ask his advice. He and Mrs. Ost came to this country as bride and groom seventeen years ago and with the exception of one year of furlough, have been here ever since. They first had charge of a mission orphanage that was established on Golovin Bay for the children, most homeless following a terrible measles epidemic. As these children grew old enough to take care of themselves and have homes of their own the need for the mission came to an end, and Mr. Ost took up the itinerant work in this part of the country. But as well as preaching, baptizing, and burying, he has built homes and shelter cabins and staked trails. He has many friends and many enemies, because through it all he has remained "a pig-headed Swede" with a strong temper. But he has certainly done much for the people up here.

His eight children are a capable, independent, and shy family—very fond of each other and anxious to help. John, the oldest, speaks Eskimo like a Native. He is almost as large as his father and is an excellent woodsman and dog musher. When scarcely twelve years old, he made the trip to Golovin and back alone, driving his own dog team and returning with five hundred pounds of freight.

About my first job there was to take three stitches in a nasty cut in Joe's (the third boy) big toe. He had attempted to cut ice with an axe and had hit right through the ice and into his toe. He was a brave youngster, scarcely making a murmur for fear it would disturb his father.

The next day I visited the bureau school and met the Nylins. Big, deaf, white-haired Swede father, tiny nervous, ex-opera singer English mother and six-year-old nervous, spoiled, precocious Junior. My visit with them was cut short by the arrival of several patients to see Mrs. Nylin. She had had two year's training as a nurse during the war and has worked under Dr. Don Nickolson, the fine nerve specialist in Seattle. I met him at the Orthopedic.[22] But the following day I talked on hygiene to the school and later spent the afternoon and evening with the Nylins. They are very interesting and enjoyable hosts, have taught five years in the Arctic before coming to Elim, and have a most interesting collection of Eskimo implements and carved ivory. I quite enjoyed them.

Mrs. Ost, although terribly crippled with rheumatism, manages to help the villagers, care for her family of ten, teach her children regular school work four hours a day, and keep all travelers passing through Elim, since there is no road-house. I helped her make a down quilt for her ten-month old baby, Denny. With his pink skin and white downy hair and dear smile he reminded me of little Sam as we saw him last Christmas.

As the storm of Tuesday and Thursday cleared away I decided to start home. Friday morning John was my driver, and with nine dogs in our team we started out, following the two mail teams. We were fortunate indeed to have the trail broken for us, for six inches of snow had fallen the night before so that now the snow was at least three feet deep and in many places drifted much deeper.

All the way along John told me the legends the old Natives had told him about the fishing and hunting, mountains and streams. We caught up with the mail teams at the shelter cabin and waited there for them to lead out. Ahead, one of the drivers broke trail on snowshoes so that it would not be so hard for the dogs. As the sun came out of the fog about noon I attempted to get some pictures—should they prove good I'll send you some in the next "number."

The most thrilling part of the return journey was our slide down McKinley Hill. Imagine, if you can, three dog teams—the first fifteen dogs, the second twelve, and the last nine—racing frantically down a steep grade almost a mile long. Even with brakes set hard in the snow and ice, the heavily loaded sleds almost crashed into the dogs dashing down the hill. Many times I expected to hit one of the stakes that marks the trail or a log half buried in the snow. But each time John dexterously swerved to one side and we sped on down and down. It was real sport.

Late Monday, January 17. To continue my account of the Elim trip. From McKinley Hill on we took the lead since our dogs were freshest. The moon came up just as we reached the bay, so we had six good miles over the crusted snow and ice by moonlight. At the roadhouse we found Mr. Jackson (the banker I had met in Nome) and a friend of his who were on their way to Nenana to get the railroad for Seward and boat from there to Seattle. Since they had encountered heavy trails and had a big load with only twelve dogs, they decided to lay over a day in Chinik before attempting to climb over the hills to Elim.

Saturday morning we watched the mail teams start out for Nome and Elim and bade good-bye to big Irish Tom Gaffrey, representative from Seward Peninsula to the legislature. He was making the long trip with only six dogs so he was not delaying any more than absolutely necessary.

The trip home, this time right across the upper Golovin Bay, directly towards White Mountain, was an easy and delightful one. The dogs were eager to go, the weather clear and warm, the ice covered with just enough snow to make the sled slip along easily and to show fox, rabbit, and ptarmigan tracks. We scared up a flock of about thirty ptarmigan in a thicket of willows at this end of the bay and met three dog teams on the way. But the rabbits and foxes were not in evidence, merely their tracks.

Today I visited all through the village and was greeted with hearty hand shakes and "Qui Anna—qui anna! You come back. We think maybe you stay Elim. Qui Anna!" At one home I was given an old stone axe and an arrowhead found in a washed-out grave on the beach. The handle of the axe is gone but the grooves where the thongs held it in place are quite plain.

At another home I was admiring a beautiful white skin— down an inch deep and thick and soft. Maggie told me it was a swan skin with the long feathers plucked out, and then added "I give him you" and put the skin in my lap.

Now it is ten minutes of twelve and my alarm is set for 6 A.M. There are just dozens more things to tell you all, but I must go to bed. Just before the lights blinked out at 9:30, Mr. McCallister called me down to his house to answer a phone call from Chinik. As a result I am going down early in the morning to see an old Laplander who had a paralytic stroke. So I guess I'd better pack my bag and get forty winks before I start.

You asked how long we were without a cook—about six weeks. No, there was no bread mixer, but Mrs. Neeley, and Mrs. Mac, and I mixed fifty pounds of flour with the other ingredients in a wash tub and kneaded down on the pine-covered table, working to the tune of "He shall die— die— die" or some other equally tragic tune. Our dining room girls wear white caps and aprons that they made in sewing class, and they have great fun teasing the cook about his ruffled cap.

My "fern" died before Christmas. Too little sunlight to make it thrive. I also tried a carrot hanging basket, but that, too, gave up the ghost. The seeds I sent you I gathered long after all flowers had ceased to bloom and no one here knew what they were, so we will have to wait for blooming time again before we know.

January 20, 1927

Just there I was interrupted by the arrival of a dog team from Council bringing a man with far advanced TB Poor chap, he thought he could come down to see me for a few days and go home cured. Would that I had such healing! But he is so far advanced that I fear care even in the best sanitarium would do him no good.

March 1, 1927

Guess my yarn had better begin with January 27 since that day was the McCallister's wedding anniversary. We planned on a little party in their honor down at the Burlingame's home (they have the biggest house).

Mrs. Neeley and I were to make the ice cream and sandwiches, fresh assorted cookies had been brought from Golovin, and Mr. Griggs was to supervise the making of the coffee. I hustled through my morning work, made my visits to the village before noon, and had just started making the ice cream after lunch when a knock came at my dispensary door. It proved to be a boy who had cut his hand eight days before while butchering reindeer at the Lomen plant below Golovin. Now the hand and arm were swollen almost beyond recognition. Needless to say the ice cream had to wait while I lanced and dressed the hand and put it in a continuous bath of bichloride.

In the meantime, Mrs. Neeley had come over and had finished freezing the ice cream and started to make sandwiches. She stopped long enough to help me open my hospital room which I had in a state of fumigation following its occupancy by an advanced TB case. We scrubbed and dusted and made the bed and were just returning to the kitchen when one of the dormitory boys came running in with the news that Jackson had broken his leg.

Jackson is a Native from Kotzebue, a hunchback who is also crippled from infantile paralysis. He had been out to the Seattle Children's Orthopedic hospital for a year and is greatly improved, but he still limps. He had been sliding down hill and another boy jumped on the sled and broke Jackson's right leg—his weak one—just above the knee. Fortunately for me there was already made an iron splint for some previous victim, so in about an hour Mr. Burlingame and I had the splint in place and were just getting the boy into bed and fastening the splint to a frame when two small girls arrived with a note. "My sister need you now quick. Clara." I knew what that meant so, grabbing my obstetrical outfit, I left Mrs. Neeley and Mr. Burlingame to finish Jackson and I ran to the farthest house in the village.

The children were hurried to the nearest neighbor and fourteen-year-old Clara poked up the fire and put on water to heat and then informed me that the husband had started to Nome the day before, expressly against my pleadings and arguments to the contrary.

A lovely 9 ½ pound girl arrived in due time and I had a very anxious hour following waiting for the placenta to come in small pieces and trying to check a hemorrhage. It was now 9 P.M. and old Comayak came in with her blind husband on their way home from church. She agreed to stay with the mother during the night but must first lead her husband home. When she returned I had the mother and baby quietly settled and apparently all right, so I dashed home to find both of my boys asleep and Mrs. Neeley on guard. I washed up and put on a clean uniform to go down to the party! For the first time in months we had the lights burning until almost midnight. Then there was one more excursion over the ice to see the new baby and home to bed.

Just yesterday morning I took the last drain out of Roy's hand and sent him home to Elim. Jackson is still in bed and will be for at least three weeks more, since his right arm is not strong enough to allow him to rise on crutches. I now have another patient, typhoid, whom I had to put into my own bed since she naturally could not be put into the same room with Jackson.

Today is his birthday and we are celebrating with the tiny pink candles you sent in the Christmas box, stuck into pink and white cookies. I made pineapple ice cream and, just by chance, one of the village women brought me a big bowl of frozen salmon berries and huckleberries. They are really very good and considered quite a treat by the Natives.

All this last week Mr. Range, the district superintendent, was here on his annual inspection tour. He is just returning from a trip to Seattle and has stopped at many of the bureau schools along the way, all those in this part of his district. The outcome of his visit is that Mr. and Mrs. Neeley have asked for a transfer to Unalakleet, and I for Tanana. The government has turned over old Fort Gibbons there to the Bureau of Education for a government hospital. It has been entirely remodeled and will be used as a general hospital for both the Natives and the whites. It will eventually be converted into a sanitarium for Natives. There is not a single sanitarium in all of Alaska at the present time, and now the Native with TB simply stays at home, spreads the disease among his relatives, and dies. My salary there will be the same as here. The other members of the staff are a Dr. and Mrs. White and another nurse whose name I do not remember. Mrs. White is taking post graduate bacteriology at the University of Washington at the present time. The *Martha Angeline,* the Yukon boat, also draws its staff from this hospital—so I may still have a chance at that. Mr. Range was not at all sure that I would get the appointment since Tanana is outside his district, but he is willing to write to Mr. Wagner recommending it.

If I do not go to Tanana I am asking for Unalakleet. That will give me the same kind of work as here, but I will be much more in contact with other people. Unalakleet is the division point for all northern mail routes and therefore winter trails. All mail comes down the Yukon and over the portage to Unalakleet and from there is distributed through the various routes to Nome, Kotzebue, Point Barrow, and all intermediate points. It is located on the Bering Sea, at the mouth of the Unalakleet River, about forty-one miles north of St. Michaels. Besides the teacher, there is a missionary, a trader, and several white men with Native wives. The tiny hospital there was built by popular subscription, and up to this time the nurse has been maintained by the Swedish Lutheran Church.[23] However, this year the bureau took over the hospital since the mission could no longer support it.

I shall enjoy working with the Neeleys, but I am asking for Tanana as first choice as I think it will be good for me to work under a doctor's orders again. Also, I still have a hankering for that hospital boat.

We have been having gorgeous weather. Early in February we had a warm southeast wind like the chinooks in Montana. It sent the thermometer from -40° to 44 above in two days. The snow vanished rapidly and is now covered with a heavy crust. We have had zero weather or about ten below since then but no more snow, just bright cloudless days. It is amazing how the days have lengthened out this month. Instead of four or five hours of daylight we now have eleven or twelve hours, and the sun is really getting more than a few inches above the horizon. I have been tempted to get out my camera again. I want to get pictures of some of the old people of the village and also of the four babies I have introduced into this world. Little Gregory, my first, is quite an adorable, round faced, smiley Eskimo by this time. He has no teeth yet, however.

April 5, 1927

Tonight a strong east wind drives the snow before it and piles drifts around my door. Instead of the merry calls of the boys outside playing ball on the school grounds, I hear the low delirious whimper of my little typhoid-pneumonia patient, the whistle of the wind as it rushes down my chimney, and the throb of the electric motor plant.

Next morning

The signal "lights out" came just at that point, and I hastened to get everything in readiness for the night before I should be left in darkness. Now the long night is over and the storm still blows—it really looks more like a winter day than it has at any time during the past months.

My little patient is not so well this morning and I'm wishing, as I have many times during the winter, that I had a doctor to rely upon. The responsibility is terrible.

Jackson, who has been with me ever since he broke his leg two months ago, will be leaving me soon. His leg is as strong as ever, but his father is worried about him so that plans have been made for a dog team to take him to his home in Kotzebue sometime this month. I shall surely miss the boy, for he has been good company—never complaining of his pain or his long days in bed, and since he is out of bed he has been a real help. I have been trying to teach him bookkeeping.

This month has been a busy one, but uneventful—just the usual round of interruptions and nothing in particular accomplished. The chief topic of conversation now is "how to reduce." Since I weigh 143 pounds and my waist has increased two inches since I came, you may be sure that I am vitally interested. I'm the shortest of the women but weigh four pounds more than Mrs. Burlingame, who tops me by half an inch. We carefully remind each other that "this or that" is "fattening" and calmly go on eating. I am sure that my fault is too little exercise, for I seldom get away from my house except for a hurried trip to the village and the rush to the dormitory for meals. I'm eating no more than I always did but am exercising about one tenth the amount.

The breakfast bell has just rung; guess I'd better eat so I won't get too thin.

April 10, 1927

After ten days of blow from the north, east, and west, the wind has quieted down, leaving great drifts of sparkling snow dry as sand and as difficult to navigate. Mrs. Burlingame, Mrs. Neeley, and I put on our snowshoes this afternoon and, leaving the men to run the affairs of the village, we went over onto the flats about three miles on the trail to Nome. All went well until Mrs. B attempted to walk without the snowshoes and sank into the snow up to her waist. We almost had to dig her out, but we came home warm and glowing from our two hours' out-of-door exercise, and I, for one, feel much better tonight.

My little patient has successfully passed his pneumonia crisis but is still fighting his typhoid symptoms, aggravated by an abscessed tooth and ear! Poor youngster. I don't wonder he sometimes cries just because he doesn't know what else to do. His mother usually comes up and stays with him for an hour or two in the afternoon while I make my rounds in the village.

April 27, 1927

When Mr. Range, the district superintendent, was here some three weeks ago, I gave him my resignation to take place July 1. I'm shipping my trunk out on the *Victoria* and plan to come overland via St. Michaels, Yukon River to Nenana, government railroad to Seward and then to Seattle. Will probably spend two weeks on the coast and then home. All plans "subject to change without notice." Then, when I get home sometime in August, we will talk about the future plans. I've written to Sister to watch for my trunk since it will reach Seattle about a month before I do.

June 17, 1927

Dear Home Folks:

The long wait for mail is almost over! The *Victoria* is reported near Nome so in another eight or ten days the mail should be sorted, sent on to Golovin, re-sorted there, and sent to us. And you have no idea how welcome it will be! The last letters, written March 12, reached here May 1, and since then there has been positively no news. Even our telephone line to Golovin has been down much of the time, and we have had to depend upon "mukluk telegraphy" for every kind of news.

The report that has worried us all has been about the *Carpenter.* She is the first freighter in and brought not only our freight but eleven men and three women passengers. When only about ten miles from Nome she encountered heavy ice and lost two propeller blades, so she had to anchor in the shelter of Sledge Island. There the ice closed in around her and she waited three weeks for an opening in the ice and a tugboat to get her out. The eleven men walked the ten miles across the broken ocean ice to Nome and the following day the wind blew in from the south, taking the great ice pack and the *Carpenter* with it up through the straits. Nothing has been heard from her since, although she has a wireless.

The *Silver Wave,* a little launch owned by Lomen Brothers, and a mail boat from Nome to Kotzebue arrived in Nome two days ago, but her partner, the *Donaldson,* which brings our mail and then goes on to Unalakleet and St. Michaels, has not yet come through the pass.

How you would all enjoy our wildflowers now—they are like those of Mount Rainier, multiplied by millions! I never saw so many miniature fragrant blossoms so closely packed together. One can scarcely walk along the open hillsides without treading on them at every step. I have listed thirty-five different varieties in bloom now within a half-mile radius of my house, and every day brings new kinds. Usually I take some of the girls walking in the evening and invariably we find new beauties. Many are our old friends of Montana and Washington in miniature—seldom more than two inches high with blooms like lilies of the valley; rhododendrons not more than six inches high with half-inch fragrant blossoms, three or four to the cluster; millions of forget-me-nots; purple and white crocus; pink and white heather; pink and white mountain phlox; bluebells; shooting stars; buttercups; elephant trunks; saxifrage; salmonberry blossoms big as a wild rose on bushes three inches tall; blueberry; strawberry; wild roses; violets purple, white, and gold—and many, many others whose names I do not know.

The country is beautiful, beautiful, now—the hills always clothed in purple or blue, the flats a delicate green of fresh willow buds, huckleberry, and new grasses. Even the spruce trees are gay with tiny red buds like infant cones tipped on every twig. Our river had dropped about eight feet since the high water that took out the ice and now runs smoothly and quietly, reflecting the ever-changing colors of sky and cloud and the fringe of stately spruce and fairy willows.

Now I can understand why it is that an Alaskan is not considered a "sourdough" until he has seen the ice go out. No matter how many summers or falls or winters he may have spent here, they do not count unless he has actually seen the ice go out in the spring.

All winter our river, eight hundred feet wide at this point, has stretched east and west like a great white highway. As the warm spring days came on, we watched for the first signs of a break in that great sheet of ice. We even had a pool at a dollar a bet on the day the ice would first move in front of the dorm. The snow on the southern slope melted early and ran in hundreds of little streams down the hillside to the river, so that the overflow on the ice was knee deep in many places before the water below rose enough to break through the sides of the sheet. For several days small pieces were breaking off and floating down the open water at the northern bank of the river, but it was not until the evening of May 28 that the first big crack split right across the river and the whole ice mass slowly started downstream. You should have seen our excitement! We all rushed down to the bank to watch the ice crack and break. But to our great disappointment, it broke ten rods down the river before it stopped. For the next two days it crept slowly in one great sheet down towards the bend at the foot of White Mountain.

At about 7 P.M. on the thirtieth we heard a dull crackling and crashing and almost before we could realize what was happening, huge chunks had broken off the sides of the main mass, and the center sheet started its journey, the current carrying it more and more swiftly until the whole river was one mass of crashing, swirling ice. Once started it moved very rapidly, and in an incredibly short time the river before us was clear of every vestige of ice and looked as calm and serene as on its most placid day last fall.

But the end had not come—we had seen merely the prelude to the great event. The little island above us had formed a partial barrier, and against this the ice had been packing and jamming for several days.

About ten o'clock that same evening (the sun had not yet gone down) someone called that this second jam was moving. There it came—like some gigantic creature pushing out into the smoothly flowing waters of the stream. The ice that had gone before was calm and sluggish in comparison to this. It raged and crashed and fought. Great slabs would rise up out of the pack and come grinding down upon others in front of them! They seemed like things alive, each striving to beat the other on its mad rush to the sea. The whole mass seemed impelled by some mighty force behind it that urged it on to greater and greater frenzy.

The setting sun touched the clouds and distant hills with mauve, lavender, pink, and gold and other pastel shades too delicate for name. The ice below surged, caught, and reflected these tints as a million prisms might. We watched the waters rise two feet in almost as many minutes, flooding the lower shore, carrying away caches, and poles on which fish nets were spread to dry and leaving in their place gigantic cakes of honeycombed ice. Little mice scurried to higher ground. And still the stately ice came sweeping down past us, pounding against the rocky base of White Mountain and surging around the bend of the river out of sight in its eager haste to meet the icebergs of the sea. The majesty and power of it all was awesome, but the beauty of color and form made me reverent. The sun sank lower and lower; the hills looked as though a veil of pale blue and lavender chiffon had been draped over them; the ice, gleaming in a myriad of iridescent lights, still sped onward. At last, a little before midnight, just after the sun had sunk below the northern hills, the ice cakes became smaller; great stretches of open water appeared between them; the water began to recede almost as quickly as it had risen. Soon all but a few ice blocks had passed from sight around the mountain. The calm expanse of the stream reflected the fading glory of the sky, the dark green of the spruce along its banks, and the white and gold of an occasional lone ice cake moving like some stately swan. Once more the great Epic of the Ice had been acted and now Alaska waits for summer.

Today for the first time we have been troubled with mosquitoes. I went down to the river about 6 P.M. to wash some films I had been developing, but my visit was heralded by a singing horde of winged elephants. Tonight a breeze has sprung up so I sit on my front steps while writing to you and have not acquired any more bites. Enough? Well, I guess!

Heavy clouds rolling in from the east give promise of rain. That will make our garden grow—lettuce, turnips, onions, radishes, marigolds, pansies, California poppies, shirley poppies, peas (started indoors), cosmos, and nasturtiums. You should see them grow in twenty-four hours of sunlight.

I'm yawning widely although the sun is still well above the horizon, and my watch tells me it is 9:30 P.M. Good night and sweet dreams.

Gertrude.

Endnotes

1. Newsome and Betty Baker, interview by Elfrida Nord, 11 January 1999, Clallam Bay, WA.

2. News items, Seward Peninsula District, U.S. Bureau of Education, 16 May 1927, Nome, Alaska.

3. *Great Falls Tribune* (Great Falls, MT) 10 July 1927, "Great Falls Young Woman Caring for Eskimos as Health Nurse, Writes of Her Experiences," 1.

4. Memorandum for the Secretary, Department of the Interior, Bureau of Education, Appointment Form, 29 August 1927, RG 75, Box 195, Appointments, Nurses. National Archives, Washington, D.C.

5. Memorandum for the Secretary, Department of the Interior, Bureau of Education, Appointment Form, 17 May 1928, RG 75, Box 195, Appointments, Nurses. National Archives, Washington, D.C.

6. G. Scott, Order No. 1648, Office of the Secretary, Department of the Interior, Acceptance of Resignation, 6 October 1928; RG 75, Box 195, Appointments, Nurses. National Archives, Washington, D.C.

7. *Jersey County News* (Jerseyville, IL), 20 December 1928.

8. *Port Angeles Evening News* (Port Angeles, WA), 18 September 1966, "Clallam Bay's Country Doctor Saga," 8.

9. Ibid.

10. Gertrude Fergus Baker, Letters to her family (1926–1927) from White Mountain, Alaska. Alaska Nurses Association Collection, Series 14-1, Box 35, Files 561–562, Archives, Elmer E. Rasmuson Library, University of Alaska Fairbanks. Gertrude Fergus Baker submitted these letters in 1956 at the request of the AaNA committee.

11. Robert Fortuine, *Chills and Fever: Health and Disease in Early History of Alaska* (Fairbanks: University of Alaska Press, 1989), 156–157, 177.

12. Dr. Schwartz had been a doctor at the Department of Interior Native hospital in Noorvik.

13. The Lomen family was a prominent Nome family during the first half of the 1900s who were involved in a variety of businesses: reindeer herding and harvest, storekeeping, and photography. The elder Lomen was an attorney and judge (Carl Lomen, *Fifty Years in Alaska* [New York: David McKay, 1954], 60–72).

14. The *Boxer* was a Bureau of Indian Affairs Department of Education service ship.

15. Vilhjalmur Stefánsson, *The Adventure of Wrangell Island* (New York: MacMillan, 1925). The survivor was Ada Blackjack, Eskimo seamstress and cook.

16. This is Lula Welch, the nurse contributor of Chapter Three.

17. The variety of dialects in the area served by Fergus is verified by Steve Langdon in *The Native Peoples of Alaska* (Anchorage: Greatland Graphics, 1989).

18. Indian Head: a firmly woven cotton fabric with a texture similar to linen.

19. Care in typhoid fever was a challenge that demanded skilled nursing. Fergus was adequately skilled to meet this need. Her care of Edward documents the twenty-four-hour vigilance of a hallucinating person, the care of infectious linens and excreta, and special feedings (such as ice cream) for a period of several weeks. See Bertha Harmer, *Textbook of the Principles and Practice of Nursing* (New York: MacMillan, 1923), 488–497.

20. This is a reference to the *Nome Nugget,* a weekly newspaper.

21. The Osts were missionaries for the Swedish Mission Covenant denomination, a group that had its origins in the Swedish Lutheran Church. Ruth Ost is included in H.W. Jones, *First Ladies of Alaska* (Escondido, CA: Americana Printing, 1967), 142–145.

22. Orthopedic: This is a reference to Children's Orthopedic Hospital in Seattle, Washington.

23. The Unalakleet hospital had been maintained by the Swedish Mission Covenant Church, now the Evangelical Covenant Church.

7

That Takes a Lot of Guts:
Mildred Huffman Keaton

U. S. Government Field Nurse
Southeast Alaska, 1923–1932; Yukon River, 1932

MILDRED HUFFMAN KEATON WORKED in Alaska longer than any other nurse in this collection. She was born March 20, 1898, to John Preston and Ella Jane (Huffman) Keaton in Carter County, Kentucky. In 1909 the family moved to Snohomish, Washington, where Mildred attended grammar and high school. She started her health career as a nurse's aide for Three Lakes Lumber Company (Washington); then after considering medicine or music, she entered nurse's training at St. Peter's Sisters of Charity of the House of Providence Hospital, Olympia, Washington. After graduation she became a surgical assistant at Snohomish Hospital and private duty nurse at Providence Hospital, Everett, Washington, in 1922.[1]

In 1923, Keaton moved to Kake, Alaska, as a village nurse for the Department of Interior, Bureau of Education. In 1927, she became territorial school nurse for Juneau, Douglas, and Thane, until 1928. She served as surgery nurse at St. Ann's Hospital, Juneau, and supervised the Juneau American Legion Baby Clinic, then again as surgery nurse for the Alaska Native Service Hospital, Juneau, from 1929–1932. During the summer of 1932, she served as the nurse aboard the *Martha Angeline*. After that she became a field nurse for the Alaska Area Native Service, covering Kotzebue Bay and the Seward Peninsula by dog team in winter and Coast Guard cutter in the summer from 1932 to 1936.[2]

While in the villages as traveling nurse, she was expected to administer all manner of medical attention within her ability: hold clinics for mothers and their babies, deliver babies, advise the village midwives in modern practices, examine school children, treat minor ailments, render first aid to accident victims, arrange for necessary hospitalization of patients, carry on immunization programs, and help and advise the village teachers on medical matters. The villagers looked forward to the arrival of the nurse and were most cooperative and appreciative of her services.[3] She was bold and skilled and not one to rely on protocol when a patient's life was at stake.

In 1937, Mildred Keaton was featured in an article in *Collier's* magazine entitled "Angel in Furs."[4] She was described as a tomboy, yet feminine in voice, manner, and sympathies, with the extraordinary gentleness and sureness of a born healer. "She is of Irish lineage and is pugnacious with a

7.1. Mildred Keaton. Courtesy of Mildred K. Ruthruff, Snohomish, Washington.

great mop of wild black hair. She is a real Southern lady with a love of strong tobacco and she drinks her bourbon neat."[5] Often in remote places she was judge, interpreter, marshal, and commissioner as well as nurse.[6]

Keaton became temporary superintendent of Old Presbyterian Hospital in Barrow while a doctor and nurses were being recruited. She then became field nurse for Pt. Lay and Wainwright, making yearly eighteen-hundred-mile dog team trips from Pt. Barrow to Demarcation Point, contacting nomadic Eskimos and collecting vital statistics from 1936–1941.[7] It was reported that she was "probably the only person who knows every Native along the Arctic coast by name."[8] In December 1941, she became emergency superintendent of Barrow Hospital due to lack of medical staff and taught home nursing and emergency first-aid courses there until August 1942. She participated in the evacuation of the Native population in the Aleutian Islands at the outset of World War II and then became field nurse for St. Lawrence Island, 1942–1943, followed by Nome, 1943–1946.

She served as a nurse aboard the M.S. *North Star* [see Figures 7.2 and 7.3] from Pt. Barrow to Seattle during the summers of 1945–1946.[9] This service consisted of the doctor on board and Keaton going ashore to hold makeshift clinics and provide health care as time and facilities permitted while the North Star delivered supplies to the village. Going ashore meant descending a ladder from the main ship at anchor and jumping into an open boat to be ferried ashore, because there were no wharves or docks. This could be a daring feat in rough seas and inclement weather.[10]

Mildred Keaton retired from government service in 1949 and moved back to Washington state for family reasons. In Washington she worked with intense dedication during the polio epidemic years for the Visiting Nurse Service of Puget Sound. In 1951, Keaton returned to Alaska as ship's nurse on

7.3 Mildred Keaton with ship's officers. Courtesy of Mildred K. Ruthruff, Snohomish, Washington.

7.2 Clinic patients at the North Star. *In this photo patients from Savoonga are being brought to the ship in umiaks for treatment or X-rays. They will return riding with cargo destined for the village. Alaska Nurses Association Collection (Clara Gaddie #75-167-440). Reprinted with permission of Alaska and Polar Region Archives, Elmer E. Rasmuson Library, University of Alaska Fairbanks.*

the Coast Guard Cutter *North Wind,* followed by a two-year assignment to Nome as welfare agent assigned to the lower Kuskokwim and Yukon Rivers. Then she was in charge of the White Pass and Yukon Railroad Hospital in Skagway for two years. For the next nine years, she was a volunteer school nurse for the Copper River School at Glennallen.[11]

A member of a large family from Snohomish in western Washington, she returned to them from time to time, and in 1972 to retire. She died in Snohomish May 15, 1980, at age eighty-two.[12]

Her recollections in this chapter are extracted from an autobiography, untitled and never finished, deposited in the Nursing Archives at the Elmer E. Rasmuson Library, University of Alaska Fairbanks.[13] The selected excerpts portray some of her early experiences.

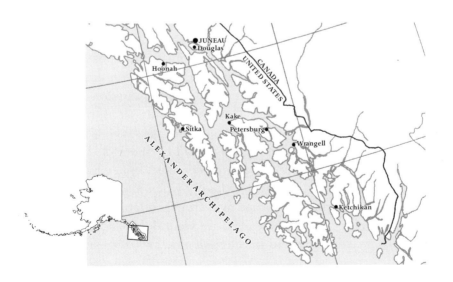

Excerpt from Mildred Keaton's Autobiography

It all began in the fall of 1922 when another nurse and I were working at the old Providence Hospital in Everett, Washington, she in maternity and I in surgery and emergency. We were working the night duty, and in those days a duty was a full twelve hours of 7 P.M. to 7 A.M. I had graduated from St. Peters School of Nursing in Olympia, Washington, in June of that year.

Along in the first week of November we scanned the morning paper as usual, looking for positions for nurses anywhere but where we were, and chanced to see where Civil Service examinations for nurses were to be held at the local post office on a certain date. The announcements were for positions on islands and possessions. After much discussion we decided to go down and take the exams. Islands, to us, meant those off the coast of Washington state, and possessions could be most anything. Neither of us had been out of the state of Washington except I having been born in Kentucky and come to Washington with my family when just a child, and my companion having come over from Scotland with her parents when yet a babe. However, we went down and took the Civil Service exams and in the rush of heavy duty and sleeping days, we soon forgot all about having taken them and began scanning nursing positions again.

About ten days after taking the exams I received notice, or rather a directive, which I later learned meant "get on the ball," to report to the director of insular affairs in the L. S. Smith building in Seattle for assignment. A few days later my nurse friend received much the same notice. We had said nothing to our parents about having taken the exams and certainly had no idea of going very far afield even with all our big talk, so did nothing about it; we sort of covered up our heads, hoping it would all go away. A few days later we both received quite terse letters, meaning "do it now." We took the old electric interurban car and jolted our way down to Seattle, all of thirty miles, to the office of Superintendent Lopp who, in the process of explaining things to us, advised that one position was for Alaska and would have to be filled as soon as possible, and the other was for Hawaii but not so urgent. Then he asked us which of us would take the Alaska assignment and which Hawaii. We, being in a state almost bordering on shock, were unable to decide, so finally, no doubt weary of our indecision, he took from his desk a couple of matches, broke one, and told us to draw. We did, and I got the long match which he said was for Alaska. We were a quiet, thoughtful pair as we shook and swayed our way home on the old interurban. Now the die was cast and we had no alternative—our parents must be told. As we passed Tony's newsstand back to the hospital, with a smugness we did not truly feel, we told him where we were going. "Well," he said, "I don't know nothing about Hawaii, but Alaska now, that takes a lot of guts." And that, I was later to learn, was the understatement of the year.

Mail came thick and fast for the next two weeks, and all too soon my ticket to Petersburg, Alaska, the nearest steamship dock to my station of Kake on Keku Island.

On December 15, 1922, my dad and I, with my trunk—
and I may add that was the last time I ever lugged a trunk
to Alaska—boarded the Great Northern local train from
Snohomish to Seattle and took a taxi to the Alaska S.S. dock
on pier 54 where I boarded the S S. *Jefferson*, commanded by
Captain Glascock. My dad, who had always had itchy feet,
was a good prop for me during the last few minutes before
going aboard. Going through my mind was the fact that it
was just ten days until Christmas, always a festive time in our
big family, and I wondered where I would be on that day. It
was fortunate that I did not at that time know.

The next day, our second out of Seattle, the stewardess
came and asked me to see an old timer, since she was concerned about him. Seems he had come aboard in Seattle well
inebriated and had immediately gone to bed. The cabin boys
thought he would just sleep it off as they had seen many
others do. However, finally when they were unable to arouse
him, they became alarmed and reported him to the steward
who conferred with the captain, and since the stewardess
was not a nurse and there was no doctor aboard, they sent for
me. One look was sufficient to see he was either developing
pneumonia or already had it. The captain immediately got in
contact by wireless with Alaska Steamship's doctor in Seattle,
and I talked with him, giving him all objective symptoms,
and he directed me in the man's care. The cabin boys almost
drowned me with coffee and goodies, probably to be sure I
would stay awake that night since the captain had asked me
to special [care for] him until we reached Ketchikan where he
could be taken to a hospital. I later learned that he had recovered and was able to take ship on the next northbound steamer two weeks later. The Alaska Steamship Company sent me a
check for twenty-five dollars and a letter of appreciation.

Petersburg is a small town whose population is predomi-
nately Scandinavian, and more kindly people I had never

met. The few days I was there I made many very fine friends
and was invited for coffee in many homes. Coffee there is second only to afternoon tea in England. However, due to heavy
snowfall the streets were something to navigate. There were
narrow paths along where the sidewalks should be, with high
banks of snow on either side. On advice from several people I
purchased lined, knee-length rubber boots and a long, lined
mackinaw.

On December 23, Captain Hemnes of the mail boat *Trigve*
came and told me that winds were moderating and to be
ready to leave next morning at five o'clock. He had already
moved my trunk aboard. Next morning after a good breakfast
at the hospital a young lad came to escort me down to the
small boat harbor where I had my first view of the *Trigve*,
and almost did not go aboard. She was about a thirty-five-foot
cabin cruiser and loaded down almost to the dock. However,
she was my only means of getting to Kake and that was my
destination so I had no choice, but I made a mental resolution that when once there I would stay put for the full duration of my tenure in that village. The deck hand, whom the
captain addressed as John, only he pronounced it "Yon," (and
I never did hear his last name) was busy storing all things
aboard. My trunk was placed so it could be used as our table
and was used as such for the entire trip. About seven o'clock
we got under way and headed I knew not where. In the pilot
house was sort of a long bench with a wide backboard where
passengers were supposed to sit. Behind this board was a
bunk, which Captain Hemnes said would be my bunk in
case we did not reach Kake before nightfall. The trip usually took about eight hours. I had gotten a pair of coveralls
in Petersburg and these, with my boots and mackinaw, I felt,
would be ample for any type of weather.

We wallowed along in rough seas and fog with water
swishing over the deck until I thought surely we would

capsize. About noon we ran into a heavy snowstorm, strong winds and heavy seas, so the captain ran into Portage Bay where many halibut fishing boats were anchored riding out the storm. Hardly had the captain dropped our anchor when dories were lowered from the halibut boats and their captains came aboard to visit and get any news the captain could provide. We swayed and rolled all night at anchor, a miserable sensation, as swells came into the bay.

Next morning the captain had our dory lowered and said he was going ashore for fresh water and that I could come along, which I was glad to do and get away from the boat swaying and rolling. He loaded the water cans, a shotgun, and me into the dory and rowed ashore. The snow was very deep ashore and I soon found my boot tops full of the wet stuff. We trudged along through the snow, crossed a small stream about ankle deep, then a bit further we found a larger freshwater stream where he filled the water cans, left me with them, and going a bit farther shot a couple of geese.

All of this took some time so that on our return trip the tide had raised the shallow stream we had crossed too much above my boots. So the captain took the water cans across then came back for me where I stood in the wet snow, holding two geese in one hand and a shotgun in the other. He told me to get on his back, which I did, and about halfway across it struck me funny and I began to laugh, but when he said, "I tell you it's no yoke," I soon sobered up. Trekking along through the snow back to the dory with Captain ahead carrying the oil cans, I clutched the geese in one hand but sort of dragged the shotgun along beside me since my fingers were cold. I stumbled over a root or some such thing, fell down, and the shotgun discharged with a bang. Captain put down the cans and ran back to me asking if I was hurt, to which I replied yes, but on clambering up I found that I was perfectly all right. The shot had not come anywhere near me. Poor

Captain, I'm sure he was disgusted and probably hoped that I had been shot dead.

We returned to the mailboat cold, wet, and miserable, and when we got alongside I took hold of the rail but my hands were so cold I could not hang on, and since I had sort of kicked the dory away from the boat, down I went, miles it seemed to me, but probably only a few yards before I was hoisted up like a fish with a gaff hook in the back of my coveralls. The captain gave me a suit of heavy wool long-handled underwear, wool socks, and a pair of wooden deck shoes and said, "Now you will stay aboard." The coveralls he gave me were much too big and the woollies itchy, but I said not a word, believe me.

All magazines, newspapers, and even the calendar on board the mailboat and all the halibut boats were in Norwegian, and I had not thought to bring along any reading material, so time dragged a bit. Christmas Day the halibut fishermen came aboard, so I spent the holiday learning to play pinochle, drinking gas boat coffee (in a class by itself), and eating Norwegian goodies that they brought over with them. After several more days swinging at anchor the seas calmed a bit so Captain pulled anchor and we continued on our way and arrived at Kake village in the early evening of New Year's Day. What a grand feeling to at last be on land. I didn't even mind the eighteen inches of fresh snow I had to walk through but staggered up the beach to the school house, just happy to be on land again.

There were two teachers in the village and the husband of the senior teacher, all living in government teacher's quarters. I was assigned a room and after an evening meal fell into bed and immediately asleep. Shortly after midnight I was awakened by someone ringing the clinic bell, which also rang in my room. Going down to the clinic adjacent to the main building, I was greeted by a seventeen-year-old lad who asked me to come with him to the home of the chief, whose daughter was very sick.

I dressed and went with my escort to a huge log house known as a "pit house," home of the chief and his relatives. The building was one huge room with an earthen floor in the center part, and about four feet from the earthen floor was sort of a balcony around the entire room about six feet wide, and from this balcony were ladders reaching up to yet another balcony around the room where relatives of the chief lived. In the roof of the building was an opening of about eight feet square called the smoke hole, and directly under the smoke hole on the earthen floor was a bonfire where all cooking was done. It was also the only means of heat. When my vision adjusted to the darkness of the room, since only two lanterns were lit, I saw a tent tightly tied down around an improvised bed. Around this bed were three medicine men and one medicine woman all chanting and shaking charms of this and that. In the bed under the tent was a very pretty girl of about twelve years of age, gasping and panting for air, her pulse was racing and obviously with quite a temperature elevation.

The chief signaled the medicine personnel to keep quiet, and when we were able to hear each other, through the chief's son as interpreter, I explained that the child had pneumonia and must have air, so the tent was removed. I gave her a tepid bath and aspirin and told the chief that if she could be moved someplace where she could have peace and quiet and plenty of air I was sure she would recover, but I doubted that she would under these conditions.

Next morning early I was much surprised to see four men carrying the sick girl on a litter to the Presbyterian manse where Mrs. Tamare, the mission lay worker, lived. I went over immediately and was delighted to see Alice, the patient, in a nice clean room in a clean bed in one of the rooms in the manse and with plenty of fresh air. Mrs. Tamare was most cooperative so we nursed her day and night and within the week she was able to walk to her own home.

A few days later the chief sent for me to come to his house, and when I arrived I was directed to stand between him and his wife in front of his home on the boardwalk, which I was later to learn was an honor. He had a number of his relatives and about a dozen young men around about. Four loaded canoes were on the beach at the water's edge in front of us. At a given signal the eight young men walked out to the canoes, two men to each canoe. Some sort of signal was given, then the three medicine men and one medicine woman took their place in an assigned canoe; another signal was given and the eight young men gave each canoe occupant a couple of paddles, then shoved the canoes off the beach and the occupants paddled away. Later I was to learn that when the chief gave a potlatch it was considered an honor and courtesy for his young men to wade out into the water and help the visitors bring their canoes to the beach, but when a canoe was shoved off the beach it was an order that the occupant never return to the village. I could not help but wonder that should his daughter not have recovered would I have been shoved off the beach with nowhere to go.

The chief had the Kake canoe-maker make me a lovely canoe and paddles all painted with Native dye. This canoe was almost my undoing. The chief's wife gave me a lovely pounded silver bracelet with the head of a crow etched on it. She belonged to the Crow tribe,[14] and in their custom all children follow the tribe of their mother, so I became a Crow.

Kake, a Tlingit Indian village of about four hundred people, was like a picture, with the irregular beach having here and there sandy beaches and many huge rocks jutting out of the water, especially at low tide [see Figure 7.4]. Behind the village about a quarter of a mile were quite high hills covered with green timber. Across the water from the village proper was the Indian burial ground on a small island. This island was surrounded by sandy beaches and no doubt there were an abundance of clams on the beach, but no one ever was allowed to dig clams there or even go to the island except for funerals or to decorate family graves on the day set aside for such ceremony.

Keku Trading Post, which also housed the post office, was on the beach side on sort of a point. Here the contour of the sea curved around the point then swept inland, making a small bay before extending on around the mountains to seaward. The government school and home of the personnel were next to the Keku Trading Post about one hundred yards farther along the little bay; it faced the main street of the village. About one block farther along the little bay was the Presbyterian manse, a lovely old building built by

7.4. *The village of Kake from the air. Reprinted with permission from the Alaska Nurses Association Collection (#74-167-196N), Archives, Elmer E. Rasmuson Library, University of Alaska Fairbanks, Fairbanks.*

Presbyterian missionaries many years ago. It was a one-story building with a large living room and huge stone fireplace. There was a kitchen, a den, and three bedrooms and the inevitable shed for wood since, of course, the kitchen range burned wood. The government house was of two stories, with a large living room, a dining room, a kitchen and bathroom, and a store room. Upstairs were four sleeping rooms. Directly in front, attached to the living room, was the clinic with entrance from outside off the porch and also through the living room. It was a nice clinic with many windows facing the main street of the village.

There were two other trading posts in the village besides Keku Trading Post. One, a large wooden affair with living quarters on the second floor was owned by an elderly Scotsman, a remittance man. This Scotsman did very little business and kept a very small amount of supplies. He was a very quiet man who liked to read and play the upright piano he owned. Each morning about ten he could be heard playing and also in the evening. He ended each concert by playing "The Bluebells of Scotland." The German who owned Keku Trading Post was just the opposite. I have heard him give a ten-minute dissertation just over a stamp.

The third trading post was the cooperative Native store, a small building just off the boardwalk on the ocean side. This store was very interesting, since during fishing and cannery season practically all the men and women were away from the village, leaving only the elderly Natives and some small children who were left in their care. The storekeeper, always elected to the job by the people, would lock the store then hang the key outside of the door just out of reach of children. The idea and practice was that if any of the fishermen or cannery workers would come to the village for supplies, etc., they could unlock the door, go in and get what they needed, and if they knew the price leave the money in a cigar box on the counter; if not, they could leave a slip from the pad on the counter. But if they could not read or write they then left a small stick with notches cut on it as having purchased something. Each stick had notches that designated the person doing the buying. In the late fall when I would help the storekeeper audit his books we were never short. They were truly an honest people. I always enjoyed this auditing with all the cash in the cigar box to be counted, the slips of paper to decipher, and most of all those notched sticks, which the owner would come in to claim and then tell us what he had purchased.

At first I wondered just what I would do to kill time but very soon found out. No one had been immunized and that program had to be set up. When the chief evicted the medicine men and woman he issued an edict that everyone was to cooperate with the nurse, so that hurdle was over, for which I was truly thankful. The Presbyterian choir needed help, the ANS [Alaska Native Sisterhood] organization wanted some help with their sanitation and home health program, and the older school boys were most anxious to have a basketball team and be able to enter the southeastern conference. So there was plenty to keep me busy.

The ANS organization soon was functioning nicely, and the Presbyterian choir doing about as well as I ever got them to do, but the basketball team was something else again. I had played basketball in high school but that was quite some time ago. I certainly had never been a coach. However, the boys sent for all the equipment and a coach's manual of instructions, and each morning before school and evenings after school we all went down to the town hall and went through the motions at least, and each night I studied the coach's manual. We finally came up with a creditable school team and developed a town team of older young men known as the "Town Team," thus having a team with whom to compete.

Years later, two of my school boys' original team made the All Alaskan team roster.

One lovely summer day in 1925 about noon, a young lad came in from Rabbit Island where his parents owned a fox farm. He was looking for help. Seems his father, while trying to pull up a scow, had a stroke and his mother and he were unable to get him up to the house, a distance of about a quarter of a mile and up quite a hill. They had managed to get him on a ladder and pulled him up above high water but could go no farther. Since fishing season was on and the cannery running, there were only the elderly remaining in the village. I told him I would go back with him, so we made a very quick trip across to the island. Then, try as we may, we could not carry the man up the hill since he was quite a large man, and heavy; so we finally put a mattress on the after deck of their launch, and by using a ladder for a stretcher and all our strength, we got him aboard.

The mother insisted on taking him to Juneau where she had relatives and to a doctor of her choice there. This trip would take from twenty to thirty hours. She could navigate the launch while the lad and I would act as engineer and deck hand. The weather was clear and the sea quite calm. That evening we came to a small island and dropped anchor, put the dory overboard, rowed ashore, and tied up to a tree and had our supper and a bit of sleep. When we tried to get the anchor aboard we were unable to do so, and having no winch we were stymied. We were finally able to get it into the dory and towed it behind us all the way to Juneau. We traveled along the remainder of the night and all the next day, eating in snatches and not sleeping. I thought sure we had had it when we got into those rip tides about thirty miles south of Juneau and the engine stopped as we bobbed about broadside, head on, and completely turned around a couple of times. But finally the lad got the engine going and we arrived at the Juneau small boat dock about midnight that night. Willing hands on the dock helped us secure and then took the patient up to St. Ann Hospital, where he died two days later. Two of my brothers, Bob and Ted, were living in Juneau and working at Alaska Juneau Mining Company and, as news gets around quickly, they were horrified that I had made such a trip and insisted that I wait for the steamer going to our cannery and return on her, which I did, and was, if the facts be known, glad to do so.

The previous December of that year they brought me a young lad from trapping camp who was obviously suffering from a ruptured appendix. The weather was much too stormy for any of our boats to make the trip to Petersburg, our nearest doctor and hospital. We had no wireless communications then and of course no antibiotics in those days. So in desperation, I finally opened his abdomen[15] and put in a drain, which flowed profusely. Three days later we were able to take him to Petersburg where Dr. Rogers later removed his appendix and he made a good recovery. We had a new doctor come to Wrangell and of course he heard about me opening the patient's abdomen, so he wrote to Dr. Rogers of Petersburg and Dr. Dawes of Juneau, wanting them to assist him in removing my nursing license since I had practiced medicine. I knew nothing about all of this until Dr. Dawes told me when we took the man to Juneau. Both Dr. Dawes and Dr. Rogers wrote the new doctor asking him what he would have had me do, or what he would have done under similar conditions. He did not answer them and the petition, if that be what it was, died there. Sometimes it truly is pitiful how some persons hew to the line whether it will mean saving a patient's life or not.

About noon on August 25, 1926, I noticed smoke coming from the trading post run by the Scotsman, and very soon a blaze. I was then living in Keku Trading Post, running the store and the post office. The government ship *Boxer* had been in a few days previous with our supplies and gasoline and oil for all the stores, which the ship's crew had unloaded on the beach in front of the village. An Alaska steamship had been in and taken some of the cannery crew out, among them the radio operator. The mailboat had been in, just left for Petersburg an hour or two before. The younger men and women in the village and the teacher and his sons had also gone fishing, so only the elderly, the incapacitated, myself, and the small children were there to do what we could. We rang the school bell as hard as we could, hoping the women in the cannery would hear it and come up, but the machinery in the cannery made so much noise they could not hear it.

We dashed from house to house on the front street as they became involved in the fire and saved what household things we could, but it was not much. The tide was way out and the only other water available was the town pump back on Second Street. The wind came up a bit and blew the fire away from Second Street as it was off shore, but all the houses on Front Street were very close together and made mostly of logs and dry as tinder, so the fire just went from house to house. We took a couple of very old men and got them into a canoe and shoved them off shore and they paddled as best they could away from the village toward the manse in the cove a good distance from the village proper. One elderly bedfast woman we carried in a blanket litter to the manse and put her into a bed there.

As the wind shifted to off shore it was obvious that the fire would soon set fire to the oil and gas drums on the beach from blowing dry shakes and shingles, so I ran over to the trading post and got everything out of the post office and the cash box out of the trading post and any books I could find. Finally help came running up from the cannery, mostly women and girls, but we had no way of contacting our fishermen who were well down in Cape Ormany fishing, and with the wireless operator gone there was no way of sending out messages.

Soon the Keku Trading Post was ablaze, and one by one the gasoline drums exploded, as did the oil drums. Both the Scotsman's store and the Native cooperative store burned, as did Keku Trading Post, so the only food supply in the village was the annual supply that the *Boxer* brought in and stored in the government house. All night long people were digging in the ashes of their homes, hoping to find something of value. We slept people in the homes on Second Street; the town hall, which, being so far away, did not burn; and in the manse.

During the early morning the weather changed abruptly, first to rain then a very heavy wet snow, but it did bring the fishermen in from the fishing grounds. After their first shock, they made plans and pooled all the gas remaining in their boats and put it into the fastest boat in the village, made up a crew, and they left immediately for Wrangell to buy food, bedding, lumber, gasoline, fuel oil, clothing, and tents. There was no lack of money—just nowhere to spend it. When our boat got to Wrangell, of course, a message went out to the Coast Guard about the fire and the next day they anchored in the roadstead. We just did the best we could until they arrived. They came ashore and put up tents, and gave the people blankets and some food stuffs, so we had a tent village. The weather continued bad with snow but a bit colder, so we did not have to move about in so much slush. Bad weather held our boat in Wrangell longer than we had anticipated, and before they returned a boat under Red Cross charter came in with more supplies and bedding, etc.; also drugs for the many colds in the village.

When our boat returned it was loaded to the water line with lumber and building supplies and towing a barge from the Wrangell Lumber Mill, also loaded with more lumber, gasoline, and fuel oil. Within hours the sound of hammer and saw could be heard throughout the village as houses were going up. Then came the mailboat, and news of the fire having gotten to the States, box after box of contributions, many of which were something else again. For instance, there was one huge box full of women's hats. I'm sure many closets were cleared out of disposable things, and more inappropriate things for Kake I have never seen. It was a pity to pay postage on such boxes. However, the boxes received from Alaska towns were indeed gratefully received since they, of course, knew what to send.

Two babies were born during this hectic time but made it all right. On the next mailboat the new nurse for Kake, my relief, came in as I was being transferred to Juneau.

I was very glad to see her since she had worked in other Native villages and knew the score, and within a few days had the picture well in her mind. The Keku trader also returned and took over the mail situation. When it was time to leave all the people came down to the beach to bid me goodbye, and I'll admit to a lump in my throat.

Juneau, 1926–1932

The ship came into Juneau at night and a more beautiful sight I have never seen. All those lovely lights, not only in the town proper, but way up on the side of Mr. Roberts where there were many homes, and the many, many lights of Alaska Juneau Mine hanging on Mt. Roberts' side. It was breathtaking, and since it was a clear, cold night there was a lovely orange glow from it all. My brothers, Bob and Ted,[16] met the ship and took us up to Gastineau Hotel where, wonder of wonders, one could just, by turning a tap, get water to wash without having to send a boy with a bucket to the pump, and still more wonderful, just the flip of a switch, lights; a far cry from pumping up those old gas lamps or

lanterns and being so careful not to put the match through
the mantle. I never did get used to lighting them, or of the
fear of them blowing up, and whenever possible got someone else to light them for me. We spent the evening bobbing
about a foot off our skirts and next morning went up to the
home of Judge and Mrs. Paine and pressed them. The Paines
often visited us at Kake when down on their fox farm, so we
knew them well. Donie[17] was to live with them the first few
years of her teaching in Juneau. Feeling a bit more present-
able but almost indecent with such short skirts, we went
down to the Christine Halvorson dress shop and had a shopping spree.

I was assigned to the Department of Interior Hospital down
on Willowby Avenue as the surgery nurse. This little hospital was established for the care of Alaska Indians, Eskimo,
and Aleuts. The main or general hospital was on the second
floor, with the general outpatient clinic room, general office,
and quarters for living-in personnel and kitchen on the first
floor. There was also a forty-bed TB annex adjoining the main
building on the first floor. Doctors from uptown did what
surgery was needed and held daily clinic for outpatients,
since at that time we had no resident physician. While working at government hospital I often acted as relief surgery
nurse at St. Ann Hospital on my time off.

The next year we were transferred to the Indian Service
and our Alaska office was changed to Juneau, a director for
Indian Services in Alaska was established, and Dr. McCauliffe
and his wife came to the department hospital, he as the resident physician and she as chief nurse. Juneau proper had at
that time five physicians, two of whom did surgery. Three
had been practicing medicine in the territory quite some
time before Alaska had a medical board. These physicians
were just waived in without having to take the medical board
exams.

Across Gastineau Channel at a distance of about three quarters of a mile was, and still is, the little town of Douglas, nestled down toward the beach on Douglas Island. The very rich Treadwell gold mine operated on this island for many years, but since they were operating well out under the waters of Gastineau Channel, the sea broke through and flooded the pits and the mine has been idle for a good many years. Transportation between Juneau and Douglas had to be by water since there was no bridge at that time. The little ferry *Teddy* made many trips between the two towns with passengers and sometimes a bit of freight and mail. Many men working in Alaska Gold Mine on the Juneau side commuted to their homes in Douglas daily.

Juneau had two steamship docks and two small boat docks besides the small boat harbor behind the huge rock dump that protected them from strong Taku winds from the south. There were narrow floats about four feet wide to which the small boats could tie up. Alaska and Pacific Steamship companies each brought in a ship once a week, and Canadian Steamship Company one every ten days, so the dock was a busy place most of the summertime, but in wintertime the number of ships to dock were much fewer. Just below the docks and sort of wedged in between the docks and the big cold storage plant was an area known as "Roberts Row" where the ladies of the line plied their trade, and I learned that it was not by trapping that they got their mink coats and capes. All Alaska towns had their "line" and even the more prosperous mining camps out in the bush had their "Mother Hubbard establishments." It was an accepted way of life and no one thought anything about it. The "Roberts Row" buildings had for the most part false fronts advertising tobacco.

The docks were very busy during tourist season: Indian women sitting about with their beading work to sell, tourists milling about, and tons and tons of freight being unloaded.

Then, too, almost always one would see old Gold Medal Joe from Sitka Pioneer Home there doing a sort of dance shuffle. He got the name Gold Medal Joe because his vest was almost covered with old medals people had given him and bottle caps he had put on it himself. He always managed to get to Juneau during the summer and usually tried to miss the last boat to Sitka in the fall, and when the weather became on the nippy side he would try to get into St. Ann Hospital's old men's ward. The new wing of Sitka Pioneer Home having not yet been finished, St. Ann Hospital still maintained a large ward for about twenty old prospectors. These men were well cared for and did a lot of rocking chair mining, but usually when they had a poker game someone cheated and the battle was on, so the orderly had to come up and quell them. Joe kept asking to get into this ward, but it was already full and the sisters told him so. One day when it was pretty cold he went downtown and bought a bottle of milk and a loaf of bread and sat on the hospital steps in the cold to eat his supper. Of course the sisters had to take him in that night but they saw to it that he got to Sitka on the next boat going there.

During tourist season the town maintained a little information booth down on the dock for tourists. We had very little to show them except the town clinging onto the mountainside, the governor's mansion, the territorial museum where Fr. Kashaveroff was curator, and if time allowed, a trip out to see the glacier. Sometimes the mine allowed them to go through the mine mill, and the cold storage plant would take them through the receiving sheds if fishing boats were in unloading onto the conveyor. There were some very odd tourists and also some very fine ones.

One day it was my turn to man the information booth. Along came a lady with a little black book in her hand and told me that she wanted some information. Said she was a fifth-grade teacher from Iowa. Number one, she would like to know just how many thousand feet above sea level we were. I could hardly believe my ears, but she was serious so I said, "Lady, we are here on the dock and the sea is not more than three or four feet below us." She snapped her little black boot shut and indignantly said, "Well, I never." I never knew just how that remark was intended, but felt quite sure the answer was not appreciated.

The territorial commissioner of education called me and asked me to be school nurse for half days during the school weeks, so I became, although only part time, the first school nurse in the territory.[18] My office was in the high-school building adjacent to Mr. Keller's office. Most of the work consisted of doing a bit of first aid and being on hand during physical education in the gym and on call during basketball practice, since it seemed that a few accidents that had taken place in the gym had been poorly handled, and the school board wanted someone to give instruction in first aid to the teachers and older high-school students and be available in case of illness in a classroom. I would report to school at one P.M. after my morning's work at one or the other hospital as surgery nurse. It was a rather unusual nursing duty, but interesting.

For some time I had wondered why teachers often mentioned the fact that they would have to go to PTA tonight and disliked it heartily. Seemed to me that was not much of a chore, one night a month. However, I found out since now I was expected to go,[19] and never once did I go that some mother did not come to me and at length, and I do mean length, inquire why her daughter or son was not gaining weight since she had been given a balanced diet, or could her son or daughter be moved nearer the window since they were not able to see the blackboard. And many times they would want to know why the students, or perhaps the teachers, did not like their child. So I, too, disliked PTA.

One day a teacher came to me and reported that two children in her room from the same home had ugly looking scabs on their faces. When they came to the office it was easy to see that they had impetigo and a real mess of it. Regulations were that I should give them a slip for their parents to take them to their family physician. Next day they reported to the office with a slip from their family physician, who, by the way, was one of our physicians who had been waived in, and on the slip, his Rx pad, was this diagnosis: "Miss Keaton, this is not contagious or infectious—just seems to be going around." To this he signed his name with MD following. Sort of gave one the idea that it was perhaps being carried about in a basket and passed out here and there. For about three weeks I treated those children daily and finally got them cleared up.

One summer during the peak of the cannery season, our local health officer received a wire from the superintendent of the Port Althorp Cannery at Port Althorp, stating he was sending him one of their workers who had some spots on his face and many of the other workers were worried about it. The lad arrived and it took only one look for the doctor to see that he had smallpox, and so the doctor wired the superintendent of the cannery. The superintendent wanted to know what he could do since he did not want to close the cannery at the peak of the season. The doctor contacted all registered nurses in Juneau, six in number, excluding hospital staffs, and since I had had smallpox many years ago it was decided that I should go to Port Althorp and vaccinate everyone there. A few days later, fortified with the vaccine, I boarded the motorship *Estabeth*, a sixty-foot cabin cruiser boat that carried freight to canneries and mail and supplies to the villages in that area. Her captain was big Jim Davis, quite a colorful free-wheeling character, well known around the country. We had an uneventful trip out to the cannery and on arrival there the superintendent had everything in readiness for me to do the immunizing. I vaccinated everyone in the area that night, and the next morning the superintendent had a cannery tender take me to the village of Hoonah, since many of the men from this village had been working at the cannery where the smallpox case had been.

That day I vaccinated everyone in Hoonah and was just finishing packing up my gear to take the evening boat *Estabeth* back to Juneau, since she was due that evening, when we saw the captain coming up the small dock with one of the sailors sort of guiding. I was in the school room where I had worked during the day, and the teacher and wife and Presbyterian minister were there to give me some mail they wanted taken to Juneau. When the captain and deckhand came in, the deckhand told us that captain had swung down from the pilot house on one of the lines by his left hand and just at that time the boat had dived into a huge wave trough which left the captain hanging with all of his weight on the left arm and it was obvious he had dislocated his shoulder. The captain, knowing no other medicine for pain than whiskey, had well fortified himself with it. The deckhand and other sailors had brought the boat into Hoonah. We placed the captain on a chair and tried to reduce the dislocation, but he not only was unable to sit up, but was most uncooperative, and his vocabulary was something to hear. Finally we put him on the floor, with the teacher trying to hold his head straight while his wife poured ether through a towel, sometimes on his nose and other times in his hair as he moved his head about. The minister, a very small man, in attempting to hold on to his right arm, made mileage up and down the floor as he thrashed his good arm about. I had my heel in his left armpit pulling with all my strength. All in all, we must have made quite a picture. Finally we got the shoulder in fair position and the lads took him back to the boat where he took another generous helping of his pain medicine and went to sleep and slept until almost noon next day.

The missionary kept making tut-tutting noises all during the shoulder setting and trying to stop the colorful language, to no avail. We departed from Hoonah a little after noon the next day and on arriving in Juneau I took captain up to the doctor who X-rayed his shoulder and said it was in good position, so I guess we did a fairly good job of it. I told captain he should clean up his language just in case he should ever again need have the Hoonah missionary give him first aid. He laughed and said, "Well, a few off-color words might be good for him."

The Piggly-Wiggly store brought pennies to Juneau in 1930. Many people had never seen them, especially the younger people who had been born in Juneau or Douglas, and were willing to pay many times their value just to have them for keepsakes. Senator Tom Devigne, a trader from the Yukon River area, proudly showed me five pennies he had been able to purchase for five dollars to take back to his trading post, since very few in that area had seen a penny. A few years later when I spent the summer on the Yukon River I saw those five pennies, all shined up and mounted on a lovely piece of birch hanging over the counter in his trading post at Ruby.

I had been transferred to the Yukon River on the medical boat *Martha Angeline* for the next summer, then would be transferred to Kotzebue for the next three years, so we broke up our home in the fall of 1931 and my brother Bob and family moved into our home until our lease expired. The other boys found rooms elsewhere, and I moved down to the government hospital to live until time to leave for the Yukon River early in the coming spring. It was difficult to leave our home and many Juneau friends, and as I look back on the years I lived there I find the memories very good. Each time I have visited Juneau since having moved away I am able to find a number of long ago friends and we always enjoy a wonderful visit.

Nenana, 1932

On June first we began provisioning the *Martha Angeline*, and a more peculiar boat I have never seen. A long, shallow draft, flat-bottomed riverboat. A bit of deck on the bow, and a bit more astern where the little dory could be placed, but only about a foot of deck on either side, just enough for the deckhand to walk along when pike poling off sand bars. A door on the after deck opened into the galley, which ran full both sides of the boat. There were shelves with all our food stored either on them or in bins under them, a large table, a coal-burning cook stove, and a huge coal bin beside the stove. A door from the galley ran midship through a narrow passageway by a small room on the right, having of all things, a huge bathtub. Forward of this was the clinic, with a door opening onto the forward deck. A ladder of six or eight rungs on the afterdeck went up over the galley to another deck where there were six staterooms, three on each side. Each stateroom contained a cot with mosquito net hanging from the ceiling down and around the cot, a chair, and a well-screened port hole. Climbing another four steps was another deck with a dental clinic toward the rear and the pilot house to the bow. The boat was powered by two Red Wing engines and overall looked like a huge crab floating on the river [see Figure 7.5]. Came the day when the river pilot returned from his trip down river which he made each year in a small boat after breakup, as each year when the ice went out new channels were made and new sand bars piled up where they had not been before. The pilot sounded out the channel and placed white painted barrels here and there along the river bank to indicate the channels.

The next day after the pilot returned we took off down river. We had no dentist that year and were to pick up our cook at Tanana village, so there was only the doctor, the captain (a veteran on the river), a deckhand who had made several previous trips, and myself.[20] Since I was the only woman aboard, I had to fall to and do the cooking. I at once served notice that anyone who criticized the cooking could put on the apron. We were going nicely down the Tanana River so I decided to make an apple pie and had had it in the oven

7.5. The Martha Angeline. *This medical service boat made one round trip a year on the Yukon River. Photo from the National Archives, Alaska Region.*

about ten minutes when, wham!, we hit a sand bar with our bow high and dry, and the river current put the stern also on the bar, which made us lying at about a forty-degree angle, bow to stern. Almost all the food fell from the shelves onto the galley deck, as did the coal from the bin. Fortunately, the dishes remained in their racks. The crew launched the dory and outboard and with it pulling, them pike poling, and a cable run through the boat bow to stern right through the galley, they finally got us afloat again. When all the galley mess had been cleaned up and medicines in the clinic put back on their proper shelves, I made a lunch of sandwiches, and served the pie, which was sure a masterpiece. On the high side of the oven it was just two pieces of crust baked together, and on the low side a huge bulge of apple filling. It was, however, done, and to my disappointment no one made a comment, just ate it.

We had been advised in Nenana that all the people in Minto village would be down the river farther fishing, so we did not stop at Minto but continued on down river and tied up at their fish camp where we immunized and Doctor saw a few minor cases and I extracted a couple of teeth. We crossed the Yukon River at the mouth of the Tanana River where it flows into the Yukon. The stern-wheeler *Yukon* of Canadian Transportation Co. was tied up to the Tanana float. It came weekly from Whitehorse to Tanana with passengers, and like all other river stern-wheelers, pushed a long barge carrying freight. The Yukon Transportation Co. runs two stern-wheelers from St. Michael to Tanana every week with passengers and cargo. These stern-wheelers burned six-foot wood, which was picked up along the river at wood chopper camps. Since the huge mosquito net that covered the part of the boat where the wood was stored had to be lifted while the boat was loading wood, it was not unusual to see the passengers lined up helping to get the wood aboard so the boat could get

out into the middle of the river and away from the millions
of mosquitoes. Then in midstream the mosquito net could be
dropped down.

After we had tied up to the Tanana village, Doctor and I
walked up to the Tanana Hospital. The resident physician had
departed several weeks ago so only two elderly nurses were
in residence besides the husband of one of the nurses who
was sort of a handyman about the place. The nurses' rooms,
dining room, the surgery, the store room, and a small laundry
were on the first floor. Upstairs in the hospital proper were
two large wards, one for male and one for female, regardless
of age or illness of the patient. Between these wards were the
portable toilet and a huge zinc tub attached to the floor with
a drainage hose attached and leading to a hole in the side
of the building where the tub could be drained. A tall pipe
with faucet attached and a pipe going to the hot water tank
in the wall was the shower as it was above the zinc tub. The
patient, by either crouching or in a sitting position, could
have a shower unless he was a bed patient. The nurses had
a number of patients for Doctor to see, so since I was free, I
went out exploring about the village and encountered a Mrs.
Senif, wife of the marshall, and she gave me considerable
history of the village since she had lived there for forty-some
years. She was busy doing her annual chore of sowing poppy
seeds about the village to cover the unsightly spots. She took
me out to Rowe Hall about two miles out of the village where
they have the Episcopal church, a recreation hall, quarters
for the missionaries, and a huge garden. It was a very pretty
place and the building comfortable, but the mosquitoes to en-
dure on the walk out there were something else again. Next
she took me to see Mrs. Call and her little orphanage where
she had about ten or twelve girls. I met her adopted daughter
Sausa and her older adopted daughter Melba, who was blind
but studying the violin and was later to become quite a musi-

cian. We supplied ourselves with head nets then walked the five miles down to old Fort Gibbons, which was used during World War I. Many buildings were still standing, including the Gould Library and the huge water tower. She said that during the first World War there was telephone communication via telephone wires strung along trees from Ft. Gibbon to St. Michael, also a fort at that time, on the mouth of the Yukon River.

We could not get all of the mosquitoes out of the clinic until we would be tying up to another fish camp and more mosquitoes. They were driving us all crazy. We wrapped our legs with toilet tissue under our hose and it would be fine for a while, then sort of wrinkle and the same old misery. I had gotten some calico in Nulato and made myself some sleevelets like the old-time storekeepers used to wear. I starched them real stiff and they worked fine, so I made some for my legs, too, with a ruffle to fall down over the foot and they, when starched stiff, worked wonderfully, too. I can imagine what a sight I made with all of that gay colored calico (I could not get any plain material) hanging down below a white uniform, but one gets beyond the caring stage. One Indian man asked Doctor why "nurse pants all time come down." Even then I did not care. I was comfortable.

At Kaltag we met the teacher, Mr. Wilson, and I dutifully delivered a pie from Mrs. Adams, the teacher at Kokrines. Here, too, the Natives were all downriver at fish camp. So we continued on downstream, stopping at all fish camps until we got to the village of Anvik, a small settlement composed mostly of the Episcopal mission and orphanage. At the request of the superior we stayed there three days and did considerable work for them, such as tonsillectomies, all immunizing, several ear and eye treatments, and I did considerable emergency dental work. One evening as we were having our dinner, a long boat with outboard came alongside and tied

up. In it was a white man with his Indian wife who had come
to have an aching tooth extracted. We told them we would be
through soon so the woman sat up on a grassy bit of hill near
the boat and I happened to look out and see her not only suffering from toothache but now and then pulling on handsful
of grass, obviously having birth contractions as she looked to
be full term. I lost no time eating and took her up to the dental clinic and extracted the tooth, then sent for the mission
nurse, Mrs. Swick, and we hustled the woman into their boat
and went with them with a medical bag with us downriver to
their log cabin several miles downstream. The man had a fish
wheel and a fish cleaning table on the beach near the cabin.
The woman lost no time in getting up to the cabin where she
took two sharpened sticks, one in each hand, sort of squatted
over a nest of moss and down, and working with her contractions soon delivered a big, husky boy, who fell down into the
nest. I took the babe, severed the cord and tied it, and Nurse
Swick remained with the mother until the placenta dropped.
Then the mother got up and walked to her bed in the corner of the room and went to bed. I put the babe in with her
and we called her husband, who came in and shoveled up
the contents of the nest and put them into a piece of tarp,
took them out, and buried all of it. We remained a few hours
until we were satisfied that mother and babe were all right,
then the father took us back up to Anvik. As we passed by
the home a couple days later, we saw the mother out split-
ting fish with the babe swinging in a little hammock from a
tree bough, well covered with a mosquito net. The father was
removing fish from his wheel and brought us a very nice one
for our dinner. As we left, both the father and mother smil-
ingly waved us good-bye.

Again we stopped at a number of fish camps, then came
into Holy Cross where the village people told us to go around
the bend and tie up at Holy Cross Mission[21] and they would

come to us there. This we did and it was quite a sight. A lovely garden right down to the river edge, the priest's house near the garden, and up higher on a hill was the mission, school, and orphanage. There were both girl and boy dormitories and nearby a children's house where the preschool children lived and had their schooling. They ranged in age from two to five years. Farther along the hill was the little infirmary overseen by Father Epipham. The main building containing the kitchen, dining room, and recreation rooms was large and airy. I asked the sister who was cook how long she had been here and she replied, "I have worn out two cook stoves and this is my third." These were the Sisters of St. Ann. This mission also had cows and several horses. They were way over the hill grazing in a very lush meadow. Most of the mission children, being orphans, remained at the school the year round. I saw some of the older boys carrying what I thought were armloads of wood from the priest's house basement and mentioned that it was quite a way to hand carry so much wood, but was informed that they were carrying bread, since it was always baked in the stove in the basement of the priest's house. They also had a small sawmill for cutting lumber to be used in their buildings. Several months before our arrival a seven-year-old lad had fallen on one of the saws and severed his leg, amputating the foot and several inches of bone above it. Sister, with the help of others, had done a fine job of stopping the bleeding and had sewn the flap over the stump and it had healed, but ends of bone were now protruding from the incision, although there was no infection. She just had not left enough flap. We prepared the youngster there in her little dispensary, and Doctor and I, with Sister giving whiffs of ether, removed about two more inches of bone and brought more flap over the stump. We did several tonsillectomies, and Doctor treated a number of ears and eyes and some skin rashes, all of which was greatly appreciated.

When we left after three days there they gave us some very lovely fresh garden stuffs, fresh milk, butter, and cottage cheese, which we all enjoyed very much.

From Marshall we made a one-day stop at Pitka Point fish camp then went on down to Mountain Village. This village had one trading post, owned and managed by two brothers, a post office, and a very small sort of rooming house for river transients who might become storm-bound there. We carried on our usual program of immunizations, and Doctor saw a few other patients. We were there three days. Now began the long, slow haul upriver with the current against us. We made slow headway, with many overnight tie-ups to the willows at night. The mosquitoes were about gone but the gnats and no-seeums were thick in the willows and could make life as miserable as the mosquitoes. We stopped briefly at Marshall, then enroute on to Holy Cross, we had a bit of engine trouble and had to beach the boat on a sandbar so the captain could repair a knuckle joint or some such thing. When we finally arrived at Holy Cross, some of the men gave the captain a hand doing the repairs, and they again showered us with fresh garden stuff, milk, butter, and cottage cheese. We remained there a couple of days and the doctor checked up on the lad with the amputation. He was healing nicely. He also saw a few more patients. Our next stop was Anvik Mission where we stopped briefly and picked up a fourteen-year-old lad with a hot appendix to take to Tanana Hospital so Doctor could operate on him. We put him to bed in the extra stateroom, watched his diet, and since our little refrigerator was capable of producing ice, kept it on his abdomen and kept our fingers crossed. We stopped at Kaltag only briefly and the teacher, Mr. Wilson, gave me a lovely moose steak to take to Mrs. Adams, the teacher at Kokrines, who had sent him the pie. This couple were married that next winter, so perhaps we played a part in the romance.

Arriving at Nulato, we found the village quiet since all the Koyukuk Natives had returned to their homes up the Koyukuk River. However, we stayed a couple of days so some of the men in the village could give the captain a hand in doing better repairs on the motors. At Ruby, our next stop, we remained overnight since Doctor and I had to attend a woman who had had a partial miscarriage, and we wanted to be sure she was out of danger before we continued upstream.

The store, or trading post, was on the first floor and their living quarters and sleeping accommodations for travelers upstairs. We were invited up to visit with them, and a little old prospector called Pete gave me his poke of his summer's diggings and asked me to take it to Fairbanks to the bank for him since I was scheduled to go into Fairbanks from Nenana. I asked him if he had any idea how much was in the poke, to which he replied, "The bank will know." I asked him to tag it with his name and address and he said, "I put 'Pete' on the poke, and the bank will know where the gold came from." That poke worried me to no end, and every night I looked to be sure it was under my bed where I had put it.

We stopped briefly at Kokrines and I delivered the moose steak, then we headed for Tanana, arriving there in the late evening. We put the lad with the appendix in a little isolation room, then the deckhand and I started clearing out the surgery. Since the surgery had not been used for quite some time, it had been used as a storeroom for food supplies and clothing, and there were clothes lines everywhere where the laundry was dried. We worked most of the night getting the place cleared out and wiped down with Lysol, and next morning, with Nurse O'Brady[22] giving ether, Doctor and I removed the appendix. It had not ruptured, but in another few days would have done so. The two nurses took over patient care of the post operative with the doctor remaining within calling distance, so I was free.

Now it was late August and that definitely is fall on the Yukon. Nights were quite cold and the moon something remarkable to see shining through the beautiful birch trees, all lemon-colored, or many even bare with great silver-colored trunks and limbs. As we rounded the bend of the river at Rampart Rapids, the most narrow part of the river, the captain suddenly turned the boat toward the right and went in and tied up on the south side of the river. He pointed out to us several big buck caribou on the north side of the river, sort of walking about, seemingly testing the approach to the river. Suddenly they jumped in and swam across to the south side. Very soon, what seemed like a huge river of brown bodies came down to the river's edge on the north side and without a moment's hesitation, plunged into the river and swam across to the south side, the does swimming downstream from their calves. This was the fall caribou migration. We stayed tied up to the willows on the south side two days and nights before the whole migration had passed. It was a sight I shall never forget.

Our final stop was at Beaver, the cleanest and most beautiful village we had seen on the river. All the Native homes were of logs and practically all of them had nasturtiums vining over them.

We were two days in Beaver, then began the trip downstream to Tanana where Doctor was to remain. Jessie, our cook, would also debark there, then go on to wherever she was to teach school that winter. As we passed Purgatory, the Yanart boys gave us a salute from their devil-with-pitchfork effigy. We did not stop. We stopped very briefly at Stevens Village and not at all at Rampart, but continued on down to Tanana, since it was getting a bit nippy to be on the river. Only two days were spent in Tanana, then the captain, the deckhand, and I headed up the Tanana River to Nenana. We had a one-day stop at the little village of Minto. We arrived at

Nenana late the next afternoon and tied up to the float. Since I was to come out over the Richardson Highway,[23] I shipped all but my warmer clothes to Juneau. I stayed on the boat that night, then next day at noon took the train to Fairbanks and stayed at the Nordale Hotel the next two days, or until the so-called bus (a Packard touring car), would be ready to leave. Meantime, I dutifully delivered the gold poke to the bank and they said, "Oh, yes, that is Pete's and the gold comes from around Rampart." So I never did find out his last name.

September 12 at 8 A.M., with the bus loaded with supplies for roadhouses along the route and I the only passenger, we got away from Fairbanks.[24]

Endnotes

1. W. B. Courtney, "Angel in Furs," *Colliers* (November 20, 1937): 80.
2. Tewksebury's *Who's Who in Alaska* and *Alaska Business Index* (Juneau, AK: Tewksebury Publishers, 1947) 1C:43.
3. "Salute to Women," *American Revolution Bicentennial 1776–1976*, 48.
4. Courtney, "Angel in Furs," *Colliers*: 80.
5. Ibid.
6. Ibid.
7. Tewkesbury's *Who's Who*, 43.
8. "Throughout the Territory," *Alaska Life* (1939): 12.
9. Ibid.
10. "Salute to Women," 48.
11. "Fifty Years of Nursing Recalls Lifetime Heroism," *NewsWheel* 7:5 (Glennallen, AK: Copper Valley School, 1968), 1–2.
12. "The End of the Road," *Alaska Magazine* (August 1980): 62.
13. Mildred Keaton, unpublished manuscript [no date], Alaska Nurses Association Collection, Series 13-4, Box 33, File 520 and related materials in Series 14-1, Box 36, File 592, Archives, Elmer E. Rasmuson Library, University of Alaska Fairbanks. The pages are not numbered. (See note 24.)
14. Keaton certainly intends Raven, not Crow. Raven is a social division among the Tlingit. To be made a member of the tribe was a great honor.
15. As an operating room nurse and surgical assistant, Keaton had probably assisted with this procedure many times.
16. Mildred Keaton had two brothers in Juneau and eventually was joined by a third. In 1928, the four Keatons and two unrelated young single men rented a house on Sixth Street, near St. Ann Hospital. Much of Keaton's writing about

this period relates to the social life of this young crowd. The three brothers eventually married, two to St. Ann nurses.

17. Donie Taylor had been a teacher in Kake and moved to Juneau at the same time as Keaton.

18. The distinction of first was held by "sanitation teachers." Mildred Keaton may have been the first school nurse employed by a territorial-run school.

19. Counseling families is an important aspect of all community and school nursing. See "Public Health Nursing Responsibilities in a Community Health Program," *Public Health Nursing* 41: 67–69.

20. These were Captain Milligan; Doctor Carter; Jessie Harper, a schoolteacher who served as cook during the summer months; and an unnamed deckhand.

21. This school operated from 1888–1955. Beginning in 1941 they had their own nurse, Sister Mary Edward (Margaret Cantwell and M. G. Edmond, "Continued Growth: Holy Cross." In *North to Share: The Sisters of St. Ann in Alaska and the Yukon Territory* [Victoria, BC: Sisters of St. Ann, 1992], 137).

22. Golden Olive Brady, field nurse, was working out of Nulato at this time. This reference is possibly to her.

23. The Richardson Highway runs between Fairbanks and Valdez and was the main overland route into the interior of the territory in 1932, with the exception of the Alaska Railroad.

24. Keaton completed the work for the benefit of her family. Entitled *No Regrets, the Autobiography of an Arctic Nurse*, it is available from her niece, Annette Tucker, 914 Fourth St., Apt. 14, Snohomish, Washington, 98291-2858. Send $22 (includes shipping).

8
I Experienced the Lord's Providing: Alma Alvida Carlson

U. S. Government Traveling Nurse Western Alaska, 1929-1947

ALMA ALVIDA CARLSON WAS born in 1896 in Moose Lake, Minnesota, to Swedish immigrants O. E. and Johanna (Sjoberg) Carlson. She attended teacher's training at State Teachers College, Duluth, Minnesota,[1] and taught for three years in Minnesota. Through her contacts with the Swedish Covenant Church, she got word of the need for and was accepted as a teacher for the Bureau of Education in the Native village of Elim, Alaska. She quickly discovered that among the Eskimos a teacher had to know much more than the three R's. Many of the villagers were almost untouched by the white man's civilization, and the Native's needs for modern medical care and simple hygiene lessons were much more urgent than academic knowledge.[2] After three years of teaching, Alma realized she would be of greater service in Alaska as a nurse, so she went back to school. She graduated from Swedish Covenant Hospital School of Nursing, Chicago, Illinois, in 1928.[3] Following graduation she spent one year at Eveleth, Minnesota, as a staff nurse and then returned to Alaska to work as a traveling nurse for the Northwest District of the Department of Interior, Office of Education, Alaska Native School and Medical Service.

In the new headquarters hospital at Kotzebue built in 1930–1931,[4] a definite program was formulated under the advisory board of R. E. Smith, MD, Alaska Native Service physician, and George Morlander, superintendent of schools of the Northwest District. Equipped with a dog team, reindeer clothing, and a sled of medical paraphernalia, Alma Carlson became the first traveling nurse in the Northwest District above the Arctic Circle. She held this position from 1930 to 1937. By 1940, the role of itinerant nursing was well established, largely through the efforts of Carlson and a few other dedicated nurses.

8.1. Alma Carlson at Noatak: "slept and ate here." Alma Carlson's Noatak home also served as the dispensary. Reprinted with permission from Alaska Nurses Association Collection (#78-27-16N), Elmer E. Rasmuson Library, University of Alaska Fairbanks.

In 1937, Alma Carlson went outside Alaska for public health nurse training at Simmons College in Boston, Massachusetts, returning to Alaska to continue service to Native villages, this time to Mountain Village[5] and Hooper Bay from 1938 to 1940.[6] She then received further training at Henry Phipps Institute in Philadelphia, Pennsylvania,[7] returning to work among the Eskimos of Akiak and Bethel in 1941–1943.[8] She was transferred to become an itinerant field nurse headquartered at Fairbanks in 1944.[9] While working out of Fairbanks she received a pay raise and personal commendation from the acting secretary of the interior, Michael W. Straus, for helping in control of an influenza epidemic in Wainwright in October 1945. Straus wrote, "Without thought of your own health and with no physician in the village, you assumed virtually the sole responsibility for diagnosing and treating the illness of the patients."[10]

In 1947, Alma Carlson left Alaska to renew her ties at home in Minnesota. To the general superintendent of the Alaska Native Service, Carlson wrote, "It is over twenty-five years since I first went into Alaskan service. I definitely feel that this is time to quit. I am going to adjust myself to work in the States, most likely not in Indian Service."[11] She resigned from the Alaska Native Service and went to work as a staff nurse at Miller Memorial Hospital in Duluth, Minnesota. She was described as "mild mannered, soft-spoken and retiring."[12]

The readers of *Jessen's Weekly* (Fairbanks) honored Carlson the year after she left Alaska by nominating her as a citizen of the Alaska Territory who had performed distinguished service. A Jessen's Weekly Distinguished Award for 1948 was presented to Alma Alvida Carlson for "unselfish service and spirit for the good of Alaska."[13]

In 1951, the Duluth *News Tribune* wrote a feature article about her and her Alaska experiences.[14] Alma Carlson died in 1975 at the age of seventy-nine. In the last year of her life, at the request of her family, she recorded her Alaska experiences onto a tape. A few of her letters had been saved and are presented here, followed by a transcription of the tape recording.[15]

Letters written by
Alma A. Carlson 1934–1947

Some team might soon be going to Kotzebue so I better get my writing as nearly completed as possible. We have had cold freezing weather, not very much snow but just barely enough for sleds. Here at Noatak the Native men are out now for reindeer corralling, marking, and counting the deer. Someday when they are in the midst of it I am planning on going out to the camp; it is only about twelve miles from the village. All the years I have been in Alaska I have not been out to the corrals when the reindeer marking has been in progress. I should not allow myself to miss out on that.

Two days ago we had a little four-year-old boy that had a close rescue from being drowned. Someone happened to look out and see an object in the river and got him out; he was unconscious but revived.

Kotzebue, Alaska, February 13, 1936

Dear Folks:

Two months or over has passed by since I last wrote you. Not only that but it was over two months that I did not have any mail until I got back here to Kotzebue three days ago. I was moving about out of reach of mail much of that time. I have covered considerable territory since last I wrote: visited three villages. Each winter I think proves busier than the one before. This one certainly is taking the prize of all of them I think. I have stayed two weeks in a village, busy from the minute I land until I pack up and am off again. The day or two on the trail has seemed good rest and relaxation. When I tell you of some of the travel experience this year though, I know you can't feature any rest about it.

It seems I am getting some experience I have not had before, some that my travels up here really would not be complete without. For the first time I have been out when the drivers have got lost and not found the village as intended, and I have had to sleep out in the open without tent or even camp stove. Going from Selawik to Buckland we had that experience. The trip should have been two days and proved four. The weather got cloudy and misty and rained part of the time (my parkey cover froze stiff like a board). For a day and a half, until it cleared, the Native driver did not know where we were. Just as soon as it cleared, landmarks told them direction. Two nights for shelter a hole in the snow was dug, sled cover thrown over for a roof. I had my sleeping bag and my feather quilt so I slept as warm as in any hotel. That quilt is a lifesaver; I can sleep in thirty-below weather without anything else over and be perfectly comfortable. I don't even go inside my sleeping bag—use that for bed and mattress. Then the skinlined coverall suit I have is certainly a good one for travel and for sleeping out. I sleep with this suit right on.

Cooking over an open fire with no camp stove was another new thing. We were fortunate to have willows to use for fuel. At no time was I uncomfortable. The weather was not cold and the trails moderately good.

At Kotzebue I plan to stay about two weeks, after that I have three northern villages to make before I am through. Spring travel is not bad; days long and pleasant.

I have now received leave of absence for one year so I am definitely planning and arranging to come out this early summer. I cannot yet state the time; maybe in June some time. I will not leave later than the first boat which is in mid June. I may, if I get through earlier, take a plane by way of Fairbanks and come earlier. My plans still are for making the trip to Sweden, and I plan if possible to get a boat from New York latter part of July—that is if war does not start to make such trips inadvisable. I look forward to that trip; it's only too bad that it all has to be so much along the travel line. I get so much travel, travel, and more travel that I can almost get a bit fed up on it. But of course this will be a different type of travel.

It is not going to be altogether easy to pull up roots and leave here; it seems I am so rooted that it will be hard to unroot. Each year I am getting more and more so, too. But I believe it is time that I do so now, that is, to pack up and leave.

This year we have more snow, higher drifts than I have ever seen. We have had lots of windy stormy weather. Some drifts are up as high as the upstairs windows. To go out anywhere in the village is like going mountain climbing. One does not care to go out just for walks.

Marshall, Alaska, August 18, 1938

Dear Folks:

It may be about time that I give you all a call again. I have not since I got back written any circular letter. Now I shall give you all a copy and after that I do not promise to give any more than I get. For about one year at least now, I know I am going to be so occupied that to settle down and write may not always be so easy although I suppose I ought to have some new things now that I am in new territory. At present I am out on my first tour, doing my first village, and does it seem good to be doing a job of my own again, with my own plans and my own program.

I arrived at Mountain Village August 1; made the trip in
better time than I had dared count on; and at that I had to
stay in St. Michaels three days waiting for a riverboat. The
whole trip went smoothly. I enjoyed it. We came through
Nome, spent one day there, so I had time to visit some of the
people I know there. On the boat we had some very enjoyable
people: we had a tourist from New York who is a radio singer
and sings religious selections over the national broadcast; with
him was a New York millionaire. I saw quite a bit of him too
but did not know he was a millionaire until the last two days.

When I got to Mountain Village I pitched my tent.
Quarters are crowded at the hospital; I would have to have
stayed at the roadhouse, so better than that I pitched a tent.
Without a doubt I will be using my tent a good deal up here.

There is a very good doctor at Mt. Village, a rather young
fellow; the only trouble with him he is newly married and
has a most spoiled impossible wife; she is very discontented
with the country and will no doubt be leaving; that of course
will mean that he too in time will be going. He is good and I
would like to see him stay with us.

We had a visit from Dr. Worley, the medical director,
which was of interest; he is a very fine person. I feel glad to
have met him and to have so favorable an impression of him.
He gave me recognition for the work done and gave me liberal
leeway for working out my district programs.

I have been in Marshall four days. I came here by mail boat
and expect to get away tomorrow again by the mail boat on
up farther to Anvik and points between. The mail boats are
very comfortable to travel on. They have a cabin and comfortable quarters so no hardship about that travel. The two mail
boats meet here for the upper and lower Yukon. The villages
along the Yukon are very very small, just a few Native families in each; not many whites either. But the Natives that I
have seen are really more advanced in their methods of living

than are those in the North; they speak good English, most of them have two-roomed cabins, quite clean. So to me there is nothing primitive about this section; but I am told that I have that coming down in the Hooper Bay country. I plan to go there in about a month from now: go there by boat and then stay until I can get out by dog team. I can go by river channels from Mt. Village to Hooper Bay; I am going with a trader's family.

When it comes to the work, to the Natives, and the conditions in general, I do not feel any different about it than I did at Kotzebue. In about a day's time I have made working acquaintance with the Natives and can be in full swing. The Natives here are as keen as any to have physical examinations, to have teeth pulled and fixed. If you can pull a tooth without too much hurting you are all set, you can count on getting plenty of customers.

We have had a lot of rainy weather since I got here. It is not at all cold, almost as warm as rainy days in Duluth. I have been going around with just a sweater when I go out. I believe I am going to notice a little difference in climate between here and Kotzebue. There are heaps of blueberries this year. Coming here on the mail boat we were anchored one evening about seven o'clock. So I took a gallon pail and went up on the hills and picked berries and filled my pail in about 1 ½ hours. There are a lot around Marshall but it has rained ever since I got here, so I have not been out. Gardens grow quite well here; at Mt. Village the soil is less favorable so the gardens do not amount to so much.

If I tell you how I am living at Marshall you will have a shock. I am sleeping and eating with one old widower and having my office and working quarters with another; both are old timers in the country. They are tickled to have me favor them by using their quarters, I think. There is a so-called hotel here, run by white folks, but that would cost me about

$4 a day and there would be no freedom to do the Native work around there, so I prefer to get a simpler hang-out. The fact that I am an old-timer, as they say, gives me the prestige of doing almost anything without shocking the public. There is a place here I expect to board after this, but the wife is not at home just now—this is Eric Johnson's place.

The Yukon as far up as I have gone so far is not forested except for quite sturdy willows, and around here there are cottonwood and some birch. On up farther I understand there are supposed to be fir trees.

I think I am going to like the country around here. I have met with greatest courtesy so far. The Marshall folks, there are a few whites here, have been most accommodating. There has been some discussion of making this place the nurses' headquarters. The villagers are very desirous of having it so, so maybe there is some cause for all the courtesy too, playing up to me. I am supposed to make a decision for headquarters this trip. I doubt I want it here since there are too few Natives right here; I would rather have it at Mt. Village where the hospital is. There is no building at Mt. Village so maybe I'll get to work and have one built for myself: have a log cabin made.

Enough for this time.

Kwiguk, Alaska, January 5, 1939

Dear Folks:

I do not feel very letter ambitious tonight but the mail plane is expected to pass through here tomorrow so I better get a little written and sent. It may be some time before I get a chance to send again, not till I get back to Hooper Bay.

I am out on one of my winter tours. I left Hooper Bay one month ago, December 5. I have covered a lot of ground in this time; am now on the return back to Hooper Bay.

Christmas I spent with the teachers, Starritts, down on the lower Yukon. Mrs. Starritt is the teacher who worked with me last summer; we lived all summer together in my eight-by-ten-foot tent. So it was a most pleasant place to spend Christmas, the place I preferred most to be at. I had a pleasant time although I was busy most of the time; I was there two weeks.

A tour in this part of the country is rather strenuous. It is not the trips that prove so hard; they are shorter and easier than up North. But the villages are so small I can plan to stay only about a day, then move on. Often I get in in the afternoon to a place and go right to work seeing the people, treating, and teeth pulling. Often I go on the next day and same routine. This soon taxes one's pep and strength. I shall be glad to get back to Hooper Bay where I will be staying still for a few weeks, probably a couple of months, before traveling again.

This is proving a very sickly winter; the measles is sweeping the country. I seem to be tracking right behind it; I get the after-effects to contend with. The TB patients seem to succumb quickly; there have been a lot of deaths all over the districts. I hear it is in Hooper Bay now so I will get back there in time for the aftermath, too. Practically everybody under forty years gets it, but those over forty do not. Indications are that the last measles epidemic was in 1900.

The weather has been ideal to travel; I have not had any bad trips all this time; not much snow either and very little wind. So in that respect I have been fortunate to date. I have had one plane trip and saved myself about three days dog teaming thereby. Twenty minutes after I got out of the plane it was forced down, out of gas, and the pilot had to walk in to St. Michaels. A few days after that the owner of this plane company was wrecked in a plane, killed. He is a pilot that I know very well and have flown with; quite a sad accident. Dog teams are still the safest in the long run, slow but sure.

This is rather short letter, but let it go at that.

Hooper Bay, Alaska, May 21, 1939

Dear Folks:

No prospect of getting any mail out for a few weeks yet, but it may be a good idea to get a starter on a letter and add on to it at a later date. The spring is late this year; it does not seem late to me here since I am used to the Kotzebue seasons which are reported a month later than here. The spring here this year seems to me about same as up there. We are having warm thawing weather now, but that has been for only a short time, so there are still big drifts. But there are bare spots and water puddles.

This is proving a very interesting stay to me. I have not yet seen Hooper Bay as it really is; I have not seen it uncovered of snow. The igloos were all snowed under when I came. They still are partially. Every day I go out the village has changed appearance: new igloos visible.

The village truly is unique, something different from what I have experienced before. Except for a very few log cabins, the igloos are sod and mud. They remind me a lot of those moss houses we children used to construct in the early spring. The construction is a lot on the same plan; the windows are skylights. How much of the dwelling is underground and how much above I cannot yet tell since the snow is still packed rather deep around them. To me they are fascinating. As to cleanliness it varies, on the whole far better than I had been prepared for. Some are quite clean, a few still rather messy. But when the women put forth the effort to do a cleanup they can do it pretty well. I have started a project of having health visitors go around on Saturday. They make inspection on sanitation and so on; this helps to get them to clean up at least once a week. Had I to live in the same amount of space with as many occupants I wonder how much better I would do. There are in places eight to ten persons in one small room, smaller than most of our ordinary bedrooms.

But except when it storms the majority of the family spend their time outdoors and only go in to eat and sleep. Even for sleeping there is what they call a "kasheega" the "men's house." This is a large public gathering place for the men. Here the old widowers, bachelors, and others who have no room spend their time, sleep, and so on. It isn't such a bad place, large and roomy and in fair condition. The men too go here for baths. I wish the custom was for women and children, too, to have a community house to bathe in.

There are quite a number of new things to see and observe. The other day I was called to treat a hot water burn; when I got there first aid-application of blood from a seal had been applied. This is a new Native treatment I have not heard of before; to me it appeared a rather good one at that: there was a coagulation protecting the scald underneath. I am on my sixth week here now; I am afraid time will come too soon when I have to start out on my travel tour again. Although I really have no white associates, I have not missed that phase a bit. I have enough Native visitors daily to keep me from getting lonesome or finding the place too quiet. The Catholic priest I see about once a week, occasionally he comes here and at times I go to call on him. He has a radio sending set so we have outside communication.

Oscar Andrewak, the Mission missionary, got married recently. He married a widow from Mt. Village, a very fine person. Oscar was married to Elizabeth Wilson but she left him and got divorced. He is a very fine agreeable person. Today I had the family for afternoon coffee.

Hooper Bay, Alaska, October 21, 1939

Dear Folks:

I do not know if mail will go out soon or not; the government boat is probably coming in a day or days. Boat season is a bit longer here than up North, they can still come unless it gets too stormy. We have snow on the ground and small streams are frozen but the ocean is still clear of ice.

I have been back here nearly three weeks; I came the second. Now this means back home, I presume, since this is my headquarters. I moved all my things from Mountain Village here. Seems nice to be where my things are, even though I have not a house as yet to put them in. Imagine landing here with not a place to put things, besides what I have personally. The office sent me a full supply of furniture, stoves, bed, dresser, dishes, rug, and no provision for a house.

The new school building is under construction, a large fine building; but it does not include nurses' quarters in the plans. There is a room, however, that may be allowed for my use eventually.

At the present time I am living in a ten by twelve tent. I may have to live in it for some weeks yet if it proves possible to do so. It is well constructed, has a frame affair, floor, door. So with continual heat it has so far been comfortable. I have an oil heater so heat is continuous and even. I have it quite cozy. I even got a radio but so far have not been able to get it to work; I bought it second hand. It may be the aerials that are no good. The village is responsive, with a little help in teaching them how to do things and how to use resources, they go ahead at a good rate. The soap-making project has done a lot I think; they can bring in their oil and get just as much soap as they choose. With soap this way clothes have shown themselves much cleaner.

I continue to like it here as well as ever, in fact I think I like this place the best of the villages in my district.

There is a school population of close to eighty children, so you see it is a field to work in. All the villages along the Yukon are very small and getting smaller too. Schools formerly open have closed in places and more may close I am afraid since the children are so few. But surprisingly enough, off in the district that is comparatively more primitive, the population is increasing by leaps and bounds.

I do not know how large or small a territory I will have to cover this year; another nurse is supposed to come and take half of my district but to date no one has come. It is hard to get public health nurses for Alaska it seems.

I have had no mail for a long time, five or six weeks. It may be some time yet before any gets here too, all depends on the season if it freezes soon so dog teams can travel.

Hooper Bay, Alaska, April 23, 1940

Dear Folks:

No chance that I know of at present to get mail out but it is not a bad idea to have a letter started and add on to it now and then. There too could be the possibility all of a sudden of a plane coming in: I never know when I may have to call for one.

We have Hooper Bay quarantined for diphtheria—should I run short on antitoxin I would have to wire for more.

I wrote you from Nelson Island, at that time waiting for a plane to come. It took four days before the weather was such that the plane could fly. By that time three of the diphtheria cases had died and the two remaining were on the verge of going: the antitoxin saved one but one died in spite of it; it proved too late. The one that made it did so by the closest margin possible. I thought he was going when suddenly he began to rally. One more case developed the day after the plane came, but I had antitoxin and that proved an entirely different course of affairs.

April 6 a plane brought another nurse to relieve me and the plane took me back to Hooper Bay since there were suspicious cases here. Two days after my arrival cases began to sprout and I had to clap down a rigid quarantine of whole village. To date we have had eleven cases since I came back, and there had been a few, probably about four I figure, before I got here. It appears we have the cases cornered in five homes—I hope we can keep it thus. I have antitoxin to give at the onset so all has gone easily and smoothly. The eleven here have not caused me the alarm and trouble each one did at Nelson Island.

The Nelson Island experience is something I hope to never experience again. It worked like wildfire; patients bad and gone before you knew what was happening. Two children struggled all night for breath like drowning persons before death relieved them. Out of the four deaths three were in one family; this family had five children to begin with; in six days only two left.

We have been unable to trace any source of the infection. no villages or camps around have had similar cases. Hooper Bay got it from there. A Native was over there from here visiting about the time it started there. He was sick two days after he returned here.

Now I have another big worry and problem: I fear Scammon Bay too has cases. I sent one team over to get reports; ten were having sore throat and swollen glands but no one then had been alarmingly bad. But symptoms indicate the same thing.

This is the stand-still period—almost no travel of any kind possible. Planes with a doctor from Bethel have tried to come to investigate Scammon Bay but have not been able to make it. A plane arrangement was all made and they were to come and pick me up and we, doctor and I, fly to parts of my district that might be affected, but landing conditions stopped this plan.

I have a Native that has gone by kayak now: he was to go along the edge of the shore ice. He has not yet returned and we are all anxious for reports.

This has been a strenuous epidemic year: first measles with its heavy toll and now this.

To keep a village like Hooper Bay quarantined is a strain; their huts are so close together and such a mob of them. I have restricted all home visiting or group playing; every family near his own door step. It is two weeks since we clamped down, and as a whole it is working quite smoothly now. I had to use a few severe measures before I got the upper hand but believe I got it. I actually locked a number up from leaving their house at all and put one boy in a locked shed a while—let others understand that the shed would be used if quarantine was not observed. The mass of them took warning so no more lock-ups were needed. The doctor told me I could go to any extreme I wanted to to enforce quarantine.

Orders are to keep quarantine until sixteen days after the onset of the last case. This is the fourth day since last one, and we never know when there may be more beginning. These five homes still have many that may get it.

Dr. White at Bethel has a radio phone so he keeps daily contacts. I can send a message at noon and he replies at 8 P.M. so this proves a great help.

Oh, yes, the teacher at Nelson Island got the diphtheria the day after I left. It would have been to all of us a terrific worry and tragedy if he had come down during that spell when weather did not permit planes to come—he got sick one day after the arrival of the antitoxin. He had an acute onset, and I fear there might have been tragedy without it. In all there were eight cases over there—four out of the eight dead.

I gave myself toxoid in 1934, and this probably has been a saving feature for me. I know I must have swallowed plenty of germs, the way I was coughed at by those acute cases. I sat one whole night by the boy who pulled through, holding his nostrils to control nose bleed. The only way I could control it was to sit and hold it with my fingers.

We are having the earliest breakup the country has had for twenty-one years. The big Tanana breakup occurred two days ago. That is the one that has the big pool—$90,000 this year to the nearest guesser, who proved to be a woman from Anchorage. She guessed by one minute off. Very little snow left here, weather warm.

May 17

More than three weeks have passed since I started to write. Never did I realize what was close before me then. Good thing we do not know beforehand. Here I am at the Bethel hospital and have had my first day out of bed for seventeen days; I have been here at the hospital eleven days. May 1 I developed diphtheria myself. I had put most of the Schultz family in bed with it just previous, including Mrs. Schultz. Mr. Schultz, Grandma, and one little girl are the only ones up and about.

I saw that I could not carry on and had to go to bed; I had a bad pulse before I gave in to go to bed so I sent a call to Bethel for nursing relief. The doctor came over. He stayed four days. At the end of that time the Schultzs were all responding well, but I knew I was not. I had had two nights with heart attacks when I was as close to going as I ever expect to be and still remain. My pulse was just the barest little trickle, breathing the greatest labor, and I had a sinking out feeling. Had I not had antitoxin taken I am positive as can be that I would never have made it, but no doubt I had not taken large enough dose to support me.

Doctor had to go back so I suggested I be taken to the hospital. I felt I was not doing well although he could not make out anything specific on me and thought I would be all right. But I kept having sinking out spells every time I would relax, my pulse soft and slow, varying in volume. It all was too much like mamma was to suit my fancy. Absolute rest and quiet and hospital care I knew would be my only saving feature. It took eight days in the hospital before my pulse changed and as soon as it did I felt like a new person come to life. For four days now I have been fine, pulse good, so I've been up for a while and felt fine.

This sick experience without a doubt has been a good lesson. I know life a little better from the patients' point of view. I know what it is to not have one speck of strength left of your own—I was carried out of Hooper Bay on a stretcher to the plane. And I know too the grand and glorious feeling of strength returning.

Bethel hospital is new opened this winter; it has forty beds. For Alaska it is quite a fine little hospital, better than any of the others. There are four graduate nurses, besides some Native helpers. After I have come to feeling better I have had quite an interesting time with the nice group of workers here. One of the nurses is a sincere Christian, comes from Moodys. The mission at Bethel is the Moravian; I have met two of the missionaries, seemingly very fine, sincere type of people.

From here when recuperated I plan to take a plane to Mt. Village, then on into lower Yukon fish camps for the summer work.

While my heart was acting up so badly I had visions of myself through with hard work. I feared I would be left a bird with a broken pinion—but from all indications now I am not at least yet showing anything for chronic alarm.

Hooper Bay, Alaska, September 22, 1940

Dear Folks:

Within the week no doubt we will have a chance to send out mail; we are expecting a mail boat soon. We may even have a plane possibly. Mrs. Schultz's mother is supposedly on her way back and would have to fly here we think.

Hooper Bay school is in progress. This year they have three teachers, Mr. and Mrs. Schultz and a new teacher, a half-breed woman who came as assistant. There are over seventy children in school. It surely is fine to have three teachers.

This new teacher has been married and has a six-year-old boy with her. Their food supplies have not come yet so they have been cooking and eating with me. I am enjoying having them; she is a very fine person to have around, interesting and helps me a lot: does most of my cooking for me. She reminds me a lot of Nelly Dexter when she was with me.

There is always plenty of work to be found to do in Hooper Bay. I spend some of my time in sewing activities both with school groups and with the women [Figure 8.2].

To teach and supervise sewing is about the last thing I ever expected myself to do. But I find myself able to do quite a bit along that line when I need to. These people need just that type of training: their clothes have been miserable appearing. To make a little go a long way we need to show them how to sew more. We have them sewing most of the boys' overalls for example. They can make two pair for what one pair costs ready made. They are getting so they look fairly neatly and cleanly dressed around here. We simply will not tolerate too much filth. That is the only way to get effect, namely, not to tolerate it otherwise.

The Schultzs surely are a God-send to this village. The more I work with them the more I appreciate them. I would not trade them for any others, their temperaments and mine match up very well, and our ideas of work coincide. They are fine Christian people so we have common grounds there too. It is always a home-like atmosphere around here. When I have been away a few weeks I look forward to getting back.

Without a doubt we still have the diphtheria going here. There have been mild throat cases right along this summer, but none acute enough to cause alarm. But now recently I have had a few very acute throats to care for, the very same kinds that caused deaths last spring on Nelson Island. I have had antitoxin to give which has given immediate effect. One woman was so bad when I was first called I did not think she was going to live, but antitoxin without a doubt pulled her through.

We have put on a regular campaign to get at the cause of continued cases. By going after sanitation I believe we are going to tread it down. If sanitation and control of cases does not do it I figure there must be active carriers that keep it going, in which case I intend to howl enough and loud enough to get authorities in here to find the trouble makers.

If cases continue and no help is sent, I simply will not carry on by myself, it is too much risk. I have so far been Schick negative, no doubt due to the antitoxin I took, but if this wears off and I find myself Schick positive and there are active cases going on I will not take the risk of staying. I have no desire to risk going through again what I did last spring.

8.2. Sewing class. Courtesy of Robert Stevens (Ann Taube Album), Seattle, Washington.

But I have good hopes of having it under control with the measures we have taken. There have been eight very definite cases since I came back here, in one month's time. That is too much to suit me. I do not wish conditions to turn out so that I should have to feel that I should not risk staying. I know I would not be out of here long before I would be yearning to be back again.

I have been getting my health and former vigor back quite readily. I am at present the best I have been since I was sick. I still take a little precaution not to overdo but as a whole I am in pretty good shape, and I surely wish to remain so.

With my best regards to you all.

Bethel, Alaska, July 30, 1941

Dear Folks:

I have had letters from some of you since I last wrote, from Dad, Annie, and Agnes. Mail comes once a week here at Bethel. I am still at Bethel. I am helping out in the hospital since they are short a nurse and have been somewhat busy. So I have not yet seen my home-to-be in Akiak.

I thoroughly enjoy this hospital duty for a change. It seems so much easier and has so much less responsibility in connection with it than does the work when I am out in my own field. I actually wish I could spend a year staying in a place like this and not travel, but I know such a request would not be granted. It is too hard to get field nurses.

I am perfectly happy to be back here when I hear of the heat in the States. I appreciate the coolness here. It proves comfortably warm; however, I have been using my summer coat most of the time. For over a week's time we have been picking ripe blueberries so you see the season is not late; imagine berries in July. I doubt Minnesota has blueberries by now.

We have our new doctor here now, Dr. Langsam.[16] He transferred from Juneau where he has been since last March when he came from New York City. We are most pleased with him. He gives the impression of thoroughly knowing his field of work, is very ambitious and hard working, and has a pleasing personality. However, the best part to me is that as far as I can judge him he is a sincere Christian. He does not say a lot, but his actions speak more than words. He neither smokes nor drinks and takes an interest in going to church. I assure you it is to me a treat to have that type of a person to work with for a change. There are so many of the other kind always.

The Moravian mission work here I find very much to my liking. There are some mighty fine missionary families in this field, about the best in type that I have met up with in the Alaska work, good sincere evangelical people. One family I have met are Norwegian; some of them I understand are German. Dr. Langsam, I have been informed, is of German descent. He is Lutheran. In my district I will have some villages that are Greek Catholic, some Roman Catholic, and some Moravian.

Much to my dismay I find that diphtheria is not all gone out of the district. We have at the hospital now a case that was an acute type, just like those that I had in Hooper Bay last year. I have seen two mild cases, so mild they were not diagnosed as diphtheria but which I recognize like our mild cases we had over there. I assure you I am now glad I went out for my own immunization and that I had two negative Schick tests. It sure makes me feel a lot more at ease around here. I had expected this infection gone by now, and it was to me most disappointing to find it is still here. I am so tired of these throat cases, to have to have the thought ever in mind with every case of sore throat that it might be diphtheria, and to have to try to judge whether or not it is so—this

without being able to take cultures as can be done in the
States. Some cases are so very mild while others develop like
wildfire.

Love to you all.

Tape Recording (July, 1975) by Alma A. Carlson

IF A PERSON IN ALASKA has an ambition to write I have often
said such a writing should be made during the first year
or so while up there. ... I did what I considered it my duty
to do. But my brother Arvin and some other family members
have urged and pressured me to make a record, thus to pre-
serve some of the narratives about my experiences, especially
those relating to my work as a U.S. government traveling
nurse. I do recognize now that I did have some rather unique
ones. To me it was, at the time, merely an urgency to meet the
needs of the people who had no one else to resort to for help.
Instead of writing, I have consented to put the data on tape.
To me, it is easier to talk than to try to write a book. David,
my brother, has the machine and a tape and is willing to
coach me. It will be my first attempt to try to do this, relating
about Alaska experiences. I kept no diary, so I have to write
from what I remember. It will not be in a chronological order,
but rather according to subject matter.

What motive did I have for going to Alaska? The only such
that I can recall was that Christian work in general was my
desire. Teaching, at the time, was my profession. I had had
three years of elementary school work in Minnesota. Elim,
Alaska, one of our Covenant mission villages,[17] needed a
government teacher. It was preferable to get someone mis-
sion-interested, if possible, in order to have better harmony.
If the teachers and missioners were not like-minded, friction
situations often resulted. Reverend L. E. Ost was our missionary at Elim. It was Reverend Axel Ost, a brother to L. E. Ost,

who first approached me—he thought I would be a suitable teacher candidate. He wrote to the Alaska U.S. Service recommending me and urged me to give the matter prayerful consideration. This I did. At that time I was teaching in Braham, Minnesota. I know what it feels like to have a pressuring call from the Lord to do something. I, too, experienced that. As soon as I proved willing and mailed my application for the teaching job, all hindrances were removed. I got the appointment and in the early fall was on my way to Elim.

Elim was a very typical small Eskimo village on the Bering Sea coast. The school was a two-room elementary one with grades one through six. I had a half-breed Native girl as assistant. My sister Annie was there as missionary assistant to the Reverend Ost through the first winter. This was a help to me to get myself adjusted to Alaska living. She had had some practical nurses' training, so while she was in Elim she did the needed health services in the village. Teachers were supposed to do this, besides the usual classroom teaching. After she left, the responsibility was mine. Teachers were given a medical handbook on first aid[18] and some medical supplies to use and dispense. I had no training for this, so I cleared out the medicine shelves of all bottles and boxes I did not know the use for. I picked out the few things I did know, such as iodine, Mercurochrome, and laxatives such as castor oil (Eskimos like castor oil), cascara[19] pills, and liniment. Cod liver oil was dispensed quite freely. And cough medicines. I studied the book.

After three years of this I decided to come home to the States and take the nurses' training course at the Swedish Covenant Hospital in Chicago. I enrolled in 1925 and graduated in 1928. My aim was to go back to Alaska as a teacher, better prepared for the duties involved. The three years of teaching at Elim proved to be a valuable aid for what ultimately I now consider as the most important contribution I may have made to Alaska. The U.S. Bureau of Alaska Native Affairs offered me the appointment to return, not as a teacher, but as a traveling nurse. Appeals had come from Kotzebue from the superintendent of the government schools, with a petition from teachers asking for a traveling nursing service.

I was to have headquarters at Kotzebue, where there would be a doctor stationed. My district was to be composed of twelve villages. The Natives had offered to provide dog team transportation free. My salary of $125 a month for an eight-month's term was paid out of educational funds at first. Eventually, after the travel program proved itself a success, medical appropriations from Washington, D.C., were made to cover my salary, travel expenses, and a $3 per diem. The Traveling Nursing Service was expanded to include more villages, and two more appointments were made for nurses to the Arctic.[20] The Lord, I recognized, was definitely leading, guiding, and giving me His protective care. Without Him I would not have been able to meet the challenges I encountered. Now I shall relate some of the more impressive experiences.

Here is one experience that has left a strong impression upon me. I'm going to call it "Eskimo Wisdom." In Alaska, one of my projects as a U.S. public health nurse was to give instruction classes to adult Natives about diet and foods. One impressive incident happened at Wainwright, a village above the Arctic Circle in polar bear land. My aim was to encourage the Natives to make more use of their own available foods. I was stressing liver because of its vitamin value. The Eskimos positively refused to eat polar bear liver. I believed this was only a Native taboo that had been established, so I asked for a volunteer to bring me a piece of polar bear liver and I would eat it. One man volunteered. But the next day he came and told me that the village council forbade him to bring me the liver because such liver would make the hair fall out. It was a poison. I did not get to try it and I said no more about it. Just recently, in 1974, I was reading the *Encyclopedia for Healthful Living* by J. I. Rodale regarding vitamin A. I quote, "Polar bear is richer in vitamin A than any other substance. Foolhardy explorers in Arctic regions who have ignored warnings and eaten polar liver have suffered from vitamin A poisoning. Becknell and Prescott, in their book *Vitamins in Medicine,* tell us that three quarters of a pound of this liver may contain as much as seven to eight million units of vitamin A." Eskimo wisdom that I heeded possibly saved me from the tragic experience that some of the Arctic explorers had experienced.

The Eskimos' thinking needs to be on conservation, not to be wasteful. This was true even of water. They had no piped water faucets, so rain, rivers, even melted snow often was their source of supply. They could not dig wells because of the permafrost. During one of my summer visits to a village, I was occupying the teacher's residence. It rained and the attic roof developed a leak. I asked an Eskimo man to go upstairs and put a tub under the leaking area. He returned, and when asked about the job done he said yes, he put the tub as I had asked him to do and, he said, he had made the hole larger for me. I had many humorous-natured stories intermingled with the more serious ones. Life in Alaska was not all drab.

Water is a very essential part of life for all of us. Our very existence depends on it. In Alaska it was difficult to get it in many villages, especially those along the coast if there were no freshwater lakes or streams. The very sanitation of the homes was affected without water and soap. How could clothes be washed and the floors scrubbed and baths be taken? Hooper Bay, located in the lower Yukon on the coast, had, at the time of my first visit, the reputation of being the dirtiest, smelliest village in Alaska. I found the village to be just as bad as the reports indicated. I asked myself, "why?" I soon recognized that soap and water was needed. Soap was almost a luxury article. It was a two-day trip to the nearest trading post and the price of soap was high. Solution—I found a whole case of lye in the school attic. The Natives had plenty of seal oil. On the lye cans was a formula for soap making. I practiced until I got a suitable soap result. It was a soft soap. Lysol was added to it. Now the Natives could bring seal oil in exchange and get lye and Lysol. Soap was made by the tubfuls at school. Immediately, a change in cleanliness resulted.

Now for a better water supply. They had to depend on the melting ice and snow in winter and rain in summer. They were carrying water in small pail buckets. Even to melt the snow and ice was a problem. Hooper Bay is a barren, treeless region. Driftwood was the main fuel supply and their stoves were just small oil drums cut in half. I sent a letter to government headquarters in the States, requesting a supply of empty oil drums to be brought to Hooper Bay on the next summer's first boat, one for each home. My request was honored. Now snow and ice could be constantly refilled in these tanks, be melting, so there need be no excuse not to have water. The Natives were asked to do some village improvement work to make them feel they had paid for the tanks. The teachers and I supervised sewing classes so the mothers could come and use sewing machines we had secured for the schools. These were hand-operated machines. Even boys' overalls were made.

Every child was expected to have at least two changes of clothing so they had one to wear while one was washed. The raggedy situation of the school children improved: cleaner clothes and also cleaner homes. A program for delousing was also attacked. Some children's heads were crawling with lice. From the school dispensary we furnished kerosene for shampooing the hair. This kills the lice. To begin with, we did the delousing right in the schoolroom, including cutting the hair.

Periodic head inspections were made. Eventually, the parents were made responsible to send the children clean to school, including the heads. Since I left Alaska someone gave me a gratifying report that Hooper Bay is one of the cleanest villages now. Soap and water was the solution.

One service that became a very major part of my work while traveling in the Native villages was the large number of decayed teeth [see Figure 8.3], aching ones, that had to be extracted. This was a service I had not expected and that I had had no previous training for, except that I knew aseptic technique, which of course is, even in pulling teeth, an essential part. The need faced me immediately upon arriving in Kotzebue and in the absence of the doctor. When he came back to Kotzebue he helped to prepare me with instruments—forceps for extractions and an elevator to pick out any broken-off roots, as well as the use of Novocain for pain. The conditions of teeth seemed related to the availability of grocery store foods. Villages that had such stores selling white flour, sugar, and candy had far more decayed teeth than the villages that had to go by dog team one or two day's travel to get the supplies of flour and so forth. In one village located on the Arctic Coast that had no store within reasonable reach, the teeth were almost perfect. Practically no one needed extractions. In most villages, on the average, I would have several hundred teeth to pull, especially the first few years, until I got the mess cleaned out. One year I kept count of teeth extracted. I got up to the number two thousand, then I quit counting. Dr. Smith had me supplied with dental cement and taught me to put in simple fillings in teeth that had only small holes. This, too, probably helped to save on future decayed teeth and toothaches. From the very beginning I stressed the use of the Native foods in preference to the store foods.

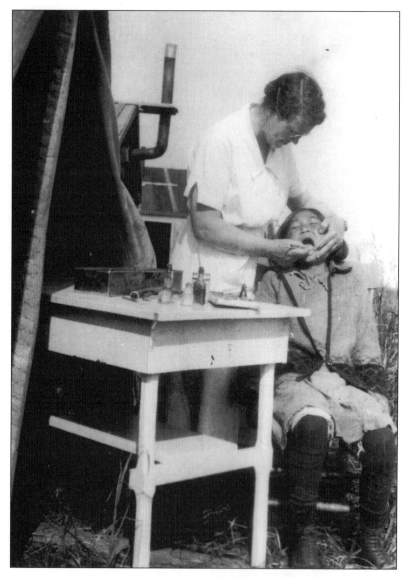

8.3. Alma Carlson giving dental care. Reprinted with permission, Alaska and Polar Region Archives, Elmer E. Rasmuson Library, University of Alaska Fairbanks, Alaska Nurses Association Collection (#84-051-745).

We had a progressive program of having health classes for all ages, adults as well as the school children. In one small village on the Kobuk, the trader, a white man, had been a blacksmith before coming to Alaska. I found that occasionally, when a Native had an intolerable toothache, the trader had a pair of pliers he pulled teeth with. He seemed to be a reliable first aid helper so I supplied him with a better instrument to use—a dental forceps. The Natives did have some crude methods of their own to get a tooth out or to stop pain. I never saw it practiced, but one method was to stick a red-hot pointed instrument, for example, a heated nail, into the cavity of the aching tooth. Apparently, this stopped the pain because it killed the nerve. The very old people had better teeth than the younger generation. They had eaten only Native foods during their childhood. The women's teeth could be almost perfect except some of them had teeth worn down to the gums from chewing skin to make mukluks.

Now I shall relate one event. This one should be the prize winner: a baby born by cesarean section. This means taken by abdominal incision, by surgery. I had been in Kotzebue only a short time, a matter of a few weeks, getting organized to start my nursing traveling work. Dr. Smith, who was to be my medical advisor and helper, to plan my work, had been on a medical boat tour on the Yukon, and while there had himself gone through an emergency appendix operation, so he had not yet returned to his Kotzebue station. So I was a lone nurse, temporarily in charge of all medical work. A Native mother went into birth labor and she had complications. She could not deliver the baby. The situation became very critical. Time and time again I experienced the Lord's providing when desperate needs arose. The promise, "Call upon me and I shall deliver thee" was one I found frequent need to resort to.

Usually, no plane service was available to depend on. Occasionally, some small plane would arrive to bring in some passenger. That is what happened. A plane bringing in a teacher couple whose destination was an inland village had to be landed and left at Kotzebue because of freezing conditions to await dog-team travel after the inlet waters would freeze up. Who was this teacher? A messenger came running to tell me—the teacher is a Dr. Gazelle. On a most critical day, here I was provided with a doctor, was given the opportunity to get some medical consultation and help. He confirmed what I feared to be the case, that surgical delivery of the baby was a necessity to save the life of the mother and baby. We had no hospital in Kotzebue. The construction was just starting on a building for that purpose. I was using an old three-room house for a dispensary and for my living quarters. There were no usual surgical supplies to resort to.

After considerable consultation with Dr. Gazelle I asked him, "What do you think we should do?" He was very concerned, pacing the floor. He answered, "I don't know what to do. Only one thing I do know: I'm not going to let the patient die." Together we searched the place to see what could be found if we could and should attempt surgical delivery. We found a scalpel, a few forceps, some tubes of catgut—we did not know how old they may have been—and fortunately, some rubber gloves. These supplies and some more, including gowns and sheets, had been transferred from a discontinued hospital in another village, Noorvik, which is now closed. It seemed we had the very most meager things needed. Sterilization of supplies could be done in a large kitchen pressure cooker. We located a few cans of ether.

Now for making up a surgical team. The district superintendent of schools had his home in Kotzebue. I gave him a quick, short course in giving the ether anesthesia. I had to be the surgical assistant to Dr. Gazelle. Two Eskimo girls, aides, were prepared with gowns that had been sterilized in the pressure cooker. All of us who were immediate assistants had sterilized garb and gloves. We were meticulous about sterile technique to the best of our ability. One girl was made ready to hand us the instruments, and one ready to take over the expected baby. We proceeded. All went well. We had a live baby and a live mother. No complications.

The surgery confirmed what we anticipated, a placenta previa, one that could not have gone through a normal delivery without surgical help. The mother and the baby girl, after a short stay at our dispensary, went home to a happy, grateful family in Kotzebue. I am sure those of you who have listened to this related experience will agree with me. We could not have succeeded in doing what we did, or even have dared the adventure, if it had not been propelled and actually done through us under the direct guidance of the Lord. He must have had His guardian angels right there by us, directing us.

Dr. Gazelle and wife completed one term of teaching in Alaska. Before leaving, they had a baby boy born to them. I heard no more of them until about fifteen years later. I was visiting in Seattle when one Sunday afternoon I was walking in a large park with a friend, and I came face to face with a person I felt I recognized. We both stopped and stared. I said, "Oh, Dr. Gazelle," and he said, "Aren't you Miss Carlson?" We had good reason to remember one another from our mutual Alaska experience.

No better prelude could have happened than that of a successful surgical delivery of the baby and that it occurred before I started on my new assignment, serving as a traveling nurse. Naturally, this had the effect of establishing among the Native people more trust and confidence in the newly arrived nurse. It was an unusual situation and an unusually favorable outcome. Dr. Smith returned to Kotzebue soon after and

I could then leave to start out on my first traveling schedule. I went by dog-team to an inland village, Noorvik, on the Kobuk.

[At this point there is a gap in the tape. She apparently refers to the death of one or two mothers after childbirth] ... both of the mothers. She had used the same fur skin to lie on for both patients at delivery. It was the Native custom to use an old skin. The midwives had very little concern for the need of cleanliness. The teachers and the Natives were, on my arrival, very panicky about what had happened. This incident prepared the way for me to immediately start a midwife training program to attack the cleanliness aspect. What was needed was to get younger women, the more trainable kind, who would at first work with the older ones. Eventually these, the younger ones, became the recognized practicing helpers. The Natives themselves soon eliminated the old-fashioned ones.

A box was made up with the most essential supplies and was kept at the teacher's quarters, in readiness for the midwife's use. It got to be so that the teachers always knew when a baby was soon expected in a home because some member of the family would come to get the box. The box contained soap, rubber gloves, Lysol, string for cord tying, and mercurochrome to apply to the cut cord area. The Native's practice had been to put ashes on the cord, this probably was not too unsafe, ashes would be quite sterile. [The box also had] silver nitrate to drop in the baby's eyes and some clean pads for the mother. Ropes were put in the box to pull on to replace the midwife's rather harsh method of belly pushing. Very methodical instructions and demonstrations were used. Classes were held for all the women [see Figure 8.4] so that even the most ignorant person would be bound to understand the reason for this safer technique. I tried to make the germ theory understandable to them. To get them to know why and how diseases and infections are transmitted from person to person, giving them the reason for cleanliness because dirt is very apt to harbor germs. It became understandable to them why they should stay out of homes and from people-contacts when there was an epidemic type of sickness. Eventually, we had trained, reliable midwives in every village in our district. To my knowledge there were no more childbirth deaths and no serious complications.

One more interesting and unusual case was that of the birth of triplets. This was at Wainwright, one of our most northern villages, about two hundred miles from Barrow. It was in winter. There were dependable, trained midwives officiating. No one expected multiple births. I had told the attending midwife to proceed with the delivery and call me only if they met with complications. They did so after the first baby was born. They were very excited when they realized one more was coming. By the time I reached the home they had the two and excitedly said, "One more is coming!" Now we had three tiny tots. Too small to do any handling of. Hurriedly, we improvised an incubator using a washtub, lining it with furs and using several warm water bottles. Midwives remained constantly in attendance, keeping the water bottles warm and feeding breast milk with a medicine dropper. One baby, a boy, died the first night. The other two, a boy and a girl, were kept alive. By radio, a summons was sent out for plane service to come, if possible, to take the tiny babies to the mission hospital at Barrow. I realized this would be our only hope for their survival.

After two days of waiting for suitable weather, a winged plane arrived. We still had the two alive. Much credit goes to the faithful attendance of the Native midwives. We had the tiny babies ready in a fur-lined box with warm water bottles and we made sure there was a tunnel-like passage for the pilot to keep putting his hand down to them to assure they

8.4. Native midwives attended classes. Reprinted with permission, Alaska and Polar Regions Archives, Elmer E. Rasmuson Library, University of Alaska Fairbanks, Alaska Nurses Association Collection (#78-27-07N).

did not suffocate. The pilot, unattended by any helper, got the babies safely to the Barrow hospital. They lived and were cared for there for several months.

After leaving Alaska I had heard no more about them. So in 1971 I decided to write to the Wainwright postmaster and ask what the ultimate outcome had been of these two survivals. Quoting from the answer to my letter, "Now for your question. The two that are living of the triplets. They are grown. One boy is down in the Aleutian chain working for a high-paying company. He seems to be doing all right. Behaving and trying to live well. The sister to him is in Wainwright. She has three children and the last one was adopted by our pastor. This girl is not married but she is that way. We are praying for her. Their father is living yet. The mother has been long gone." It was gratifying to me to find out that two babies out of the three lived, grew up, and evidently are still alive, living in Alaska.

The seventeen years I spent in Alaska provided a great variety of experiences. One was a rather humorous situation for a nurse to tackle. There were no other designated health officers. Nurses had to officiate in the absence of any other medical authority. This was another incident that happened at the far northern village of Wainwright: dog quarantine.

There had been several dog deaths. The report given me was the sick dog acted like crazy and had an inclination to bite other dogs who then got sick and died. No person, fortunately, had been bitten so far. The village council and I had a meeting. They agreed to put on a quarantine. All dogs were ordered to be kept tied up with secure chains. They did not even allow pups to run loose. This village had possibly as many as a couple hundred dogs. Guards were appointed, each given a section of the village to patrol. [The guards were] to make rounds twice a day, carry a gun, and shoot any loose dog. This really worked, especially after one loose dog was shot, and that dog belonged to the council chief. The men could take their dogs on hunting trips, but could not go to other villages. No dogs or dog teams from other villages were permitted to come in.

We sent a head from one of the diseased dead dogs to a government laboratory in Washington, D.C. The verdict of this report was rabies. The Wainwright dog population was saved. Later reports from other villages indicated there had been a serious death toll among dogs. A tragedy, since dogs were necessary for livelihood in those days. I smile to myself now when I think that my Alaska experiences even included a dog quarantine, and it worked.

More serious quarantines became my lot in some later years. People, not dogs. Transmittable diseases such as measles, influenza, tuberculosis, gonorrhea, and syphilis without a doubt were nonexistent until the coming of the white man to Alaska. The Natives had poor resistance to those germs. No built-up body resistance had been acquired. Measles and flu epidemics in early years took a terrific death toll. Sometimes whole villages of people were wiped out. I had some experience with this, especially with measles and flu, and with typhoid on a more limited basis. By continuing to educate the people about the germ nature of diseases and getting their cooperation to stay away from the sick homes, the death tolls were much reduced. In acute cases, more rigid quarantine measures were taken.

Diphtheria proved a new and tragic experience. This was in the middle of 1940. I had never previously seen a diphtheria case. My knowledge was only book knowledge. On my first trip to a lonely isolated island, Nelson, I encountered my first such case [see Figure 8.5]. I feel that the Lord arranged my travel plans for me to be there just when needed. One home had two sick children. Another home had one when I arrived by dog-team.

I surmised this was not a usual sore-throat type. There were soon two deaths with these throat symptoms. Quick action was indicated so as not to have a tragic epidemic spread of the disease. Eskimo people are very prone to flock into sick people's homes, just from curiosity. Now I was a newcomer to these people. The white missionary was a Catholic priest. I assigned him to stay, be the guard, in the home where the deaths occurred, not to leave for even a moment except when I came to relieve him. We took shifts through the first day and night. I told the priest, "I don't know for sure what we are dealing with, probably diphtheria. You and I have no family members of our own to concern ourselves with here. You and I have to take the risk, stay right in the home." He cooperated.

Some Native men were assigned to enforce strict stay-at-home rules. Every family in its own home—no visiting and no going out to mingle until we secured medical help and had a diagnosis of what these cases might be. The school teacher had a radio sending set and he started to call SOS to Bethel Hospital.

In a couple of days a doctor came in by plane. An immunization program for diphtheria was done. A nurse was sent in to stay in the village to control and help keep quarantine. The spread of the infection was stayed. No further deaths. I needed to return to my headquarters at Hooper Bay to do the diphtheria toxoid immunization there. Eventually, we had a few similar cases in Hooper Bay. No deaths. We had them supplied with diphtheria antitoxin in case we had any acute cases.

In the course of my diphtheria work looking at the throats and so forth, one child coughed right into my face. He was just coming down with the throat symptoms. That cough in my face did it. I came down with it. I gave myself diphtheria antitoxin. At first I showed no serious indications. A doctor was brought into Hooper Bay and later a nurse was sent in to replace me. I was taken to the Bethel government hospital. I did not have serious throat symptoms, but I did develop critical cardiac manifestations as a complication. This eventually proved a necessity for me to slow down on my travel work. I recovered after staying about three weeks in the hospital. But I had some after-effects. My diphtheria cardiac attack in Alaska has left some scars on my heart valve, but it is not considered serious at present. I had had almost perfect health up to that time, but this nipped that physical perfection.

I did not limit my services to only the villages that had government schools during the time that I was traveling. There were not many parochial schools left, mostly Protestant and Catholic missions that had, in years past, been the ones to start education schools for the Natives. By now most places had turned them over to the U.S. government to finance and to provide teachers. Holy Cross, with a 100 percent Catholic village population, was an exception. They had a mission

8.5. Alma Carlson arriving by dog team at Nelson Island. Reprinted, by permission, from Alaska Nurses Association Collection (#84-051-430), Elmer E. Rasmuson Library, University of Alaska Fairbanks.

with the school where the nuns did the teaching. It was a
fine, progressive village. I was given a warm welcome to come
in with my health programs. They had no hospital or nurse so
they were acceptable to get help, the same as the other villages in general.

At Holy Cross I had one experience that was somewhat
humorous, one that I have not forgotten. It was Easter
time. Much is made of such holidays, both at Catholic and
Protestant missions in general. I was staying in the guest
room at the mission with the Sisters. Easter Sunday the
Sisters felt concerned that I would not have my type of service to go to, I being Protestant. So they asked if I would be
interested to go with them to the Easter service. I assured
them I was interested, but I felt I did not have suitable clothing. I had only my fur parka, the one I traveled in [see Figure
8.6]. The Eskimos usually made holidays dress-up affairs as
much as possible. One nun apologetically asked if I would
accept wearing one of their robes and come with them. I accepted their offer. I felt that if they could offer and permit
a Protestant like myself to wear a nun's garb, I would show
my appreciation by doing just that. I wish I had a snapshot
of myself dressed up as a nun, sitting as one of them. This
proved to me to be a very unforgettable Easter.

I am sitting watching television, seeing the U.S. Apollo and
the Russians up in space making their first hook-up and contact. Because of the taping I am doing about my arctic experiences that I had during the years 1921 to 1947, my thinking
is very much focused on the life situation of the Eskimos.
Immediately, some comparative ideas come to my mind.
I shall make note of some of these. The module the astronauts are crawling into and out of reminds me of some of the
Eskimo igloos I have crawled in and out of. They were not
snow and ice, but made of driftwood and sod, and covered
with snow in winter. The old-time typical igloo had a long,

8.6. Alma Carlson in winter clothing: "Public health uniform in Alaska." Reprinted with permission from Alaska Nurses Association Collection (#18-27-12N), Elmer E. Rasmuson Library, University of Alaska Fairbanks.

low narrow passageway into the main living room. Some entrances were so low one had to crawl on one's hands and knees to get in. The long narrow entrance was often cluttered with much paraphernalia. One had to proceed cautiously not to step on pups. The mother dog was usually lying on guard over her brood. Once inside, the one-room quarters served as kitchen, bedroom, and social hall. Do you now realize why, as I sit and watch the astronauts—the Russians and Americans in the spaceships—I see a slight similarity?

Teachers, missionaries, and now the early stage of a new program with a traveling nurse reaching up into space. We are reaching up into arctic space. The television is showing the astronauts having their meal in the module. To me it looks like a familiar scene, similar to the inside of an igloo, sitting on the floor and the food simple and nourishing. The astronauts' dress looks very much like the Eskimo parka outfit. Warm garb.

We did not have worldwide communication like they have. We were not floating around in space. But we were often mushing through deep snow, balancing the dog sled over jagged ice floes. On one of my trips the traveling was so tough the dogs got too tired and refused to go on. To spur the dogs on, if a person walked ahead of them they would exert themselves and follow. I tried to walk ahead of the dogs because the driver needed to stay on the sled bars to balance it. The snow was deep and soft and I sank to my hips and could not move. For a short distance, not very far actually, I got down on my knees and crawled ahead of the dogs. They followed. They must have decided if I could make it they would exert themselves and do it, too. We got through to our destination. God was watching over us, just as I believe the Lord has been watching over the space flight at this date, 1975.

I was offered the opportunity to go back up north to Wainwright as headquarters, but I began to feel it was time to quit, to consider my Alaska career completed for good [and] to leave it for a new force of public health workers to take over. This has been done. Health services go on in more modern methods. My aim has been to relate some of the more dramatic instances I had to contend with. Not all such, by any means. In any work—it was true in my case—it is the day-by-day commonplace things we do and how we face up to it that is the ultimate actual value of our contributions in life. I think the Lord looks at us not so much on what we do, but as what we are in relationship to Him. Has our life been an expression of Him? Has He lived and expressed Himself through us? This is what I want to be my goal in life.

The last two years, 1945 to 1947, I had an assignment to work in and around Fairbanks, working with Eskimos and Indians who had moved from their isolated villages into Fairbanks to work on labor projects such as road building and on the Alaska railroad. Adjustments for these people were difficult. Fairbanks had several hundred Native people, and the number kept increasing. I did travel into outlying settlements, not traveling now by dog team, but by plane. By train in some instances, with Fairbanks as headquarters. The nursing responsibilities were different. Conditions in Alaska in general had changed. Medical and dental services were more accessible. Plane service was increasing. I asked an old Eskimo woman—she was old enough to remember how life was like before the coming of the white man—"Do you consider that the life of the Eskimo was better before the coming of the white man or is it better now?" She wisely answered, "I think it was half good before and half better now. Our children and young people obeyed their parents better in the old days than they do now. But many conditions are now better."

It is true we have given the Alaska Natives many advantages to profit from, but there are also many vices to influence them that are not good, such as alcohol, the lure of money, and even harmful drugs.

Endnotes

1. Tewkesbury's *Who's Who in Alaska and Alaska Business Index* (Juneau, AK: Tewkesbury Publishers, 1947), 1C:11.
2. Duluth *News-Tribune* (Duluth, MN) "Nurse Among the Eskimos," 8, 30 September 1951.
3. Tewkesbury's *Who's Who,* 11.
4. In 1931, the federal government transferred the responsibility of providing medical care for Alaska Natives from the Bureau of Education to the Alaska Native Service of the Bureau of Indian Affairs.
5. The Bureau of Education built a twenty-bed hospital at Mountain Village in 1929, which was closed in 1939 (Robert Fortuine, 1971, "The Development of Modern Medicine in Southwestern Alaska, Part I: The Growth of Health Services," *Alaska Medicine* [1971] 13: 2).
6. It was routine for the Alaska Native Service to transfer nurses every two years to prevent burnout. This practice persisted in itinerant nursing until the early 1970s.
7. Tewkesbury's *Who's Who,* 11.
8. The Bureau of Education built a hospital in Akiak in 1918. In 1937, erosion from the river forced the closure of this hospital. A new thirty-six-bed Alaska Native Service Hospital opened in Bethel in 1939 as a replacement for both Akiak and Mountain Village hospitals (Fortuine, 1971, *Alaska Medicine* [1971] 13: 2).
9. Tewkesbury's *Who's Who,* 11.
10. Michael W. Straus, acting secretary of the interior, to Alma Carlson. Letter of Commendation and Notice of Pay Increase (22 October 1945), Alma Carlson file, Series 14-1, Box 34, Folder 542, Alaska Nurses Association Collection, Archives, Elmer E. Rasmuson Library, University of Alaska Fairbanks.
11. Duluth *News-Tribune,* "Nurse Among the Eskimos."
12. Ibid.
13. Jessen, E. F., publisher, *Jessen's Weekly,* Fairbanks, Alaska, to Alma Carlson. Letter (26 July 1948). Of the seventeen awards, five were given to women. In addition to Alma Carlson, Lou Herron, long-term field nurse in the Bethel area, was an award recipient. The *Jessen's Weekly* announcement (25 June 1948) stated of Carlson, "She worked out a simplified health education program for outlying villages."
14. Duluth *News-Tribune,* "Nurse Among the Eskimos."
15. Alma Carlson, tape recording (17 July 1975, 2:00 P.M.), Duluth, Minnesota; and letters to her family (1934–1947), private collection, Prairie Village, Kansas. These materials were provided by Alma Carlson's niece, Glannie

Weihe, of Prairie Village, Kansas. The daughter of Alma's sister, Annie, she reported that her Aunt Alma had paid for her education in nursing school.

16. Dr. Langsam became known to the Natives as the "talking doctor" because he learned the Eskimo language (H. Jackson-Schirmer, "Dr. J. H. Romig's Successors on the Yukon," *Alaska Medicine* 35, no. 2: 109).

17. See endnote 21 in Chapter Six (Gertrude Fergus) regarding the Osts and the Covenant Church.

18. This was probably the handbook written by medical doctors E. Krulish and Daniel Neuman, *Medical Handbook* (Washington, D.C.: U. S. Government Printing Office, 1913).

19. Cascara pills: *Cascara sagrada,* the dried bark of cascara buckthorn, used as a laxative.

20. In the mid-1930s the other two nurses were Mildred Keaton and Bertha Leake (W. B. Courtney, "Angel in Furs," *Collier's* [November 1937]: 80).

Conclusion

AUTOBIOGRAPHY, IN THE FORM of memoirs, diaries, and letters, is the "primary stuff of history" according to Tuchman.[1] While there is a tendency toward favorable self-report, a sense of reality emerges when several persons report the same thing. In this collection, six nurses recount their interactions with a harsh and lonely environment and their varied responses to roles inherently filled with personal stress because of a limited or missing support system.

In addition to weather and isolation, frequently mentioned themes within their work settings include the continual presence of infectious disease, often around-the-clock work, and problems with sanitation. Housing was poor, in tents or leaking buildings; at times these nurses gave up their own beds to patients. They cleaned, prepared food, and did laundry as necessary. As a group they quickly responded to a myriad of medical and nursing problems in both the absence and presence of medical partnership.

The lack of close supervision and an imperfect bureaucracy in the early years supported the creative ways in which field nurses interpreted their roles. The statement, "... duties for the benefit of natives or for the interests of the Alaska School Service"[2] was all-encompassing. Nurses lived at their work setting; they were working all the time. For example, they organized sports, taught sewing and soap making, and organized and taught school. These activities were marginal to traditional nursing but they all promoted health.

With the institution of formal health systems in the 1930s, jobs were described, classified, and pay scales became uniform. These systems were not ready for the obvious: expanding education, in formal and in-service programs, so that nursing personnel were actually prepared for and given explicit permission to do activities usually limited to physicians. This did not happen until the 1960s and 1970s with the establishment of short-term and standard nurse practitioner programs. An improved delivery system also included the preparation of village health aides, local residents taught to care for their neighbors, with medical and nursing supervision given, if necessary, through long-distance communication. In the meantime "autonomy by default"[3] existed.

Most of the women in this collection felt some distress related to the responsibilities of their work. In spite of this, a quality of mental toughness and endurance emerges from their letters and memoirs. In later life, their memories of the rural Alaska experience were keen and fresh, and recalled with pride.

Endnotes

1. Barbara W. Tuchman, *Practicing History* (New York: Ballantine, 1982), 87.
2. P. P. Claxton, commissioner of education, to Esther Gibson, Alaska Medical Service, Letter of Appointment as Sanitation Teacher, 30 October 1916, RG 75, Box 77, National Archives, Washington, D.C.
3. Jackie Pflaum, "History of Public Health Nursing in Alaska." Paper presented at American Public Health Association, November 1992, Washington, D.C. The nurse provided the services because she was the only provider present to do the service.

Glossary of Medical Terms

Ammonium salicylate: A salicylate salt given for joint pain, to reduce fever, etc. Rarely used now since aspirin has replaced it.

Antrum: A nearly closed cavity or chamber, especially in a bone. (It may be the maxillary sinus, referred to as the antrum of Highmore.)

Appendicitis: Inflammation of the vermiform appendix, located at the juncture of the small intestine and the large intestine. (Referred to as "hot appendix" by Mildred Keaton.) Ruptured appendix: the inflamed appendix perforates and infection spreads into the abdominal cavity.

Bichloride bath: A local bath, or constant immersion, ordered for septic wounds of limbs. The solution is that of bichloride of mercury, of 1:2000 or 1:3000 strength.

Carcinoma: Cancer (CA). An invasive malignant tumor derived from skin or lining tissue that tends to spread to other areas of the body. Cancer of the mesentery: Carcinoma spread to the lining of the abdominal cavity.

Curettage: The removal of tissue or growth from the interior of a body cavity, such as the uterus, by scraping with a curette. It usually refers to the uterus and the removal of an incomplete miscarriage.

Cyanotic (adj.), Cyanosis (noun): A bluish discoloration of the skin and mucous membranes resulting from inadequate oxygenation of the blood.

Diphtheria: An acute infectious disease caused by *Cornebacterium bacteriae,* characterized by the production of a systemic toxin and the formation of a false membrane in the lining of the mucous membranes of the throat and other respiratory passages, causing difficulty in breathing, high fever, and weakness. The toxin is particularly harmful to the tissues of the heart and central nervous system.

Dislocation: Displacement of a body part, especially the temporary displacement of a bone from its normal position, also called luxation. Reduction: The restoration of a body part to its normal position.

Empyema: The presence of pus in a body cavity, especially the pleural cavity (potential space between the rib cage and the lungs).

Enema (enemata, plural form): The injection of liquid into the rectum through the anus for the purpose of cleansing, treatment, or diagnosis.

Erysipelas: An acute febrile disease associated with a local, intense reddish inflammation of the skin and subcutaneous tissue, often of the face.

Exsanguinated: Deprived or drained of blood.

Hernia: The protrusion of an organ or other bodily structure through the wall that normally contains it. It usually refers to a loop of intestine through the abdominal wall. Herniotomy: Surgical correction of the hernia by relieving stricture. Strangulated hernia: When the flow of blood to the herniated part is arrested. This can lead to death of tissue.

Impetigo: A contagious skin infection caused by streptococcal or staphylococcal bacteria and characterized by the eruption of superficial pustules that rupture and form thick yellow crusts, usually on the face, and commonly seen in children.

Ichthyol ointment: A mineral formed by the deposits of fossil fish and containing about 10 percent sulfur. It was used as an antiseptic and mild irritant for various skin conditions in an ointment preparation.

Measles (rubeola): An acute contagious viral disease, usually occurring in childhood and characterized by the eruption of red spots on the skin, fever, and catarrhal symptoms.

Miscarriage: Premature expulsion of a nonviable fetus, especially before the end of the second trimester of gestation; spontaneous abortion. Partial miscarriage: Parts of the fetus are retained in the uterus. See curettage.

Paratyphoid fever: An acute intestinal disease, similar to typhoid but less severe, caused by food contaminated with the bacteria of the genus *Salmonella,* also called enteric fever.

Perineorraphy: Suture of the perineum. In females the area between the vulva and the anus; usually related to childbirth repair.

p.r.n.: Abbreviation of the Latin *pro re nata,* as the situation demands, usually referring to pain medication interval and/or dosage at the discretion of the caregiver.

Pediculosis: The state of being infested with lice. In this book it usually refers to head lice.

Paralytic stroke: See Stroke.

Placenta previa: A condition in which the placenta (afterbirth) is implanted in the lower segment of the uterus so that it is adjacent to or obstructs the internal opening of the cervix. It may cause maternal hemorrhage before or during labor.

Pneumonia: An acute or chronic disease marked by inflammation of the lungs. It is caused by viruses, bacteria, or other microorganisms and sometimes by physical or chemical irritants. Pneumonia crisis: A sudden change in the course of the disease toward either improvement or deterioration.

Pyroseptine: A paraffin method of dressing burns.

Rheumatism: Any of several disease conditions of the muscles, tendons, joints, bones, and nerves, characterized by discomfort and disability.

Schick test: A test for detecting immunity or susceptibility to diphtheria. The toxin for the diphtheria organism is injected into the skin tissue.

Smallpox: An acute, highly infectious, often fatal disease caused by a pox virus and characterized by high fever and aches. There is subsequent widespread eruption of papules that blister, produce pus, and form scabs that leave permanent pock-marks.

Stroke: A sudden loss of brain function caused by a blockage or a rupture of a blood vessel in the brain, characterized by a loss of function or sensation. Symptoms vary with the extent and severity of damage to the brain; also called cerebral vascular accident (CVA). Paralytic stroke: A stroke in which the loss of function of parts of the body are obvious.

Strangulated hernia: See Hernia.

Strepto-staphylovaccine: An early vaccine.

Trachoma: A contagious disease of the conjunctiva and cornea of the eye, caused by the bacterium *Chlamydia trachomatis* and marked by redness, tissue growth, and formation of granules of tissue. It is a major cause of blindness in some countries.

Trachelorrhaphy: Suture of a laceration (tear) of the uterine cervix.

Tonsillectomy: The surgical removal of the tonsils, a mass of lymphoid tissue located in the area of the palate.

Tuberculosis (TB): An infectious disease of humans and animals caused by the tubercle bacillus and characterized by the formation of tubercles on the lungs and other tissues of the body, often developing long after the initial infection. Note: During the period of high incidence of this disease in the territory, although most cases were of the lungs, many Alaskans had infections of the bones and other body systems.

Tuberculosis sinus: Draining wounds that may become chronic.

Typhoid fever: An acute infectious disease caused by *Salmonella typhi* and characterized by continued fever, physical and mental depression, an eruption of rose-colored spots on the chest and abdomen, abdominal distention, and diarrhea.

Endnotes

1. The *American Heritage Stedman's Medical Dictionary* (New York: Houghton Mifflin, 1995).

Bibliography

Selected Published References

Bixby, William. *Track of the Bear.* New York: David McKay, 1965.

Blackman, Margaret B. *Sadie Brower Neakok: An Inupiaq Woman.* Seattle: University of Washington Press, 1989.

Brower, Charles. *Fifty Years Below Zero.* New York: Dodd, Mead, 1944.

Bullough, Vern L., Lilli Sentz, and Alice P. Stein, eds. *American Nursing: A Biographical Dictionary.* Volume 2. New York: Garland, 1992.

Cantwell, Margaret, and M. G. Edmond. "Continued Growth: Holy Cross." In *North to Share: The Sisters of St. Ann in Alaska and the Yukon Territory.* Victoria, BC: Sisters of St. Ann, 1992.

Courtney, W. B. "Angel in Furs." *Collier's* (November 1937).

Fortuine, Robert. *Chills and Fever: Health and Disease in the Early History of Alaska.* Fairbanks: University of Alaska Press, 1989.

Gregg, Elinor. *The Indians and the Nurse.* Norman, OK: University of Oklahoma Press, 1965.

Gruening, Ernest. *The State of Alaska.* New York: Random House, 1968.

Harmer, Bertha. *Textbook of the Principles and Practice of Nursing*. New York: Macmillan, 1923.

Harmer, Bertha. *Textbook of the Principles and Practice of Nursing*. Revised by Virginia Henderson, 5th ed. New York: Macmillan, 1954.

Kalish, Philip, and Beatrice Kalish. *The Advance of American Nursing*. 3rd ed. Philadelphia: J. B. Lippincott, 1987.

Keaton, Mildred. *No Regrets: The Autobiography of an Arctic Nurse*. Marysville, WA: Pukuk Press, 1994.

Kennedy, M. R. "Northland Doctor's Wife." Series of eleven articles in *Alaska Sportsman*. May 1965 through May 1966.

Krulish, E., and Daniel Neuman. *Medical Handbook*. Washington, D.C.: U.S. Government Printing Office, 1913.

Langdon, Steve. *The Native Peoples of Alaska*. Anchorage: Greatland Graphics, 1989.

Loman, Carl. *Fifty Years in Alaska*. New York: David Mckay, 1954.

Muñoz, Rie. *Nursing in the North: 1867–1967*. Anchorage, AK: Alaska Nurses Association, 1967.

Parran, Thomas. *Alaska's Health: A Survey Report*. By Alaska Health Survey Team, Pittsburgh, PA: Graduate School of Public Health, University of Pittsburgh, 1954.

Rasmussen, Knud. *Across Arctic America: Narrative of the Fifth Thule Expedition*. Fairbanks: University of Alaska Press, 1999 (originally published by G. P. Putman's Sons, New York, 1927).

Reverby, Susan M. *Ordered to Care: The Dilemma of American Nursing 1850–1945*. Cambridge, UK: Cambridge University Press, 1987.

Robb, Isabel Hampton. *Nursing, Its Principles and Practice*. 3rd ed. Toronto: J. F. Hartz, 1909.

Sanders, G. J. *Modern Methods in Nursing*. 2nd ed. New York: W. B. Saunders, 1922.

Schneider, Dorothy, and Carl Schneider. *American Women in the Progressive Era: 1900–1920.* New York: Facts on File, 1993.

Smith, Barrell Hevener. "Bureau of Education: History, Activities and Organization." In *Service Monograph of U. S. Government.* Baltimore: The John Hopkins Press, 1923.

Stefánsson, Vilhjalmur. *The Adventure of Wrangell Island.* New York: MacMillan, 1925.

Stevens, Robert. *Alaska Aviation History.* Volume 1. DesMoines, WA: Polynyas Press, 1990.

Stewart, I. *Standard Curriculum for Schools of Nursing.* 4th ed. New York: National League for Nursing Education, 1922.

Stuck, Hudson. *A Winter Circuit of Our Arctic Coast.* New York: Charles Scribner's Sons, 1920.

Ungermann, K. A. *The Race to Nome: The Story of the Heroic Alaskan Dog Teams That Rushed Diphtheria Serum to Stricken Nome in 1925.* New York: Harper and Row, 1963.

Wilkins, G. H. *Flying the Arctic.* New York: G. P. Putnam's Sons, 1928.

Selected Unpublished Materials

Baker, Gertrude Fergus. Letters to her family from White Mountain, Alaska (1926–1927). Alaska Nurses Association Collection, Series 14-1, Box 35, Files 561–562, Archives, Elmer E. Rasmuson Library, University of Alaska Fairbanks.

Carlson, Alma. Letters to her family from Alaska (1934–1947), private collection, Prairie Village, Kansas.

Carlson, Alma. Tape recording, 17 July 1975, Duluth, Minnesota; private collection. Prairie Village, Kansas. Provided by Alma Carlson's niece, Glannie Wiehe, of Prairie Village, Kansas.

Fuller, Stella L. Letters and field trip reports from Alaska (1922–1924), RG 509.201, Alaska, Delano Nursing Service, National Archives, Washington, D.C.

Greist, Mollie. "Nursing Under the North Star," unpub-
lished manuscript (no date), Alaska Nurses Association
Collection, Series 13-2, Box 29, File 477, Archives, Elmer
E. Rasmuson Library, University of Alaska Fairbanks.

Keaton, Mildred. Unpublished manuscript (no date), Alaska
Nurses Association Collection, Series 13-4, Box 33, File
520 and related materials in Series 14-1, Box 36, File
592, Archives, Elmer E. Rasmuson Library, University of
Alaska Fairbanks.

Mueller, Augusta. Letters to her family and Miss Knust from
Barrow, Alaska (1922–1926), Alaska Nurses Association
Collection, Augusta Mueller File, Series 14-1, Box 37,
Folders 609-610, Archives, Elmer E. Rasmuson Library,
University of Alaska Fairbanks.

Welch, Lula. "Memoirs," unpublished manuscript (1956),
Alaska Nurses Association Collection, Lula Welch File,
Folder 641, Box 38, Series 14-1, Achives, Elmer E.
Rasmuson Library, University of Alaska Fairbanks.

Appendix:[1]
From U.S. Civil Service Commission, 8 June 1938, Concerning Nurse Positions in Alaska

Chief Nurse, Grade 11, Salary $2,600

Head Nurse, Grade 10, Salary $2,300

(Proposed Duties and Qualifications)

Duties and Responsibilities: Under the direction of a medical officer, to supervise, direct and be responsible for the entire nursing service and attendants' service in a Government hospital; to be responsible for the emergency care of patients in the absence of the medical officer; to supervise and instruct the nurses; to manage and supervise the work of the operating room, kitchens, laundry and sewing rooms; to supervise all ward attendants, maids, janitors and others; to see that proper records and reports are kept; to maintain the hospital in a clean and sanitary condition; to keep account of stock supplies, and to perform related work as assigned; to give anaesthetics.

Typical Tasks: In an Indian Service hospital in Alaska:

To prepare schedules of hours for and to assign and instruct nurses, orderlies, attendants, and other employees administering to the personal needs and comfort of the patients.

To deliver women, and render emergency surgical service.

To supervise the carrying out of physicians' orders with regard to the care and treatment of patients.

To give anaesthetics and/or assist the surgeon in operating.

To inspect charts and reports, receive complaints or service rendered and to make adjustments.

To visit seriously ill patients and to interview friends and relatives of patients; to wait on dispensary cases in the absence of the doctor; to visit sick members of the nursing and attending staff and arrange for their care and treatment.

To plan the working routine of the kitchen, laundry and sewing room staffs; to arrange menus in consultation with the cook.

To see that the supplies are cared for properly, that proper records and reports of work are made; to maintain discipline among patients and nurses and other employees.

To make reports and recommendations, to handle correspondence and conduct office work.

Minimum qualifications: Training equivalent to that represented by graduation from high school; graduation from a recognized school of nursing, requiring a residence of at least two years in a hospital having a daily average of not less than fifty bed patients giving a thorough practical and theoretical training; evidence of State registration; not less than two years' post-graduate experience in a hospital; in addition, at least three years of successful duty as assistant chief nurse in a general hospital; thorough knowledge of modern hospital nursing techniques and hospital management and administrative methods; demonstrated ability to instruct, and to supervise and direct the work of nurses, attendants, and others; ability to organize, coordinate, and manage nursing activities of the scope and magnitude represented in the hospital concerned; sympathetic understanding of the sick; tact; good judgment; administrative ability; good health.

Age: Not less than 28 nor more than 40 years of age.

Physical Ability: Of an unusually sound and robust condition. Affections of the chest, thyroid, and circulation will disqualify; also flatfeet, visual defects and uncorrected dental diseases.

Itinerant and Village Nurse, Grade 10, Salary $2300
Duties and Qualifications

Duties and Responsibilities: To plan and carry out a program of public health nursing service in a designated area and to do such medical work as will meet emergency needs in the absence of a medical practitioner. To render first aid, to instruct in home care of the sick, to make such diagnosis and institute such treatment as necessary in the absence of medical advice.

Typical Tasks: To open abscesses, deliver women, sew up wounds, set simple fractures, diagnose and treat pneumonia, influenza, diphtheria, measles, scarlet fever, erysipelas, gastro-intestinal disorders. To visit the homes, teaching simple nursing care, sanitation and nutrition, advising on family matters and home making.

Requirements: Basic education: Completion of high school. Professional education: At least three years of nurse training in an accredited school of nursing giving training in general medicine, surgery, obstetrics, pediatrics and contagious disease nursing in a hospital having a daily average of not less than 50 bed patients.

Public Health Nursing: One year of post graduate work in public health nursing course of collegiate standing, or two years of paid experience on staff under nurse supervision.

Age: Not less than 28 nor more than 40 years of age.

Physical Ability: Of an unusually sound and robust condition. Affections of the chest, thyroid, and circulation will disqualify. Also flatfeet, visual defects and uncorrected dental diseases.

Staff Nurse, Grade 9, Salary $2,000
Proposed Duties and Qualifications

Duties and Responsibilities: Under the direction of a medical officer, and under the supervision of a head nurse to carry out all of the bedside nursing care of patients; to perform the work in connection with operative procedures in the surgery, to direct the work of a native assistant, to assist the surgeon during operations and obstetrical deliveries.

Typical tasks: To care for ambulatory patients or those confined in bed in a general hospital, to maintain proper techniques of aseptic nursing in relation to communicable diseases, to assist surgeon in operative and obstetrical procedures; to maintain the hospital wards in proper condition of order and cleanliness, to give medication, observe symptoms and carry out treatments ordered by physician, to teach patients elements of hygiene and healthful living.

In the absence of the head nurse and/or physician to conduct the hospital and nursing care in a proper manner.

Minimum qualifications: Graduation within last fifteen years from an accredited school of nursing giving a resident course of training of not less than two years, in a hospital having a daily average of not less than fifty beds. Two years of successful nursing experience.

Age: Not less than 28 nor more than 40 years of age.

Physical Ability: Of an unusually sound and robust condition. Affections of the chest, thyroid, and circulation will disqualify; also flatfeet, visual defect and uncorrected dental diseases.

ALASKA

The setup of special requirements for nurses in Alaska should be safeguarded by the following additions to the present Civil Service requirements for graduate nurses and graduate nurses (visiting duty):

1. **Citizenship.**
2. **Age.** Not less than 28 years of age nor more than 40. They must not have reached their fortieth birthday on the date of the close of receipt of applications. This age limit does not apply to persons granted preference because of military or naval service, except that such applicants must not have reached the retirement age.
3. **Physical Ability:** Applicants must have such health and freedom from physical defects as will enable them to meet the physical standard which the Commission deems necessary to perform the duties of the positions as stated above.

   Persons selected for appointment will be required to pass a physical examination given by a Federal medical officer. Failure to pass such physical examination will prevent appointment.

   Submit a record of illness requiring medical attention extending over two weeks duration. Name and address of physician usually or recently employed. Non-selection may be based on record of severe abdominal or goitre operations, for a condition of thyroid hyperactivity, varicose veins and chest involvement such as pleurisy, tuberculosis, bronchitis, deafness, eyesight, flat-foot.
4. **Education:**
   (a) They must have completed at least 14 units of standard high-school work. This requirement will be waived for person granted preference because of military or naval service. (Omit waiver).
   (b) They must have been graduated within last fifteen years from a recognized school of nursing requiring a residence of at least two years in (1) a hospital having a daily average of 50 bed patients or more, omit (2) concerning 30 bed daily average.

Substitute (2) Require a statement of curriculum covered in school giving number of months' service in
each major service.

1. Surgical and operating room.
2. Medical.
3. Obstetric and delivery room.
4. Pediatrics.
5. Communicable and tuberculosis.
6. Psychiatric and Neurological.
7. Out-patient department.
8. Eye, ear, nose, throat, skin, metabolism, physio-
   theraphy.
9. Public health nursing.
10. Diet kitchen.

Determining satisfactory combination made by
Appointment Officer.

Omit waiver on daily average for one year satisfactory service in the Army or Navy Nursing Corps.

(c.) They must have been registered as a graduate nurse
in some state or the District of Columbia.

(d.) They must have had not less than two years' post
graduate experience in nursing. For Graduate Nurse,
Visiting Duty, requirement (d) must include at least
8 months of post graduate training in public health
or visiting nursing in a recognized school of public
health nursing of collegiate standing, or, in lieu of
such training, two years of full-time paid experience
under nurse supervision in public health or visiting nursing. Experience must have been in general
public health or visiting duty. Work as school nurse,
office nurse, industrial first-aid nurse, and similar
restricted experience will not be accepted as quali-
fying. (For Nurse-Technician, requirement (d) must
include at least one year of post graduate training

or experiences or of both combined, as technician in bacteriology and roentgenology, with a minimum of six months in each field, full-time basis. When activity has been in both fields over this same period of time, it must be shown that it was equivalent to a total of six months in each field; experience in one branch only will not qualify. Applicants must have had the experience in both bacteriology and roentgenology. This type of personnel has not yet been utilized in Alaska.)

Chief and Head Nurse: Three years' supervisory and/or executive experience in general hospital required.

Staff Nurse: Preference given to those having done more institutional than private duty nursing.

Visiting Duty: Requirement (d) must include full statement of obstetrical and maternity and infancy hygiene service, tuberculosis nursing service and school nursing and health education.

The setup of desirable qualifications for nurses in Alaska as set forth in Civil Service papers may be stated best in terms of the quality of basic training and the measurement of successful experience. Policies as to rating of papers or preparing lists will include the following:

For hospital duty:
1. Post graduate work in anaesthetics, tuberculosis, obstetrics, surgery; eye, ear, nose and throat.
2. Content of curriculum in nursing school shall influence rating or establish some degree of preference.

For visiting duty:
1. Obstetrical nursing (successful experience in delivering without aid of physician).
2. Tuberculosis nursing.
3. School nursing and health education activities shall be of preferential value.

An interview by appointment office may be required.
A second preliminary physical examination may be required.
A further check of references will be made by appointing
office.

Endnotes

1. Excerpt from correspondence to the United States Civil Service Commission,
    Washington, D.C., 8 June 1938, concerning appointments to the Alaska
    Division of the Bureau of Indian Affairs. Medical Service Nurses, Alaska
    Division of the Bureau of Indian Affairs, RG 75, Box 257, National Archives,
    Washington, D.C.

Index